More
Small Houses

Fine Homebuilding
GREAT HOUSES

More Small Houses

The Taunton Press

Cover photo: Warren Jagger
Back cover photos: top left, Charles Miller;
top right, Andrew Wormer; bottom, Roe Osborn

Taunton
BOOKS & VIDEOS
for fellow enthusiasts

Printed in the United States of America
10 9 8 7 6 5 4 3

The Taunton Press, Inc., 63 South Main Street, PO Box 5506,
Newtown, CT 06470-5506
e-mail: tp@taunton.com

Distributed by Publishers Group West

Library of Congress Cataloging-in-Publication Data

Fine homebuilding great houses. More small houses.
        p.   cm.
    Includes index.
    ISBN 1-56158-278-6
    1. Small houses—United States.   I. Taunton Press.
NA7205.F56   1998   98-22937
728'.0973—dc21   CIP

Contents

Introduction   7

A Compact Timber-Frame Farmhouse   8   Broad eaves and sculpted rafter tails set the tone for this home richly detailed in the Craftsman tradition

A Cost-Conscious House in North Carolina   14   On an infill lot, this home nestles into a small forest of pines without disturbing the trees or the well-rooted neighborhood

Simple, But Not Plain   18   Traditional in form and modest in budget, this small house provides a family of four with an impressive variety of spaces

A Craftsman-Style Cottage on a Tiny Lot   24   Careful planning and a patient approach add up to a finely wrought small house

A Little House in the Big Woods   30   A roof-wide skylight brings light and drama to a small house inspired by a Pacific Northwest Indian village

A Duplex With a Rooftop Garden   36   In adding a small rental unit to an existing property, the architect applied a frugal sense of space and a playful sense of color

High Living in a Small Space   42   Indian shelters, boats and airliners inspire storage and cooling techniques in a 700-sq. ft. tower house

A Small House on a Rocky Hillside   46   An owner/builder overcomes a difficult site by digging her own foundation

Building Small and Tall   50   From its foundation made with pallets and old tires to the rooftop deck 35 ft. in the air, this house makes the most of a minimum space

Sunspace House   54   Roll up the door to the solarium, and the center of this inexpensive, energy-efficient house becomes an outdoor living room

Small House, Simple Details   58   The right details simplified construction, lowered costs and led to an elegant house that's compatible with its neighbors

A Town House Opens Up in Philadelphia   62   Larger windows and a new third floor transform an inner-city row house

A Mountain Retreat   67   A designer/builder blends curved walls and windows with traditional New England shapes and materials

Shingle Style Meets Saltbox   72   With a tower, angled bays, multiple decks and a covered porch, it's hard to believe that this rural Rhode Island home is under 1,000 sq. ft.

A Small House of Concrete Block   78   Manipulation of scale and space makes the most of a small floor plan

A Redwood Remodel   82   Meticulous trim carpentry adorns a Craftsman-style cabin with cathedral ceilings and a trellised deck

Summer Cabin in the Land O'Lakes   88   Just three months from drawing board to final finish, this house was built on an island where all of the materials had to come over by barge

A Small, Affordable House   92   A veteran builder reduces cost with a wood-post foundation, plywood siding and other surprising choices

A Romantic House   96   In this hectic, high-tech age, playful detailing and asymmetrical plans make a more comfortable home

Economical by Design   100   Architects fashion a sophisticated house with a utilitarian heart for under $77 per sq. ft.

Mango House **104** Deep roof overhangs and an open design help cool a house in the Caribbean

The House in Alice's Field **108** An architect explains why he built a small house and what he had to give up to get it

Three Buildings, One House **114** Separating the parts of a home into different buildings connects the owners to their environment

Dueling Towers on the Carolina Coast **118** Designed by different architects, each of these houses maintains its own personality within a powerful collective presence

A Little House with Rich Spaces **124** High-school students assemble an island vacation cottage with prefab panels

Steep Lot, Narrow House **128** Plaster, concrete and weathered timbers come together in a cozy California cottage

The Garage as Starter Home **132** A future guest room or rental unit, living space over the garage is an affordable alternative to a fixer-upper or an apartment

Room Enough for Two **136** At 1,200 sq. ft. and $105 per ft., this compact house has the details and variety found in much bigger homes

An Island Homestead **140** Innovative timber-framing techniques make this home feel like a big farmhouse in a compact package

Comfort and Delight on a Low Mortgage **146** How one couple got the house they wanted for less than $100,000

Avoiding Wasted Space **152** A small three-story house in upstate New York gets the most from every square foot

Index **158**

Introduction

I live in a tiny, center-chimney cape in Connecticut's Litchfield hills. My house has occupied this spot for at least 200 years. I know because the previous tenant traced its ownership back as far as 1791, where the trail of ax-blazed trees and crinkled parchment dried up.

The original house measured 18 ft. by 20 ft., which is around 600 sq. ft. when you add a cramped second-floor loft. Despite three additions and a shed dormer cobbled up over the years, the place still couldn't claim 1,000 sq. ft. when I bought it, even if you counted the front porch.

Why would anyone build such a small house? Well, 200 years ago every stick of wood in the house had to be felled, hewn, and sawn by hand. And with a central fireplace as the sole heat source, I suspect nobody wanted to be too far away from the fire.

Today, of course, we have home centers that are open from 6:00 in the morning until 10:00 at night. We have central heating and the conviction that fossil fuels will last forever. We have dual incomes and an inherent belief that bigger is better. We have real estate agents threatening us with talk of resale value, promoting more bedrooms, more-car garages, and assuring us that "you'd be crazy to build a small house on that lot."

Well, maybe we are crazy, but the editors at *Fine Homebuilding* like small houses and the intimate, cradled feeling they engender. Small houses require fewer resources to build. They're less expensive to heat, cool, and maintain. And generally speaking, we'd rather see money spent on great details than on drywall acreage.

Giving in to our predilection, we've collected here 31 articles from past issues of *Fine Homebuilding* that feature houses less than 2,000 sq. ft. Written by builders and architects from all over the country, these articles cover a diversity of styles, materials, locations, and programs. But each of them explores the central issue, which is: How do you make the most of a small space?

As for my own house, it's too small so I'm building an addition that will double its size. But, you know, it'll still be less than 2,000 sq. ft.

—*Kevin Ireton, editor*

A Compact Timber-Frame Farmhouse

Broad eaves and sculpted rafter tails set the tone for this home richly detailed in the Craftsman tradition

by Jill F. Sousa and Larry E. Johnson

Tom Wake's interest in local history turned out to be the deciding factor in the approval of his building permit. About ten years ago, Tom purchased a 22-acre parcel in Washington's Skagit Valley, overlooking Puget Sound and the San Juan Islands. His plan was eventually to build a vacation/retirement home, and during the intervening years he spent many a day talking to the locals and combing through the available literature to learn what he could about the area. In due time he came to us for help with the design.

When we were ready to begin building, we found out that the water association to which Tom was supposed to have a guaranteed hookup was in a dispute with the state Department of Health. No new buildings would be allowed until the dispute was resolved. However, the association would allow construction of a house if it was replacing one that had been demolished. We only needed to prove the existence of an original house.

In his historical digging, Tom discovered a photograph of an old farmhouse on his property that had been demolished only a few years before he bought the land. In fact, rubble from the old house and barn was still piled on the site. This evidence was all we needed to get construction back on track.

Between a rock and a wet place—Tom wasn't looking for a large house, just a comfortable space for himself, his dog and occasional guests. He wished to use local materials and local craftsmen wherever possible and had selected The Cascade Joinery from nearby Everson to timber-frame the house. As Tom's architects, we designed the house in a style that echoed the vernacular farmhouses of that area and at the same time created a house that reflected Tom's growing interest in the American Arts and Crafts movement (photo facing page).

The open nature of the lot seemed to suggest a simple grouping of farmstead forms. Tom's property is in a 100-year flood zone, and parts of it stay saturated for many months of the year. So we located the house on a raised building site as far south of the line of the driveway as possible. Tom plans to build a garage and garden shed to the north and east of the house where they will create an entry courtyard without interfering with the main views from the house.

An uncomplicated design satisfies simple requirements—Tom wanted all of the main living spaces on the ground floor, with guest accommodations and a south-facing study upstairs. Given the minimal requirements for the second floor, we chose to design a 1½-story house with a simple gable roof oriented north and south. We laid the house out as a basic structural grid with three bays running north and south (floor plans below). On the main floor the entry is in the central bay on the northern side of the house. The main living area is in the western bay to take advantage of the views of the sound and the San Juan Islands. Tom's bedroom, the main bathroom and a utility room are in the eastern bay of the first floor. The kitchen (bottom photo, p. 11) fit nicely into the central bay next to the living space facing south.

We placed the second-floor study over the kitchen and a north-facing deck over the recessed timber-frame entry porch (top photo, p. 10). The deck has a small wood-burning stove to enhance enjoyment of late-summer evenings and idyllic northwestern sunsets.

We added two large shed dormers facing east and west to expand the spaces of the second

---

Timber-frame grid simplifies the layout
The posts of the timber frame divide this house into three bays that run north and south. The rooms were designed to fit neatly into these bays.

Photos taken at lettered positions.

SPECS

Bedrooms: 2
Bathrooms: 2
Heating system: Radiant floor; electric baseboard supplement upstairs
Size: 1,670 sq. ft.
Cost: $147 per sq. ft.
Completed: 1994
Location: Blanchard, Washington

0   2   4   8 ft.   North

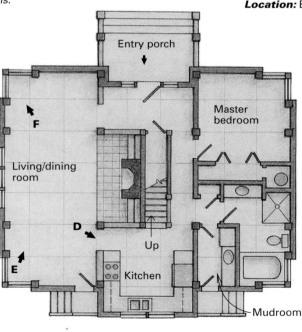

Ground floor

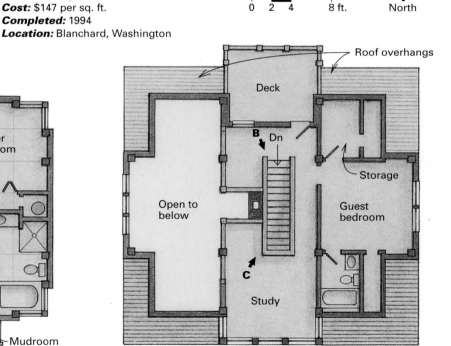

Second floor

Recessed entry sets the tone of the house. Gently curved beam ends of the timber-frame porch and deck hint at the Craftsman interior of the house. The railing on the second-floor porch echoes a theme used elsewhere in the house frame. Photo taken at A on floor plan.

Bent girts are doubled to eliminate knee braces. Doubling the bent girts, or connecting timbers, between the posts forms a type of truss system that takes the place of diagonal knee braces. The double timbers also sustain the aesthetic note started by the plates at the corners of the house. Photo taken at B on floor plan.

floor. The west-facing dormer is filled with a large two-story window (photo p. 8) that provides the main living space with an expansive view of the San Juan Islands and floods the house with light. The guest bedroom is in the east-facing dormer and enjoys natural indirect light from clerestory windows on top of the inside wall.

A massive fireplace with a chimney that reaches to the ridge is the focal point of the interior of the house (photo p. 12). The green-hued olivine stone for the fireplace and chimney was quarried in nearby British Columbia. A raised hearth finished in slate creates a small inglenook around the fireplace with shelves and display cases for Tom's burgeoning collection of hammered-copper Arts and Crafts objects. A staircase behind the fireplace leads to the second floor, where balconies look down into the inglenook as well as over the main living space and the views to the west.

Craftsman details in a timber frame—Early in the design process, we shared with Tom our library of books featuring homes of the Arts and Crafts era, in particular the works of Bernard Maybeck and the Pasadena architects Greene and Greene. Tom spent many hours walking the Berkeley, California, hills where many of Maybeck's houses are located. By the time the timber frame was ready to be cut, Tom was fully immersed in the style, and he wanted to incorporate some of the details of the period into the timber frame.

Exposed roof rafters with a decorative treatment of the rafter ends are details found throughout Craftsman-style architecture. For Tom's house we decided on a rafter-and-beam end detail that is somewhat reminiscent of the work of the Greene brothers, where the tips of the beams gradually curl up (photo p. 8). The Cascade Joinery also added this detail to the rafters where they connect to the central posts of each bent.

Many parts of Tom's timber-frame house were also inspired by the joinery of mission furniture. For example, through-tenons from corner posts penetrate the cap rail of the kneewalls that are surrounding the stairs on the second floor as well as on the half-walls that separate the entry and the kitchen from the main living space of the house (top photo, facing page). Beautifully executed open-bridle mortise-and-tenon joints were used wherever the cap rails turn a corner, and on the mantel the tenons protrude slightly with rounded ends to bring an additional Craftsman-style touch.

Corner windows mean cantilevering the main plates—The roofs of Craftsman-style homes usually feature deep overhangs, which

Top photo this page: Lani Doely

are particularly important in the Pacific Northwest, given our rainy winters. However, incorporating this detail in the house created a challenge because the stress-skin roof panels could not support themselves for the 4-ft. overhangs we wanted at the gable ends. Our solution was to support the overhanging panels on barge rafters (photo p. 13). These rafters rest on the main timber plates that cantilever beyond the walls of the house.

The solution for the overhangs was further complicated by having windows at the four major corners of the house, which meant eliminating the main timber posts typically found in the corners of a timber frame. Instead, we placed 6x6 posts on each side 4 ft. back from the corners. But the main plates, which were already cantilevering 4 ft. to support the barge rafter, would now have to cantilever a total of 8 ft. from the posts.

Mission detail in a cap rail. Through-tenons stand proud of bridal-jointed cap rail in a style reminiscent of mission furniture. Photo taken at C on floor plan.

We resolved this dilemma by doubling the main plates to give them the support they needed to cantilever 8 ft. We let the lower plate cantilever 4 ft. from the 6x6s to the actual corner of the house. There it became a corbel supporting the main upper plate that cantilevers the full 8 ft.

Jeff Arvin of The Cascade Joinery proposed separating the two plates by 8 in. and connecting them with short struts every 4 ft. The lower plate then provides a place for the second-floor floor joists to land, and the exposed upper plate acts as the baseboard. In the main living space, the double beam creates a frieze pattern that wraps around the room. The pattern is continued by the double top rail of the balcony balustrade (photo p. 12).

As a bonus, the double-plate system gives the timber frame lateral strength that allowed us to eliminate knee braces from the exterior walls. Cross bracing was incorporated between inte-

Recycled Douglas fir comes back as a kitchen. The wood used in the kitchen cabinets, window trim and timber frame itself was cut from recycled timbers. The pattern established by the window sash is continued in the panel pattern on the cabinets. Photo taken at D on floor plan.

rior posts for additional lateral strength and hidden in the stud walls. The bent girts in the second-floor gables were also doubled for extra strength (bottom photo, p. 10).

To emphasize the corners of the house, we recessed the windows on the exterior walls by the thickness of the stress-skin panels. The windows were custom-made of Douglas fir to fit between the 6x6 structural posts and a minimal 4x4 post that frames the actual corner. Each window consists of a fixed lower sash with a double-muntin awning window above. The lines of the awning windows echo the frieze pattern of the doubled plates and struts.

We interrupted the exterior plane of the frame further on the south side with a two-story bay that expands the kitchen below and the study above. On the north side of the house, the entry and the deck above are recessed, exposing the double bent girt that goes over the deck (top photo, p. 10).

Except for the south bay and the walls beneath the windows, the exterior is covered with 6-in. stress-skin panels and finished with cedar shin-

gles. On the lower walls we alternated 3-in. and 7-in. shingle courses, a pattern often seen in Craftsman-style homes. The upper coursing is straight 5-in. exposure with Arts and Crafts-inspired diamond patterns that have been woven into the gables. The walls below the corner windows, the kitchen/study bay and the north entry are clad in vertical board-and-batten sid-

ing. All of the exterior surfaces were finished with a bleaching oil that over time should weather to a driftwood color that will befit the exposed location of the house.

Concrete floors look like big leather tiles—

Initially, Tom wanted tile floors throughout the first floor, but to keep costs down, we decided on finished concrete instead. Because the house is in a flood plain, the floor level had to be at least 3 ft. above existing grade. So we had a 3-in. thick concrete slab poured on top of a double layer of ¾-in. plywood atop 2x12 floor joists. Before the concrete set up, we had a 4-ft. by 4-ft. grid pattern scored into the surface (photo facing page).

Later we colored the concrete a rich cordovan brown with an acid stain and then finished it with an acrylic sealer. An electric radiant-heating system was installed under the concrete, making the floor feel as warm as it looks. (For more on electric radiant heat, see *FHB* #75, pp. 68-72.)

Salvaged timber gets a second chance—

Tom requested that wherever possible, Douglas fir be used in building his house, not only because of its strength and rich color but also because it is the predominant local building material. Sensitive to the dwindling supply of old-growth Doug fir, we decided to use recycled timbers, in this case lumber from a huge mill being demolished in southern Washington state.

Recycled timbers are dimensionally more stable than green timbers but cost about 30% more. The recycled timbers also bear scars and stains from their previous life. But from Tom's standpoint, these minor imperfections only add to the history and character of the house. In addition to the timber frame itself, the Doug fir for the interior trim and cabinets came from the same source and was resawn at a nearby mill. □

Jill F. Sousa is an associate with and Larry E. Johnson is the principal of the Johnson Partnership, an architectural firm in Seattle. Photos by Roe A. Osborn, except where noted.

Double beams cantilever over the windows and create a decorative living-room theme. To fill the corners with windows, 6x6 posts were set 4 ft. back from the corners (photo below). A secondary plate, or beam, acts as a corbel to support the main plate and the deep roof overhangs. The double-beam pattern continues around the living room (photo facing page) and is duplicated in the balcony railing and in the lines of the windows. Photo facing page taken at E on floor plan; photo below taken at F on floor plan.

A Cost-Conscious House in North Carolina

On an infill lot, this home nestles into a small forest of pines without disturbing the trees or the well-rooted neighborhood

by Scott Neeley

Neighbors tend to take neighborhood trees seriously. Several years ago, a woman next door threatened to chain herself to the trunk of a large hackberry tree I planned to take down. The tree was centered in the only place on the narrow infill lot where the new house would fit. The woman and I later became friends, but it took her months to get over the loss of the tree.

You occasionally find similar undeveloped infill lots in old, well-rooted neighborhoods where trees form a canopy over streets. These sites are scarce, and neighbors hold them in great esteem. When such a lot came on the market in Durham, North Carolina, I jumped.

The site was full of towering loblolly-pine trees (photo facing page), and it was one of the larger green areas in this established neighborhood and had become something of a postage-stamp park. Because of the lot's place in the neighborhood, I approached the design with trepidation.

Could a new house be built within existing trees?—All of the neighbors I met on my preliminary site visits expressed concern about the

A small house in the tall pines. Although its gable rises fairly high for such a small house, the building is dwarfed by a towering stand of 90-ft. loblolly pines. Fortunately, only one tree came down to make room for the house. Photo taken at A on floor plan.

Mixing light and privacy. A high window on the east side of the house provides overhead light throughout the day. A privacy fence around the deck outside the lower windows protects the privacy of the dining room and creates a private outdoor area. Photo taken at B on floor plan.

High ceilings for the master bedroom. A western exposure and a rectangular pattern of windows in the gable wall give the master bedroom strong light, which bounces off the faceted ceiling. Photo taken at C on floor plan.

trees. Topping their list was a large 150-year-old shrub referred to variously as a grandfather's beard, a feather tree and a thunder bush. The official name is fringe tree, I learned. For a few short weeks in April and May, the tree is a stunning ball of feathery, fragrant white blossoms.

The loblolly pines, 16 in. dia. to 24 in. dia., rose to heights of about 90 ft. These trees are tall and slender with most of the branches and needles concentrated near the top. The county botanist told me that these trees have a shallow root system, and he predicted I had a 25% chance of losing a tree from construction within 6 ft.

A tall, thin house fits nicely in the pines— The 1,352-sq. ft. house I designed would be formed of two shapes: a tall, thin, two-story volume with a steeply pitched roof enclosing the bedrooms, the bathrooms and the kitchen. Adjacent to this tall gabled form hangs a shed-roofed saddlebag for the dining room (photo p. 14) and the living room (photo facing page). Positioning the living and dining rooms to the south side provided an opportunity for passive-solar strategies and allowed a framed view of the fringe tree. The tall character of the house also would reflect the visual character of the lofty pines. And fortunately, only one tree would have to come down. The footprint encompasses two offset rectangles, 12 ft. by 40 ft. and 14 ft. by 28 ft.,

running east-west (floor plan below). I calculated that a 4-ft. overhang along the south side would block high summer sun but let in low winter sun. At the front of the house, I added a porch. At the rear, a secluded deck provides an outside space.

The simplest way to create maximum volume within this small envelope was to finish the rafter bottoms, which would be simple for the large downstairs room. The ceilings follow the slope of the roof and impart a lofty feeling to a house that might feel claustrophobic with standard-height ceilings. On the second floor of the house, the bottoms of the collar ties were finished in the bedrooms to give a 12-ft. ceiling height (photo left).

Careful use of stock materials gives the house custom appeal—For an exterior skin, I chose ⅝-in. resawn-fir plywood siding with 1x2 battens at 8 in. o. c. I centered all openings with respect to the battens to produce a crisp look.

I held the eave and the rake tight to the side of the house with just enough of a projection for a strong shadowline. Along the eaves, a 2¼-in. rafter projection allowed for the continuous soffit vent and a 1x3 frieze board. T-111 siding grooved 4 in. o. c. sheathes the overhang and the front porch, where 4x4 finger-jointed fir columns support 4x6 yellow-pine beams.

SPECS

Bedrooms: 3
Bathrooms: 2
Heating system: Electric heat pump
Size: 1,352 sq. ft.
Cost: $66 per sq. ft.
Completed: 1995
Location: Durham, North Carolina

First floor

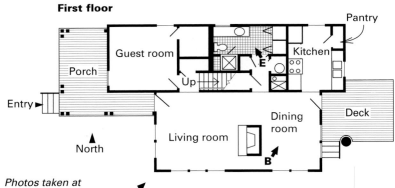

Photos taken at lettered positions.

0 2 4   8 ft.

Second floor

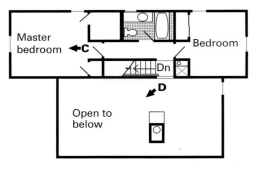

A small house that feels big. A large, open area under a shed roof comprises the living area and is punctuated only by a fireplace wall that soars to the 18-ft. ceiling. Elsewhere, rooms and ceilings are of a more modest scale, although ceilings in the master bedroom and study rise to the level of the collar ties.

Drawings: Mark Hannon

I selected white paint for the exterior of the house, but I added a small amount of gray to decrease glare. I used matte-gray spray paint to unify the chimney's base flashing, the exposed metal of a skylight and the store-bought lighting fixtures and mailbox.

Simple detailing carries over inside—I kept the inside of the house clean and simple. The tub and shower surrounds in the two bathrooms began with stock 4¼-in. square glazed ceramic tile. I chose five closely valued colors for each surround and arranged the inexpensive tile at random (bottom photo). The ¼-in. wide gray joints set off the tiles nicely.

I used the same moldings for baseboards and window and door casings. They are milled from 1x3s with a slightly stepped profile to add another shadowline to the trim. The fireplace hearth is concrete. I used a packaged-concrete mix that I reinforced with galvanized wire lath. After I stripped the forms and set the hearth in place, I mixed up a strong concentration of yellow fabric dye and brushed it onto the concrete. I then belt-sanded the concrete and applied two coats of clear paste wax to get a mottled green-gray color. ☐

Scott Neeley is an architect in Durham, North Carolina. Photos by Steve Culpepper.

Tall views of the living area. The stairway is walled off from this shed-roofed living area, except for the second-floor landing, where a frameless window opens onto the first floor. Windows on the south side of the living room frame a 150-year-old fringe tree, one of the oldest in Durham. Photo taken at D on floor plan.

Blending inexpensive tiles gives a rich look. Stock fixtures and components look lavish against the reflected image of rich ceramic tile. The ¼-in. grout lines of gray set off the five randomly mixed colors of ceramic tile in the shower surround reflected in the mirror. Photo taken at E on floor plan.

Simple, But Not Plain

Traditional in form and modest in budget, this small house provides a family of four with an impressive variety of spaces

by Ross Chapin

Susan and Rene Theberge faced a familiar dilemma when we started discussing their new house in Amherst, Massachusetts. As soon as we got around to the subject of budget, we bumped head first into the point where many a dream home has died. If the house is to be anything more than a basic box, the sq.-ft. price can get imposing pretty fast.

As an architect who specializes in small homes, I've had many clients who simply scaled back on the sizes of their houses to get costs in line. It's a good strategy, and it's the one that Susan and Rene chose to pursue. It looked like we could fit everything the family needed into 1,750 sq. ft. But designing a smaller house presents more of a challenge to the architect. The task is to serve all

of the essential requirements of the family in a house that fits its site and includes some special touches while staying within the budget—$125,000 in this case. At 1,750 sq. ft., that works out to about $72 per sq. ft.

The budget eventually rose to $87 per sq. ft. because we upgraded some finish materials and added some planters around the deck. Rising

Little gables enliven the roof. One gable roof shelters the entry while another one lets daylight into the stairwell. The diamond-shaped decoration above the window is painted MDO plywood. Photo taken at A on floor plan.

Why not have a fireplace outside? Shingle siding and a steep roof wed the house with New England tradition, but the outdoor fireplace puts a twist on the plan. This house invites outdoor entertaining. Photo taken at B on floor plan.

Bedrooms: 3
Bathrooms: 2
Heating system: Gas-forced air, woodstove
Size: 1,750 sq. ft.
Cost: $87 per sq. ft.
Completed: 1993
Location: Amherst, Massachusetts

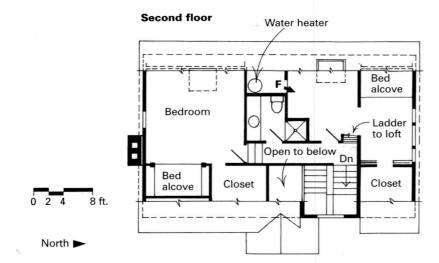

Second floor

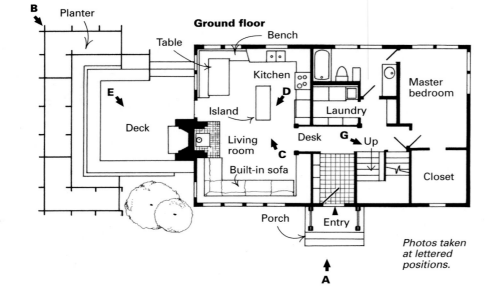

Ground floor

Photos taken at lettered positions.

A house with a fireplace deck.

The living space in this small house is doubled by the adjacent deck, which is distinguished by a dramatic outdoor fireplace. An extensive number of planters borders the deck, shielding it from the nearby road.

lumber prices added another $4,000 to the bill. But $87 is a pretty respectable sq.-ft. figure in a part of the country where construction costs are usually much higher. We kept costs down by identifying ingredients essential to the house and personalizing details where they matter most.

Pinpointing the priorities—For the house to work well, it was important that it meet the needs not just of the parents but of Stephen and Suzanne, the two teenagers in the family. Both Stephen and Suzanne needed spaces big enough for sleeping, homework and art projects, and also separate enough to entertain their different friends and to practice music (Stephen plays electric guitar). Given these activities, Mom and Dad needed a realm of their own, away from the kids. In addition, Susan needed an office for writing and study.

As they examined their daily patterns, the Theberges realized that they often hovered around the kitchen, dining table and nearby living room. They reasoned that if each family member were to have a private realm, the family as a whole would be comfortable with one large room for cooking, dining and living. This approach works because one primary room can be smaller than three separate rooms, and at the same time the primary room can leave the impression of a larger space.

After a good bit of discussion, I developed a detailed schematic design with plans and thumbnail sketches. We then met with Bill O'Bremski, the builder, to get his feedback. He gave us ballpark cost figures and suggested construction details and materials to control the cost. Though the budget was tight, it appeared that we were still in the game.

Common areas and private realms—I wanted the entry of the house to balance elegance and utility. The stairway dormer and covered porch break from the strong roofline and reach out to welcome visitors at the Theberge home (photo p. 18). The porch is large enough to provide shelter when the Theberges arrive home with bags of groceries, and for the lingering good-byes that often happen.

Inside, a wall of artwork greets you. To the immediate left of the front door, shelves, cubby-holes and assorted clothes hangers provide a place to keep order among the overcoats, backpacks and snow boots.

The heart of this house is the main room (photos facing page). It is bright and comfortable, with windows on three sides. The ceiling is 10-ft. high, with exposed beams. And a woodstove with a surrounding brick hearth and mantel is centered in the exterior wall. There are places

Drawings: Jeff Bellantuono

for most family activities to happen concurrently. While a couple of people might be around the kitchen island making food and conversation, another will be at the corner table. Still another person will be at the computer desk playing a game. Just out the door on the south side of the house is a deck with a brick fireplace/barbecue (photo p. 22).

While the main room is the center of the family life, the parents and the children each have their own private realms (floor plan, facing page). The teenagers have the whole second floor to themselves. They are separated from each other by the bathroom. Suzanne's room has a high cathedral ceiling with a skylight. Her bed is in an alcove, which keeps the rest of the room open for other activities.

Stephen's room, to the north, was going to be open to the attic loft, with Susan's study (and guest room) between the two children's rooms. During construction, this switched around. Stephen ended up with a suite of two smaller rooms (top photo, p. 23), and the study/guest room attic loft is a separate space reached by ladder from the hallway. An unplanned surprise is that the skylight in the attic fills the upper hallway with light.

Susan and Rene's bedroom on the first floor is minimal in size—a compromise to keep the overall size of the house within bounds. Large windows on two sides help open up the room. Another compromise was to share the bathroom with rest of the house.

Signature details—The form of this house is almost archetypal (photo p. 19). With its gabled roof and prominent chimney, it's the house a child might draw. It also shares a kinship with traditional New England houses—reefed in to resist severe winters and straightforward to build.

I kept the plan and the roof simple to keep construction costs down. Extraneous jogs and tricky roof planes were not even considered. The stairway dormer and the porch roof are all that break from the roof plane. All rafters spring from a common 10-ft. high plate line. The second floor is lower over the back half of the house, where the floor joists are supported on a ledger set into balloon-framed studs.

A simple building form can be brought to life by articulating its basic elements, such as windows, siding, chimney, structural beams and trim. These details don't have to cost a lot. For example, the green and white diamond ornamentation above the stairway window was made of ½-in. MDO exterior sign board. We carried the diamond theme to the accent shingles on the siding, brick ornamentation on the chimney, and to the trim at the peak of the gables. The cost of

The kitchen and living area share the same room. A 10-ft. high ceiling of criss-crossing beams and tongue-and-groove boards adds complexity to the public end of the house. The ceiling makes the room spacious, while a built-in bench (above right) and a built-in sofa (below right) take less floor space than freestanding furniture. Photos taken at C and D on floor plan.

An outdoor fireplace. The deck's center of attention is the massive brick fireplace. Held captive by a slot in the bricks, a cantilevered slab of bluestone supports the burning logs. Photo taken at E on floor plan.

the additional labor and materials to make these was minuscule.

One big element that was costly (about $6,000) was the custom-built brick chimney and Rumford-style fireplace. This is a major focus of the house, both inside and out. The brick mass surrounding the woodstove on the inside serves to temper and even out the heat. The exterior fireplace is a wonderful place to gather.

We also spent extra money in the kitchen, where the cabinets and the island counter were custom made of cherry (top photo, p. 21). Susan and Rene wanted granite counters in the kitchen, but at $40 per sq. ft. for granite slabs, the expense was out of the question. Fortunately, there was an alternative available: 1-ft. sq. granite tiles, which cost $10 per sq. ft. The resulting grout lines constitute a compromise that was easy to make.

The ceiling of the main room is higher than normal—10 ft. to the bottom of the tongue-and-groove planks. It is surprising how much this extra height adds to the spaciousness of the room. The exposed 3x4 purlins bring an interplay of light and shadow above the heavy 6x10 beams, which makes them seem lighter and higher. The beam system adds a lot of character, but it was nearly omitted because of its extra cost—$900 more than basic common joists with gypsum wallboard. And while attractive to look at, a ceiling like this transmits sound more than a conventionally joisted ceiling covered with drywall.

Storage and built-ins—For a smaller house to work well, there must be storage space. Besides having adequate closets, carefully placed built-ins make the most of a home's usable space. Built-ins mean the owners need less furniture, which frees living space. For example, the center support for the stair was framed with 2x12s and fitted with bookshelves (photo below).

In the main room, the back of the built-in sofa is framed with 2x10s, which creates a deep windowsill shelf (bottom photo, p. 21). At the opposite corner of the main room, the built-in bench in the eating corner takes up less space than a table with chairs. Before we drafted the plans for the bench and sofa, we made mockups in the studio to get the dimensions right for comfort.

Although it was planned from the start, the basement was one of the priorities that might have been axed if the budget tightened too far. It cost an additional $2,500 over the cost of a crawlspace. But besides being some of the least expensive storage, shop or studio space available, a basement cannot be added easily at a later date.

Toward the end of the project, interior designer Tina Lalonde assisted Susan and Rene with the selection of finish materials and colors, and she helped them find the best prices. One of Tina's comments about the project epitomized what can go right when a family builds a home. She recalls that Susan and Rene used the design and construction process to bring the family closer together. They involved their children in the decision making, valuing their opinions. ☐

Ross Chapin is an architect living on Whidbey Island in Puget Sound, Washington. Photos by Charles Miller.

Teenagers need room. A sloped ceiling with a big skylight is typical of the upstairs bedrooms. Instead of a single larger space, Stephen's bedroom occupies two smaller rooms, thereby separating the music studio from the study hall. Photo taken at F on floor plan.

Staircase bookshelves make good use of space. Storage is always at a premium in a small house. A bookcase in the middle of a run of stairs takes advantage of a piece of wall that often simply can go unused. Photo taken at G on floor plan.

A Craftsman-Style Cottage on a Tiny Lot

Careful planning and a patient approach add up to a finely wrought small house

by Derek Van Alstine

Harrison McCreath grew up in a beach house in Santa Cruz, California. When the house was built in 1910, it didn't overlook the yacht harbor. The harbor didn't arrive until the 1960s when the Army Corps of Engineers scooped out the nearby marsh and dug a channel to the sea. In no time the new harbor filled with sailboats, creating an irresistible scene at the heart of an already picturesque community.

Harrison McCreath and his wife, Mary, eventually inherited the little beach house. But shortly afterward, the Loma Prieta earthquake of 1989 rendered the house uninhabitable.

The McCreaths couldn't face the idea of tearing down Harrison's childhood home. So they set about to fix it. Their son Rob gutted the interior of the house. By the time the McCreaths called me, all that was left of the house was a roof, four exterior walls and a few forlorn floor joists. No doors, no interior walls, no nothing. Empty.

"We may be in over our heads," they said at our first meeting. "Can we restore our house? Can we make it bigger? Should we build a new house? Can we get permits? What will the county allow us to do on a 40-ft. by 50-ft. lot?"

Time to start over—After 15 years of designing new houses and remodeling old ones, my intuition told me that remodeling the existing house

The deck in the setback. Along the back side of the house, the 10-ft. wide space between the house and the back fence is a gallery for potted plants, vines and dwarf maple trees. The lattice crown atop the fence screens out the neighboring houses. Photo taken at A on floor plan.

would be a costly exercise that might not solve the McCreaths' needs in the long run. A new house could be larger, could take up a similar footprint and could be two stories high. A new house would, however, have to conform to current zoning standards and be set back farther from the street.

As we began to talk about designing a new Craftsman-style cottage, Mary and Harrison became excited. Their thoughts of remodeling began to disappear, and a vision of what we wanted to create began to emerge. Then reality set in as we began to negotiate the bureaucratic quagmire that is city planning, Santa Cruz style.

We first learned that the combined setbacks left a footprint of 640 sq. ft. for the house. Not only that, but the new setbacks also moved the front of the house a full 15 ft. farther into the lot from the original foundation. Incredibly, off-street parking for three vehicles had to be provided. The design had to meet the approval of the neighbors, the town planning department and the Small Craft Harbor "Special Design District." That meant the house had to fit into the neighborhood according to the subjective criteria of the planning department's urban designer.

We ran into trouble right away. Try as I might to cram a comfortable two-bedroom, two-bath house into the available space, I kept coming up

Daylight and high ceilings. A high ceiling in a big room makes a small house feel much larger than it really is. From this corner of the living room, you can see a corner of the kitchen, which is mostly screened from view by the built-in bookcase. The abundant detail is illuminated in part by the skylights and the transom windows over the French doors and the sink. Photo taken at B on floor plan.

short. The only alternative was to apply for a variance to get another 5 ft. at the back of the house and space in front for the living room's bay window and the stairway to the front door.

After two public hearings and a year of arduous discussions with the planning-department staff, we received variance approval, which increased the footprint of the house to 25 ft. by 32 ft. We had gained 160 sq. ft., and we would need every square inch of it.

Squeezing into the site—I started with the parking problem. On such a small lot the only way to get spaces for three cars would be to put one of them in the front yard, one in the driveway and one under the house. This scheme threatened to make the front of the house look like a drive-in, so I disguised the parallel-parking space in front of the stairs to look like a patio, with 3-ft. sq. concrete pavers separated by 3-in. wide strips of ground cover to soften the visual impact of the paving (photo below).

Putting a garage under the house to gain a third parking space put the house over the 25-ft. height limit. So I dug the garage into the hill, dropping the slab floor 18 in. below grade (left drawing, facing page). That move brought the ridge down below the limit. In addition to space for a car, the garage also accommodates the laundry equipment, the water heater and the forced-air furnace, thereby saving valuable space on the upper levels of the house.

The living room and the kitchen and dining area occupy a high-ceilinged space on the main

Strict compliance with a sense of style. This new shingle-style cottage in Santa Cruz, California, perches on a tiny lot while staying within the required setbacks and providing off-street parking for three vehicles. The parking space in front of the stair is paved with 3-ft. square concrete pads separated with 3-in. strips of ground cover. Photo taken at C on floor plan.

SPECS

Bedrooms: 2
Bathrooms: 2
Heating system: High-efficiency gas-forced air, plus electric in the bath
Size: 1,034 sq. ft.
Cost: $200 per sq. ft.
Completed: 1993
Location: Santa Cruz, California

Photos taken at lettered positions.

Second floor

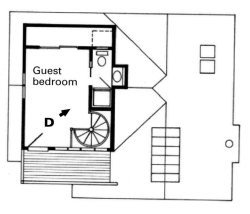

Section

Bump-out for bathroom sink

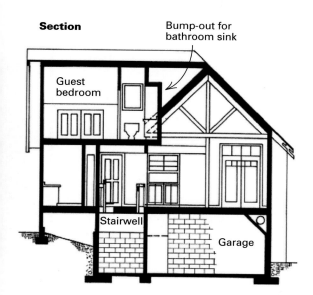

Guest bedroom

Stairwell

Garage

The bath in the guest quarters. A pocket door leads to the full bath on the upper floor. Tucked into a 3-ft. by 9-ft. slot, the bathroom gains space for the bathroom sink by notching it into the bump-out above the kitchen. Photo taken at D on floor plan.

Main floor

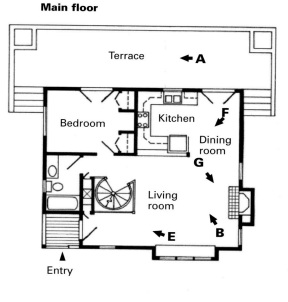

Ground floor

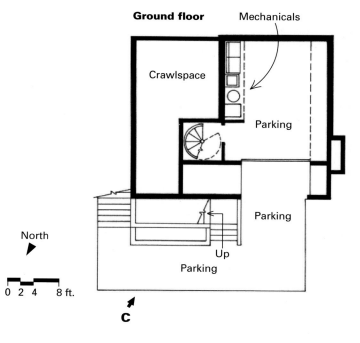

North

0 2 4 8 ft.

Finding extra space. *On a tight lot, you borrow space wherever you can find it. In this case, the author notched the garage into the site to stay within height limits. The three floors are connected by a spiral stair, which saved more than 100 sq. ft. of floor space.*

Spiraling from floor to floor. From the main floor, a spiral staircase connects with the garage and the guest bedroom. A spiral stair occupies less than half the floor space of a standard stair. Photo taken at E on floor plan.

floor (photo p. 25). The bath and one of the bedrooms take up the rest of the available space on the first floor (floor plan p. 27). The second story houses the guest bedroom and a small deck overlooking the harbor. In the backyard, the entire setback is now a terrace (photo p. 24) off the dining area.

A full bath in a pint-sized space—The McCreaths and I worked and reworked each element of the plans to be able to fit everything we wanted into the available space. We had to have a second bedroom, and the upstairs was the only place to put it. But I didn't see any way to shoehorn a bathroom into the plan. Mary insisted, however, that we find a way to include a second bath. Studying the section drawings, I realized that I could extend a soffit over the kitchen stove to provide enough space for the sink in the upstairs bathroom without encroaching on the 27 sq. ft. of floor space allotted for the bathroom. The space in front of the toilet is also the standing room in front of the lavatory and the stall shower. You enter the bathroom by way of a pocket door (photo p. 27), which keeps a swinging door out of the minimal floor space.

Because of the exposed framing below the bathroom and the no-wasted-space layout, we couldn't get ductwork for the forced-air heating system into the toespace beneath the sink.

No wasted space in the kitchen. A compact, U-shaped kitchen works behind the built-in partition in the living room. The partition includes a cavity that houses the refrigerator, and the upstairs lavatory fits into the soffit over the cooktop. The cabinets are made of vertical-grain Douglas fir. Photo taken at F on floor plan.

Layers of tile and wood. A steel fireplace insert is given the Craftsman touch with a broad border of deep green tile and a mantel of oiled Douglas fir. Photo taken at G on floor plan.

Fortunately, there are electric alternatives for just such a situation. We installed a Fahrenheat Toespace Heater to solve the problem (Marley Electric Heating Co., 470 Beauty Spot Road, Unit E, Bennettsville, S. C. 29512; 803-479-4006).

The final adjustment to get the bathroom to work was a shed dormer on the south side of the second-story roof. The dormer gave us some standing room over the toilet and a window. The result is a full bath in a minimum of space.

A spiral stair saves space—A typical stair requires a minimum of 80 sq. ft. on each floor. A spiral stair, on the other hand, takes up about 36 sq. ft. on each floor. Given that we needed to connect three floors with a staircase, using a spiral stair would save 132 sq. ft. overall while still complying with building codes. There's a catch, however. In our area, a spiral stair can be the primary stair only if it serves a living space of 400 sq. ft. or less. And because of their complicated construction and curved elements, spiral stairs also cost more than conventional staircases. The stair that we installed in this project cost about $16,000, which I figure is about double the cost of a similarly detailed conventional stair. But the spiral stair is an essential ingredient in creating a workable floor plan on all three levels, and it's a key visual element in the house (bottom photo, facing page).

Signature details—We used natural wood wherever possible, and instead of concealing steel straps, brackets and washers in trusses, we chose to highlight the hardware by painting it black. The cabinets and almost all of the millwork on the interior are kiln-dried vertical-grain Douglas fir (top photo, facing page). The trusses also are fir, and the ceilings are paneled with 1x6 red cedar. The floors in these areas are red oak. The ceilings in the master bedroom and bath are 1x4 beaded Pullman siding, painted with a satin oil-based enamel to recall the original house. Ceramic tiles surround the fireplace (photo above) and cover the kitchen countertops.

As is traditional in Craftsman houses, the windows are made of wood. The operable windows are double-hung sash. The upper lites are divided, and the lower lites are a single pane of glass.

The house is sided with cedar shingles stained driftwood gray, and windows are trimmed with clear cedar 2x4s rabbeted to accept the shingles. Head flashings on doors and windows, as well as other flashing and downspouts, are copper.

Three values of green paint add definition to various exterior details, such as the doors, the window sash and the ends of the beams and the rafter tails. Where it shows, the foundation is made of split-faced concrete block to mimic the stone foundations of the Craftsman era. In certain parts of California, there's talk of outlawing

the roof we installed. I like the cedar roof, but a dark green, three-tab asphalt shingle roof to match the green trim also would look good.

An upswept roofline—Probably the most notable design feature of this house is the sweeping eave on the front elevation (photo p. 26). I thought the house needed an unexpected line to keep it from being boxy, and I've seen similar devices used on houses with varying degrees of success. All you need is a shadowline to alter the look of a building radically. The danger is that the shadowline takes on a clumsy shape or that it looks inappropriate.

I don't like to leave such details to chance, so the crew made some plywood mockups based on the curved line that I'd drawn on the plans. Sure enough, when we tacked the mock-ups to the roof, the curve didn't look right. It had too tight a radius. So we tried a couple of other curves until we got it right. The curving fascia is composed of 2x framing lumber. It borders the eave, which is 18 in. deep. The eave, along with the adjacent bay window and inset garage door, helps break up the mass of the house and contributes greatly to its character. □

Derek Van Alstine designs and builds custom homes in Santa Cruz, California. Photos by Charles Miller.

A Little House in the Big Woods

A roof-wide skylight brings light and drama to a small house inspired by a Pacific Northwest Indian village

by Victoria Holland

A metal roof sheds leaves and pine needles. Sited close to the surrounding trees, a porch and a stone path connect the small bathhouse (left) with the main house. The steep 9-in-12 pitch helps the metal roof to shed debris. Photo taken at A on floor plan.

Peeled logs provide the framework. A sleeping loft stands over the sunken living area. A custom-fabricated skylight cuts a swath of light through the roof, brightening the vaulted interior and providing a view of the surrounding trees. Photo taken at B on floor plan.

In my childhood, I grew up in a quiet, wooded place where I became accustomed to seeking solace among great fir and cedar trees. Bellevue, Washington, has since become much busier, and although many of Bellevue's trees have been felled to make way for roads and buildings, the land my parents own there is still a refuge for me.

In 1980 I purchased a small parcel of the land, a heavily wooded site filled with cedar trees and sword ferns. For the next decade I lived in a tiny cabin there—once our playhouse—while working as a building contractor. After building houses for others and living in that tiny cabin, I finally mustered the resources to build my own home, a five-year-long process.

I knew my future house had to be an open space with a lot of light. I also wanted to capture the wonder and the sense of possibility that I had once felt as a child playing in the woods. Above all, I wanted to remain connected to nature and to explore my own ideas about materials and design. I found that considering resale value or matching neighborhood styles inhibited my creativity.

Massive logs provide both setting and structure—The traditional homes that were built by our local Native Americans were called longhouses. These longhouses had carved poles at each end that supported massive structural logs. Standing as great guardians, these poles were sources of inspiration that I drew upon for my own house.

I was also determined to set the building among the trees as unobtrusively as possible with the main siting axis following the sunlight through the clearing. Dark, gray winters in the Northwest are oppressive, and I wanted to maximize the amount of light that my house would receive.

The year before I began construction, I found four straight, tall Douglas-fir trees about 16 in. in diameter for the enveloping arms of the structure. They were cut in early July, peeled on site and then left to dry. Peeling bark with a floor scraper, or spud, is a lot easier with summer-cut logs because the dark-red cambium layer adheres much more tenaciously to the wood of fall-cut or winter-cut logs. After I let the logs dry for a year, I washed them with a bleach solution to kill a dark mold that had settled on them, giving them a beautiful silver-gray finish (photo facing page).

The rest of the building is conventionally framed around the logs. The 2x6 exterior walls are covered with 1x4 horizontal tongue-and-groove clear-cedar siding (photo left) stained

SPECS

Bedrooms: 1
Bathrooms: 1
Heating system: Propane-fired hydronic radiant floor
Size: 832 sq. ft. in main house; 220 sq. ft. in bathhouse
Cost: N/A
Completed: 1995
Location: Bellevue, Washington

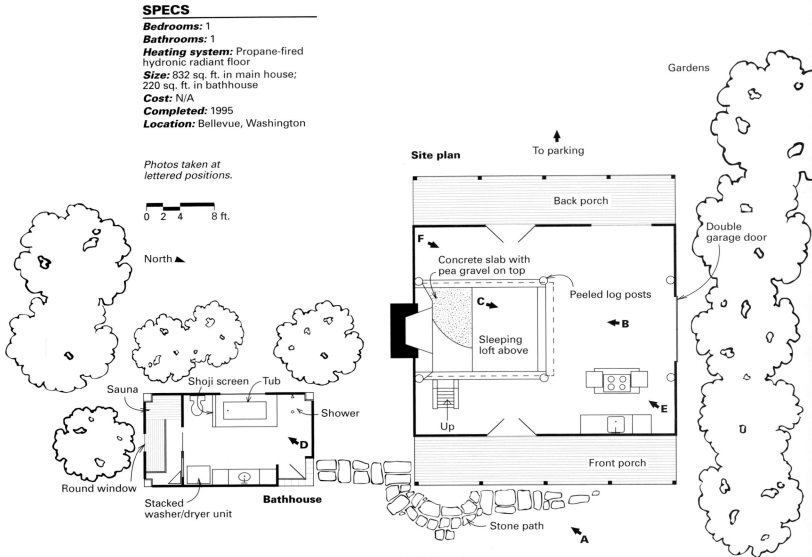

Photos taken at lettered positions.

0 2 4   8 ft.

North ▲

Site plan

To parking

Gardens

Back porch

Double garage door

F

Concrete slab with pea gravel on top

Peeled log posts

C

B

Sleeping loft above

Up

E

Front porch

Sauna   Shoji screen   Tub

Shower

D

Round window

Stacked washer/dryer unit

Bathhouse

Stone path

A

Two rooms, two buildings

Nestled among the trees, this simple home's open plan focuses on the hearth, the sunken floor in front of it and the sleeping loft above. The separate bathhouse requires a walk outdoors, reinforcing the connection with the natural world.

to match the color of aged-cedar bark on the surrounding trees.

A heated beach runs through it—Like the basic peeled-log framework, many of my other ideas for this house arose from an inspirational visit to a Kwakiutl tribal village on Vancouver Island. In native longhouse design, the raised floors along the sides are used for sleeping or private areas, and the lower central core is the communal area and fire pit.

Instead of a fire pit, I settled for a more conventional Rumford-style masonry fireplace (photo p. 31). Its shallow depth and angled sidewalls throw heat across the room, and in a power outage the fireplace can easily heat the entire building. The firebox opening is about 4 ft. high by

5 ft. wide. Although I originally intended to stucco the cinder-block chimney, I liked the understated patterns of the block so much that it remains unfinished. The line of the poured-concrete hearth continues as a horizontal wooden step around the sunken area and visually draws attention toward the fire.

Underneath the removable sunken hemlock floor in front of the fireplace is a 6-in. deep "beach" of pea gravel on top of a radiantly heated concrete slab (photo left, p. 35). In the dark of winter, the floor panels can be raised, revealing a warm beach perfect for relaxing in front of the fire.

The rest of the house, plus an adjacent bathhouse, is also heated by hydronic radiant tubing. Fed by propane-heated water, the radiant

floor offers even heat and no blower-induced drafts or noise. Beware: Don't leave Christmas gifts of chocolate on the floor under the tree!

Another therapeutic element that lifts the temperature and the spirit is the separate bathhouse and sauna (photo right, facing page). The sauna looks directly out on a great cedar tree through a round window. It is a wonderful place for reflection. There is no bathroom in the main house, which might be a real burden in a harsher climate. But I like the short walk outside and the resulting sense of ritual.

A house in the woods needs a lot of light—I originally intended to install a single 8-ft. by 7-ft. multilite garage door on the gable end opposite the fireplace. I decided that two would bring

A glass-block floor lets the light through. Mounted in a custom-fabricated 675-lb. steel grid, the glass blocks allow sunlight from the skylight above to pass through the floor of the sleeping loft and onto the living area below. Photo taken at C on floor plan.

more continuity for viewing the tall trees (photos p. 35). Stacking another fixed-panel door above the first opens that entire wall to the trees and lets in a lot more light. Less expensive than prebuilt windows, the glazed garage doors also provide the loft with a view.

In flooring the loft, I realized that it darkened the living area by blocking light from the skylight above. So I removed the wood floor and had a 5-ft. by 11-ft. steel-grid frame fabricated that would support a floor of 8-in. glass blocks (photo above left). The glass-block floor diffuses sunlight from above into a delightful, starry pattern of light and color below.

A 5-ft. wide skylight cuts a light-filled swath through the building's roof (photo p. 31). Made by Milgard Manufacturing (3800 136th St. NE,

Japanese detailing distinguishes the bath. Although located outside, the bathhouse is hardly an outhouse. A radiant slate-tile floor heats the feet, while a sauna at the far end of the bathhouse warms the body. A toilet hidden by a shoji screen and a compact washer/dryer complete the layout. Photo taken at D on floor plan.

A cast-concrete countertop completes the kitchen. Removable cantilevered cutting boards slip over the ends of the countertop and make a convenient snack area. Water stains and spots on the concrete mimic the mottled look of natural stone. Photo taken at E on floor plan.

The hemlock floor lifts to reveal a pebble beach. Three hinged floor sections allow the sunken area in front of the fireplace to be opened to the aggregate below. The warm beach is a great place to wiggle toes in front of the fire. Photos taken at F on floor plan.

Garage doors are an alternative to custom windows. Glass-paneled garage doors open the gable end to the view of the surrounding trees. The upper unit is fixed, and the lower door raises up.

Marysville, Wash. 98271; 360-659-0836) of anodized aluminum, the skylight consists of four ladderlike pieces bolted together on site. The skylight rests on a steel bar that ties the ridge boards together and is set 4 in. below the roof plane to accentuate the idea of a slice taken out of the building.

Everything—frame, attachments, supports, the screws used in securing the exterior grid bars after glazing—was electroplate-painted a brilliant magenta. Like the cosmos flowers of the same color in the garden, the bright magenta contrasts with the dark-green forest. In fact, I took a flower to the paint store for color-matching.

Once the skylight was glazed, finished and paid for, I spent the following winter under giant blue tarpaulins because I had run out of money for the roofing. But the skylight was worth every penny. It allows for less use of artificial lighting year-round. In rain, leaves or snow, the skylight provides a continuous canvas of change.

A simple design and honest materials—I wanted to avoid plastic-laminate countertops in the kitchen, so I experimented with concrete (photo facing page). I poured the tops upside down into a hardboard mold on the floor. Then my friends helped lift the 300-lb. slabs in place. I wasn't worried if the countertops didn't turn out the first time; concrete mix is cheap, and I have a sledgehammer to erase the mistakes.

I tried several sealers, but none was impervious to oil and water. After I got over the first spot, I happily watched as the marks grew into a mottled look approximating stone. ☐

_____

Victoria Holland is a designer and builder living in Bellevue, Wash. Photos by Andrew Wormer.

A Duplex With a Rooftop Garden

In adding a small rental unit to an existing property, the architect applied a frugal sense of space and a playful sense of color

by Ross Chapin

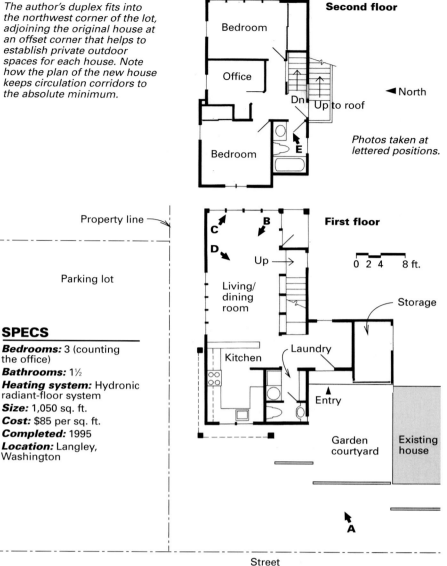

Second floor

Bedroom

Office

Dn · Up to roof

◀ North

Bedroom

E

Photos taken at lettered positions.

Property line

Parking lot

First floor

C · B

D

Up →

Living/ dining room

Storage

0 2 4 8 ft.

Kitchen

Laundry

Entry

Garden courtyard

Existing house

A

Street

SPECS

Bedrooms: 3 (counting the office)
Bathrooms: 1½
Heating system: Hydronic radiant-floor system
Size: 1,050 sq. ft.
Cost: $85 per sq. ft.
Completed: 1995
Location: Langley, Washington

A green tower. Joined at the entry, the author's duplex consists of an older remodeled house on the right and a brand new two-story dwelling on the left. The rooftop pavilion, the bump-out on the side of the house and the changes in siding patterns enliven the composition. Photo taken at A on floor plan.

340

As towns and cities become more populated, choice building sites become scarce. Yet if you have a keen eye for hidden potential, jewels are still to be found. These "sleeper" sites can pose a real design challenge, and their constraints can lead to buildings with character.

In my work as an architect on an island north of Seattle, I found an L-shaped lot with a rundown house for sale. The house was near the center of a small town, and its lot was larger than normal, equivalent to 1½ lots. Because of the denser zoning in this neighborhood, I took note that it was possible to build a duplex on the lot.

I don't consider myself a developer, but I often see the potential of a place and imagine ways to create something special. What I imagined on this property were a couple of small cottages around a shared yard, with privacy for each household. But it wasn't until I stood on the roof of the old house that I discovered the hidden jewel: a clear view over the neighboring houses

to Puget Sound, the surrounding islands and the Cascade Mountains. I was hooked.

Siting the adjoining house—My first step after the purchase was to renovate the old house (a story in itself) and get it rented. In the meantime, I dug into the paperwork necessary to put another residence on the lot.

Every site has both gifts and challenges. A successful design addresses both. On the plus side, the backyard of this property was quite lush, with several beautiful trees, including a tall, mature Chinese elm. I wanted to make every effort to preserve and highlight them. But to do this, the new house had to fit on a narrow strip just north of the old house (photo facing page). That meant the house would be hard against the site's drawbacks: a funeral-home parking lot on one side and a fairly busy street on the other.

The plan that evolved (floor plans above) is only 16 ft. wide, with an entry vestibule and a

Drawings: Jeff Bellantuono. Photo facing page: Ross Chapin

A peninsula counter screens the kitchen. The kitchen is at the west end of the house, where it overlooks a busy street. On the right, a bank of high windows over the couch lets in light, but not the view of the parking lot. Photo taken at B on floor plan.

large view of the parking lot and the funeral home, and large windows to the south would have infringed on the privacy of the original house. So I compromised with a string of high windows along the north wall of the living room, combined with the main windows on the east end of the room, next to the dining area, where they overlook the elm tree (photo facing page).

I wanted a welcoming entry that wouldn't be too exposed to the street. To accomplish this, I developed a garden courtyard with privacy fences between the two buildings and the street.

Spending money in the right places—Construction budgets are almost always tight. My situation was no different. But rather than cutting quality to bring costs down, my approach is to cut wasted, unnecessary space and keep as much quality as possible. I enjoy well-thought-out details, durable materials that age well and simple but special spaces. Of lower priority for me are the elements intended to impress others, such as formal living and dining rooms, and grand entrances.

The big-ticket item in this house is the rooftop terrace and its pavilion, which I call the Fairweather Room (top photo, p. 41). Reached by way of an outdoor staircase that runs up the side of the house, this outdoor shelter provides protection from both drizzle and sun (what little there is in the Northwest) and offers a breezy outdoor dining room that has great views. The entire structure was carefully planned to fit within the height restrictions of 25 ft. to the eaves and 30 ft. to the peak of the roof.

The Fairweather Room rated high on the "specialness factor," which brought its priority way up. I figured that it cost about $15,000 more than a simple truss-roof system. But taking the additional living area into account, it was relatively cheap space.

Keeping a building's structure simple is a fundamental way to hold down costs. Besides the fact that this little house had to fit on a narrow site, its width of 16 ft. allowed for simple joist spans, saving time and money. The walls are framed with standard height, precut 92⅝-in. studs, which saves installation effort.

I had a tough time deciding on doors and windows. I love the look and feel of natural wood, but wood windows add significantly to cost and require ongoing maintenance. Many of them use old-growth wood, a precious resource. I chose to use vinyl windows and solid fiber-core doors, which cost about half as much as their wood counterparts. What gives them substance and character is the traditionally styled, painted-composite trim (photo facing page).

I also kept the heating system simple to reduce costs. The concrete slab on the first floor is heated with a hydronic-radiant system. Because the

storage room separating the new house from the old one . This arrangement enhances the privacy that exists between the two dwellings. The structures are joined at two outside corners, which satisfies the requirement that a duplex be a continuous structure.

Strategies to make the house feel private and spacious—The living area of the house is 34 ft. long and only 12 ft. wide. The kitchen oc-

cupies the west end of this space, behind a peninsula that simultaneously helps to hide clutter while supplying much-needed counter and storage space (photo above). The living area is in the middle, and the dining table is at the south. Ordinarily, I prefer to put a bank of tall windows on the long side of a narrow room such as this one because the windows will make the room feel larger. But in this case, large windows along the north would have admitted a house is small, there is only one heating zone, requiring no manifolds or controls. The water is heated with an inexpensive 20-gal. electric water heater. As an option, a gas/solar water heater could be installed in the future. I installed electric-fan forced-air heaters on the second floor, but because the house is so well-insulated, they are rarely used. The heat from the first floor migrates upstairs.

The number of bedrooms a house has directly affects the appraisal value and rent structure. For this reason and for functional flexibility, the new duplex addition has three bedrooms. Two of them are reasonable in size; one is more like a home office.

Extracting every potentially unnecessary bit of space from a house will make it smaller, but you also run the risk of decreasing its usefulness. For example, some small houses lack storage space. I've found that storage rooms, closets and shelving are critical to the success of a small house because they allow the main spaces to be clear and functional. For this floor plan, I widened the laundry room to allow for floor-to-ceiling shelving. In a similar way, the bearing wall next to the stairway on the first floor was framed 12 in. wide to create integral shelving for books (photo p. 40). The shelf containing the stereo and TV opens into the space under the stairway, making room for their depth.

Exterior colors should suit the site and the neighborhood—Color is a significant design element and is becoming more important with the increased use of composite materials. The choices people make are often limited to shades of beige and gray. Although these colors can be beautiful, they are more often mediocre. Many more possibilities are on the palette.

Color selection is a subjective art. It takes some time to get it right, but the results can be rewarding. This was my project, and I wanted to have fun with the colors. The way I figured, if I made a mistake, I could easily paint over it.

To begin the color selection for a house, the element with the largest area is usually chosen first. Because the new house on this lot is taller than most in the neighborhood, I wanted to downplay its size with a darker color. But first I had to consider the color of the roof because those choices are limited. I found a light-gray metal roof that related well to the gray skies of the Northwest and reminded me of the old corrugated-metal roofs found on the islands. Next, I chose a dark green for the house that contrasted well with the gray roof (photo p. 36).

The vinyl windows came in two shades of white. I chose bright white because it allowed more options for color on the inside. But bright white for the exterior window trim was too harsh against dark green. I selected a light-gray trim

Creating a sense of tradition with modern, inexpensive materials. In the dining area, vinyl windows are cased with painted particleboard trim. The thin header moldings at the tops of the doors and windows are rippings from stair treads. Photo taken at C on floor plan.

color to soften the contrast while being light enough to contrast with the gray roofing.

The final color element selected should be the brightest, used in small amounts. This is the spice that brings it all alive. For this house I chose a warm shade of burnt sienna on the ornamental squares and on the exterior doors.

In the Northwest, warm interior colors counteract the gray skies—Early in the process I made a decision to use Mexican clay

tiles over the radiant-heated concrete slab and lightly whitewashed pine boards on the ceiling. These materials project a pleasant warmth that helps to neutralize our frequently gray skies. The tile floor and wood ceiling set a strong tone for the first-floor interior and gave me a place to begin selecting the wall and trim colors.

I explored varying shades of color for the walls, with white trim work to provide highlight. First, I considered warm, inviting terra-cotta hues to relate directly with the tile. These felt good in

A thick wall for plenty of storage. Framed with 2x12s, the wall between the stair and the living room is deep enough for a bookcase. The TV and stereo extend into the space beneath the stair. At parties, the carpeted stair landing serves as overflow seating. Photo taken at D on floor plan.

A great space in a surprising place. Atop the house, a gabled pavilion wraps over an open-air dining room, while most of the patio remains open to the elements. Concrete pavers bordered by planter boxes and a layer of beach stones conceal a torch-down roof membrane.

the entry and kitchen, but near the garden windows in the main room, they seemed hot. So the second approach was to look at calm greens to bring in the outside and complement the tile.

Because there aren't many south-facing windows on the first floor, I wanted to make sure there was enough daylight inside. This directed me back toward lighter off-white shades for the walls. Yet I still sensed the need for some color and contrast between the walls and the trim. After a good deal of consideration, I settled on a shade of dusty green for the trim—a definite color without being too dominant. The windowsills and doors are deeper dusty blue-green.

The carpet for the stairway and the second floor was another major element to consider. Again, beiges and browns seemed blah to me. I wanted more contrast. I found a carpet that was deep blue-green with speckles of color that matched the tile. It provided a deep base for the trim and doors. I worried some that it might darken the bedrooms too much but found that it brought in the peaceful quality that I wanted.

A bathroom with a wake-up call. Painted in boisterous patterns, the upstairs bathroom features a palette of oranges, yellows and dusky greens. Photo taken at E on floor plan.

The south-facing wall of the stairway on the backside of the bookcase comes as a surprise. It is warm yellow, which colors the reflected light that filters down the stairwell, bringing the sunlight farther into the interior of the house (photo facing page).

This color is a prelude to the bathroom, which is the real surprise (photo left). I used five different related colors from yellow to deep orange in hand-painted patterns on the walls, along with the dusty green and blue-green colors for the trim and door, black and white floor tiles, and white fixtures. There is nothing dull about it. I figured that there was no way a person could get up in the morning and not feel alive.

To paint the walls, I used a variety of brushes and a trim roller with a rough-cut edge. The patterns were planned but painted quickly to achieve a lively line quality. □

Architect Ross Chapin lives and works on Whidbey Island, Washington. Photos by Charles Miller, except where noted.

High Living in a Small Space

Indian shelters, boats and airliners inspire storage and cooling techniques in a 700-sq. ft. tower house

by Harry J. Wirth

The Indian cliff dwellers of the Southwestern United States knew how to take advantage of seasonal changes in the sun. Their shelters used natural convection for heating and cooling and were functional, beautiful and easily maintained. So when my wife and I bought 16 acres of land in Wisconsin, I wondered how to apply these principles to a modern dwelling that would have under 1,000 sq. ft. of space. Getting the most out of such a small space was something no architectural client had ever asked me to do.

After working through several designs, we thought a three-story house seemed best suited to stand among the trees on the site. The three-story design would also have the smallest footprint on the land (photos below and facing page). To free the interior of clutter, we decided to have a minimum amount of furniture; instead we'd use built-ins. Because there were no rooms —just three separate floors—all spaces would be used for many purposes.

We call the final house plan The Crow's Nest because it gives us a high shiplike lookout for bird-watching. The partially earth-bermed ground floor is 12 ft. square and houses the entrance and the utility area. The second and third

A lookout in the trees. *This Wisconsin house goes up, not out. Two 12-ft. by 24-ft. upper stories cantilever over the 12-ft.-square first floor.*

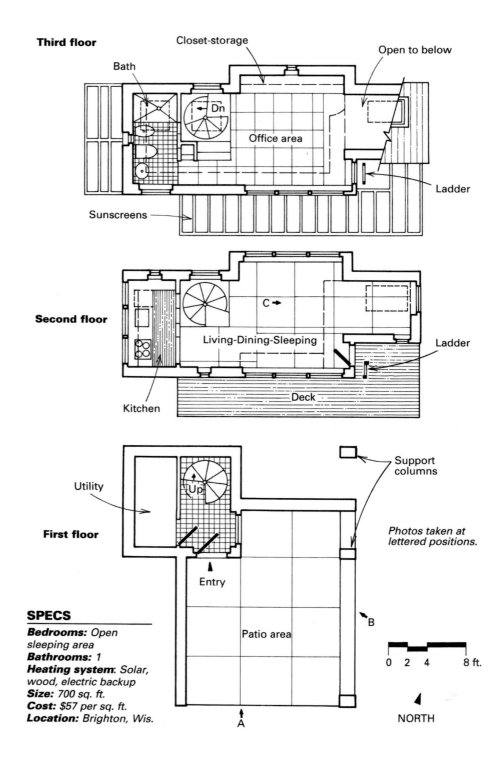

Third floor

Bath · Closet-storage · Open to below · Office area · Ladder · Sunscreens · Dn

Second floor · Living-Dining-Sleeping · Ladder · Kitchen · Deck · C →

First floor · Utility · Up · Support columns · Entry · Patio area · Photos taken at lettered positions. · B · A · NORTH

0 2 4 8 ft.

Tall, but narrow. **The design includes open living spaces inside. A roof and a patio in front of the house double as extra outdoor living spaces. Photo taken at A on floor plan.**

SPECS

Bedrooms: *Open sleeping area*
Bathrooms: *1*
Heating system: *Solar, wood, electric backup*
Size: *700 sq. ft.*
Cost: *$57 per sq. ft.*
Location: *Brighton, Wis.*

Nature provides air movement. American Indians used natural convection to cool their shelters. The author applied the same technique to his three-story tower. Yellow stanchions anchor cable railings on the first-floor deck, and floor joists on upper floors penetrate the walls to offer some shade from summer sun. Photo taken at B on floor plan.

floors are 12 ft. by 24 ft. and cantilever 12 ft. beyond the first floor on two 25-ft. long glulam beams. A galley kitchen and a general living/dining/sleeping area take up the second floor, and an office and a bath occupy the top floor (drawing p. 42). Because the interior living space totaled about 700 sq. ft., we created two outdoor living spaces that can be used year-round: a ground-level area under the cantilever and a rooftop area, complete with electrical outlets, a telephone jack and running water (photo below). We built the house for $40,000.

A roof to walk on—The installed roof trusses have a level bottom chord and a top chord that slopes ½ in. per ft. They allow 36 in. of fiberglass-batt insulation in the third-floor ceiling with 6 in. of airspace above it. The roof is vented through the north-side wall and through roof-mounted cones that are heat-welded to the roof membrane. The roof membrane is a copolymer alloy sandwiching a layer of nylon cloth (drawing below) installed over a layer of expanded polyethylene (carpet underlayment). The surface is resilient and remains supple even in winter. It's also comfortable. We sleep there in the summer and often climb to the roof to gaze at the stars or the surrounding landscape. The cones and the underlayment were provided by the roofing manufacturer (Duro-Last, Inc., 525 Morley Dr., Saginaw, Mich. 48601; 800-248-0280). The roof is accessed from the second-floor deck by two custom-made exterior ladders.

Open floor plan and built-ins—The house is small, so to avoid clutter we borrowed some ideas from boats and airliners. Storage spaces for books, blankets and collectibles were designed like overhead compartments in airliners. The 2x frames were assembled with truss plates and linked with ⅜-in. plywood floors. The assemblies were then lag-bolted to ceiling joists where wall meets ceiling and skinned with drywall. The

open bins handle a lot of material (photo facing page).

Without interior doors, all spaces become multifunctional. Spaces open on other spaces and share ceilings and vented skylights. A partial wall separates the bath area from the office, giving visual privacy but keeping the ceiling space open. Another partial wall visually separates the kitchen from the main living area. Operable skylights help eliminate dark corners. Floor joists penetrate the south and west sides of the house and create sunscreens that provide shade during summer when the sun is high and let light in during winter when the sun is low.

Detailing for comfort and energy—We selected the most energy-efficient materials and fixtures that we could find. We use two water heaters. For bathing we chose the Powerstream (Controlled Energy Corp., Fiddler's Green, Waitsfield, Vt. 05673; 802-496-4436), an electric instantaneous water heater that measures only 2 in. by 8 in. by 6 in. A standard 10-gal. electric unit delivers hot water in the kitchen.

We chose an all-electric heating design because it is simple and allows future installation of a wind generator or a photovoltaic array. The house is heated in three ways. On any sunny winter day, passive solar does the job. A double-walled woodstove on the second floor takes over on cloudy days; its 17-ft. double-walled stack extends straight up through the house.

Backup heat is provided by electric baseboard units that we concealed in the walls under the windows (drawing facing page). Two separate 2x4 walls, with a 5-in. space between them, combine to create extra-thick exterior walls. This allowed room for 12 in. of fiberglass-batt insulation and created space for the baseboard units in walls beneath windows.

Two 6-ft. openings through the first- and second-floor ceilings—one for the stove stack, the other for a spiral stair—allow natural convec-

A place for everything. Borrowing an idea from airliners, the author installed storage cabinets at the intersection of wall and ceiling to help keep clutter to a minimum. Flooring is made of ½-in. red-oak plywood squares. Angled drywall window returns help diffuse entering light. Photo taken at C on floor plan.

tion for heating and cooling. The design was inspired by the Indian tepee, which uses smoke vents at the top of its conical tent and adjustable sides to create vertical air movement for cooling. The second-floor ceiling has an electrically operated skylight, and the third-floor ceiling has two dome skylights, one directly over the three-story spiral stairwell. In summer, the skylights are opened, allowing warm air to exhaust upward. Air is drawn into the house through ground-level windows where it is cooled, then circulated upward. Even during periods of record high temperatures, that's all the cooling we need. Our total energy costs average only $40 a month.

We also applied our environmental consciousness to the bathroom, where fixtures include a low-flush, Swedish Ifö toilet that uses only ⅕ gal. per flush (Bathroom Machineries, 495 Main St., P. O. Box 1020, Murphys, Calif. 95247; 209-728-3860). Clay soils on the property did not allow a standard septic leach field, a common problem in this part of Wisconsin. So we installed a 3,000-gal. holding tank instead, which is pumped three times a year.

Finishing, inside and out—The house is sided with 6-in. clear beveled cedar, which is prefinished with weathering stain. Windows have aluminum frames and help make the house virtually maintenance-free. We specified triple-glazed Heat Mirror glass, consisting of a low-emissivity film suspended between two panes of glass

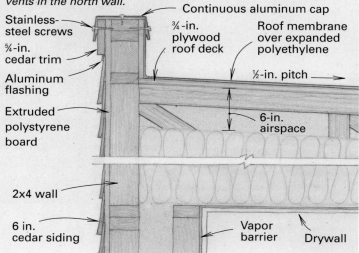

Rooftop deck. *A roof membrane of copolymer alloy sandwiching nylon cloth stays supple even in cold weather. And when installed over a layer of expanded polyethylene (carpet underlayment), the surface is comfortable enough to sleep on. A 6-in. airspace above the insulation is vented through cones on the roof and through vents in the north wall.*

Stainless-steel screws
¾-in. cedar trim
Aluminum flashing
Extruded polystyrene board
2x4 wall
6 in. cedar siding
Continuous aluminum cap
¾-in. plywood roof deck
Roof membrane over expanded polyethylene
½-in. pitch
6-in. airspace
Vapor barrier
Drywall

Room with a view. **Because interior space was limited, the roof was designed to be an extended living area. The roof has complete water, telephone and electrical service, and a flexible roof membrane remains supple and resilient, even in cold weather. Cone vents at left help ventilate space between roof sheathing and insulation.**

Drawings this page and facing page: Gary Williamson

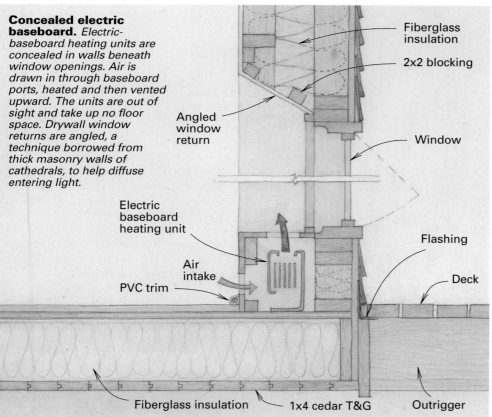

Concealed electric baseboard. *Electric-baseboard heating units are concealed in walls beneath window openings. Air is drawn in through baseboard ports, heated and then vented upward. The units are out of sight and take up no floor space. Drywall window returns are angled, a technique borrowed from thick masonry walls of cathedrals, to help diffuse entering light.*

Fiberglass insulation

2x2 blocking

Angled window return

Window

Electric baseboard heating unit

Flashing

Air intake

Deck

PVC trim

Fiberglass insulation   1x4 cedar T&G   Outrigger

(Southwall Technologies, Inc., 1029 Corporation Way, Palo Alto, Calif. 94303; 415-962-9111).

I wanted to use plain and inexpensive materials inside. We used ½-in. red-oak plywood for flooring fastened to the ½-in. CDX subfloor with drywall screws left exposed. The 2-ft. by 2-ft. plywood squares on the third floor and the 4-ft. by 4-ft. tiles on the second floor are aesthetically pleasing. And if wiring has to be altered, or if a panel is damaged, squares can be removed easily with a screwdriver. The oak is protected by three coats of gloss polyurethane. The bath-area floor is finished with 6-in. square ceramic tiles.

Baseboard and ceiling molding is actually ½-in. PVC pipe painted gray with automotive primer. Outside corners are mitered. For inside corners we glued blocks of dominoes (yes, the game pieces) into the corners, then butted the PVC pipe into that. Trim is nailed every 24 in. with 8d finish nails, and nail heads disappeared once painted. The effect is unique, soft and economical. ☐

Harry J. Wirth is a registered architect and designer and is a professor of architecture at Northern Illinois University. Photos by Eric J. Wallner

A Small House on a Rocky Hillside

An owner/builder overcomes a difficult site by digging her own foundation

by Kathleen Kenny

Twice I've been greatly affected by something I read in a magazine. First, an old *National Geographic* story about a teenaged mariner who sailed around the world provoked me to sell everything I owned, buy a sailboat with a newly found friend and sail off. For four years we cruised the South Pacific, finally returning in 1980, broke and facing the high cost of housing. Dreading the thought of a suit-and-tie, shoes-and-socks job, I temporarily settled for a barefoot, jeans-and-T-shirt job at a marina. It was there that I discovered *Fine Homebuilding* magazine. From then on, I read every issue moments after it was dropped in my mailbox, and I became convinced that I could build my own house.

So strong was this conviction that in 1983, I laid out $2,500 for a building lot in the village of Topanga Canyon, California. Topanga is a poor, but not distant, cousin to Malibu and the Pacific Palisades, where lots were selling for nearly $200,000. The lot I purchased was small and very steep, but it had a great view and was within walking distance of the town.

Six months later I enrolled at the Owner Builder Summer Camp in Nevada City, California, a school that provides five weeks of hands-on house-building experience. For about 16 hours a day I attended classes, learned about building codes, worked in shops and built a house—from the foundation to the roof, including plumbing and electrical. The most valuable thing I took home with me was confidence: I was ready to build my own home.

Three years to get a permit—The home I had in mind was a three-story, 700-sq. ft. hexagon with an attached driveway/carport, designed to fit the contours of my lot (photo above). Sectionally, the lot is a sloping two-step terrace. The top section includes a massive rock outcrop; here I planned to build the driveway/carport. Then the lot steps down 20 ft. to a relatively flat area where I planned to build the house itself.

Cliff-hanger. **Built on a canyon ledge, this owner/builder project fits the lay of the land. A carport at street level juts over a rock outcrop and joins the house at the third floor. Photo taken at A on floor plan.**

But before applying for a building permit, I was required to have a structural engineer approve the plans. My structural engineer was Kelly Wong of Engineering Design, Inc., in Santa Monica, California. I convinced Wong that my best friend, Art Starz, and I were going to do all the work ourselves. He therefore engineered a house that could be constructed on the ledge of Topanga's ancient canyon wall without the use of heavy equipment.

With plans in hand, I headed for Los Angeles County Building and Safety, secure in the knowledge that I'd soon be digging footings. How long could it take to get a permit? Two weeks? Three weeks? Try three years. My timing was bad because I applied for the permit just as L. A. County had all but stopped issuing geological approvals—part of the building-permit process—while awaiting the outcome of a law-

suit related to a landslide in Malibu. The building permit finally came through in May 1986. My spirit had survived the permitting process intact, but it was about to be tested again by the foundation.

Digging into bedrock—The foundation was built in two different phases (drawings facing page). On the lot's upper terrace, six 18-in. dia. concrete pedestal piles support the wood-frame driveway/carport. Braced above grade with reinforced concrete tie beams, pedestal piles have a spread footing—shaped like the base of a thermometer—to prevent uplift from wind and seismic forces. Because of the sloping lot, some of the pedestal piles are 10 ft. high, and all of them are at least 3 ft. into bedrock. In fact, one pile is 18 ft. below grade..

On the lower terrace of the lot, we dug trenches for a continuous-poured concrete foundation that supports the house. The foundation's 2-ft. wide steel-reinforced walls sit at least 3 ft. below grade.

But 3 ft. below grade was the exception, not the rule. Most of the excavation went deeper because both our soil engineer and our geologist wanted both the pedestal piles and the foundation trenches jackhammered 3 ft. into "competent bedrock." But competent bedrock came to mean incredibly hard granite that lies beneath a layer of sandstone. Getting to competent bedrock drove us to the brink of defeat.

We ended up buying our own jackhammer and hiring a few day workers to help us dig the trenches. We swore, dug, hauled and jackhammered every day for almost two months. Once the digging was finally finished, our help up and left, and we never saw any of them again. I can't say that I blame them.

Reinforced concrete anchors the house—Code required that our concrete withstand a magnitude-8 earthquake, so Wong engineered a steel-reinforcement system for the pedestal piles on the upper terrace and for the house foundation below. Starz and I tied all of the steel

Photo this page: Charles Miller   Drawings: Christopher Clapp

Foundation systems.

The house combines two types of foundations. Six pedestal piles braced with tie beams support the carport, while the house itself sits on a continuous-poured concrete foundation. All concrete is steel-reinforced, designed by a structural engineer to withstand a magnitude-8 earthquake.

The pedestal piles in the foreground will support a carport; in the background steel corner posts hold 4x12 rim joists. Photo taken at B on floor plan.

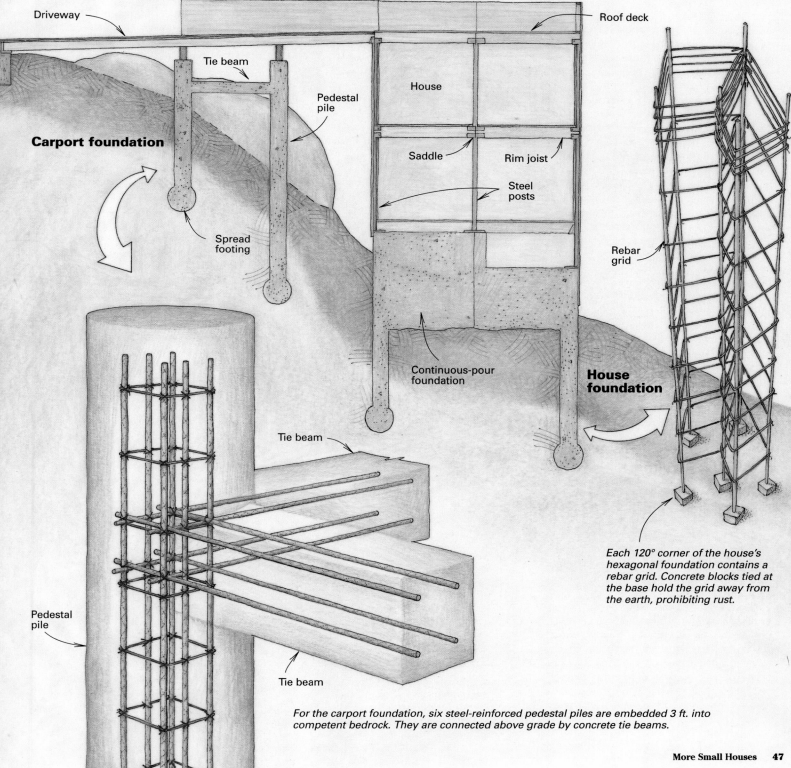

Carport

Driveway

Tie beam

Roof deck

Carport foundation

Pedestal pile

House

Saddle

Rim joist

Steel posts

Spread footing

Rebar grid

Continuous-pour foundation

House foundation

Tie beam

Pedestal pile

Tie beam

Each 120° corner of the house's hexagonal foundation contains a rebar grid. Concrete blocks tied at the base hold the grid away from the earth, prohibiting rust.

For the carport foundation, six steel-reinforced pedestal piles are embedded 3 ft. into competent bedrock. They are connected above grade by concrete tie beams.

ourselves. The pedestal piles contain vertical lengths of #7 rebar bound horizontally every 8 in. by squares of lighter #3 rebar. The steel inside the concrete tie beams, which braces the pedestal piles to one another, was also incorporated into the reinforcement system. For the house's foundation, each one of the six corners contains a massive rebar grid. Standing an average of 15 ft. tall, these grids look like scale models of the Eiffel Tower. Each rebar grid took at least one day to build.

As each rebar grid was finished, we tied a 4-in. square cement block to the bottom of every vertical piece of rebar. These blocks hold the rebar away from the earth, protecting the steel from rusting.

We got the rebar grids into the deeply excavated corners of the foundation trenches with a little help from our friends. We told three firemen we know to stop by for a beer, but as soon as they showed, we pointed to the little Eiffel Towers and asked them if they had some suggestions as to how we could get the rebar grids into place. After a bit of dragging and pulling and dropping, we had them all in. To complete the foundation's reinforcement system, all six of the cages were tied together with horizontal lengths of #3 rebar.

Placing piles and foundation—When the time came to place concrete, I did my own volume calculations, shopped for the concrete, the pumper (an independent company that pumps concrete through a hose from the truck to the forms), a deputy inspector and a laboratory. Because the piles supporting the driveway/carport required a compressive strength of 2,500 lb. per sq. in. (psi), I had to hire a concrete laboratory to work out a proper "recipe," then call it in to the concrete company. I was also required by law to retain a deputy inspector to oversee the placement of the piles. The deputy inspector, charging $80 per hour in four-hour increments, made sure that no steel was removed and that the cement went exactly where it was supposed to go. He also took numerous concrete samples throughout the job. The next day a lab representative came by and picked up the samples to test the psi strength at seven-day, 28-day and three-month intervals. The lab report showed that the piles actually have a compressive strength of 6,500 psi.

Fortunately, when it came time to pour the continuous foundation for the house, the psi requirements were low enough that we didn't need to hire a lab or a deputy inspector. We simply had to form out the foundation and place the concrete. I was so intent upon passing inspection that I took literally the county's guidelines about making sure the forms were clean. I rented

View from the roof deck. Photo taken at C on floor plan.

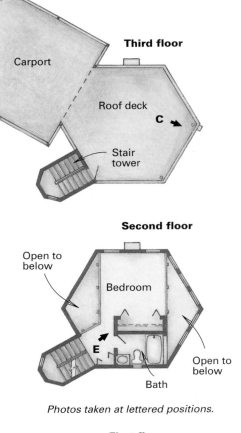

Third floor

Driveway

Carport

B ➤

Roof deck

C ➤

Stair tower

Second floor

Open to below

Bedroom

E

Open to below

Bath

Photos taken at lettered positions.

First floor

Deck

Living room

D ➤

Entry

Kitchen

A

0 2 4   8 ft.

The carport joins the house at the third-floor level, and egress is through the stair tower. The second floor is a loft, and the first-floor 2x12 joists create a cantilevered deck.

SPECS

Bedrooms: 1
Bathrooms: 1
Heating system: Direct-vent forced air
Size: 700 sq. ft.
Cost: $30,000 (materials only)
Completed: 1989
Location: Topanga, California

an industrial vacuum and got down in the foundation forms to vacuum them. The building inspector showed up while I was down there; I'm sure he thought I was crazy. But when the concrete was placed, and the forms came off, the inspector was so impressed with the foundation that he brought friends by to show off our work.

Framing the house—Engineered to be strong yet flexible, the house's framing combines steel and wood (photo p. 47). The structural heart of the house lies in its steel corner posts. The first-floor contains six steel pipes anchor-bolted to the foundation. At the top of each pipe is a saddle that carries the second-floor rim joists. All six of these 4x12 rim joists are bolted to the pipe saddles. Another set of six corner pipes for the second floor is bolted on top of the rim joists. These corner posts are tied at the top with the third-floor rim joists. After bolting all the rim joists in place, we framed each floor with 2x12s, extending the first-floor joists for a cantilevered deck. When all the framing was complete, we had what looked like a giant storage rack of steel and wood.

Although our post-and-beam house left us lots of choices for framing the walls, we opted for 2x6s throughout because we could fit more insulation between them. Two of the walls are essentially all glass and are fitted on each floor with five 8-ft. high glass doors. Elsewhere we used small, double-hung wooden windows.

The framing stage went quickly; each wall was built, lifted and then fastened to stud bolts welded to the steel corner pipes. The entire building was then sheathed with ⅜-in. plywood—some walls requiring one 8d resin-coated nail every 2 in., others requiring one nail every 6 in. The building inspector was quite particular about each nailing pattern; he showed us where we had missed three nails.

No corner boards and empty inside—What we did next was a little strange. We left the inside of the house untouched, and we completely finished the outside. We bought pump jacks for the exterior work, including the workbench, the safety rails and four support brackets. Pump jacks are a scaffolding system great for working on exterior walls. They ride up and down on poles; a foot pedal raises them, and a hand crank lowers them. We found it very easy to move from one wall to the next and loved the idea that we could pump ourselves up or down 30 ft. in just a few minutes. I must confess, though, that the odd swaying effect is unnerving, and we found only one other person willing to get on the scaffolding and stay put. Everyone else who tried it wanted off immediately. Often we were 30 ft. above the ground installing our windows, doors, siding and roof.

We sided the house with 1x6 redwood clapboards fastened with stainless-steel nails. My personal preference was not to use vertical corner boards. Instead, every course of redwood siding runs completely around the house, mitered to fit 120° corners. In addition, we color

A safe harbor. The 330-sq. ft. first floor has a large living room and a small but complete kitchen. Quarry tile covers the floor, and 8-ft. high glazed doors open onto the cantilevered deck. Note that the ceiling is open to the bedroom loft. Photo taken at D on floor plan.

coordinated every board around the house. In the end we spent far too much time up there, day after day, month after month, cutting and mitering each piece of redwood, but everyone who's seen the stratified pattern loves it.

Although I said the house's footprint is hexagonal, the southwest elevation has a horseshoe-shaped projection that contains the stair. We decided to cover its 60-sq. ft., 4-in-12 roof with standing-seam copper roofing, nicely complementing the redwood siding (Marina Sheet Metal, 5666 Selmaraine Dr., Culver City, Calif. 90230; 310-390-6682).

The roof of the house itself is actually a deck adjoining the carport (photo facing page). We devised an excellent draining system for it by ripping 20-ft. long 2x6s and then gluing and nailing these to the tops of the floor joists, resulting in a ⅜ in. per ft. slope. Decked with ¾-in. T&G, the roof is covered with EPDM membrane, a sheet of rubber, which is lapped up the parapet walls and covered by the siding. We finished off the roof with tile in a mortar bed. Two scuppers on the east wall drain into a plastic gutter.

When the outside work was finished, we had a seemingly perfect house, but the inside was an empty shell of stud walls, bottles, cans and scrap lumber. At this point we were totally burned out. It took a lot of effort to go indoors and do the electrical, the plumbing, the gas lines, the fire-sprinkler system, the kitchen and the bathroom.

Planned for expansion—By May 12, 1989, we had finished the house. Almost to the day, it had been three years since we began. It turned out to be a neat little house with about 700 sq. ft. of living space. The half-cellar (half of it you can stand in; the other half is still bedrock) contains a forced-air furnace and a pair of water-heating tanks. We regularly use the smaller 10-gal. tank and switch on the larger tank if we have overnight guests. On the first floor (floor plan facing

The bed and the head. The second floor is open on two sides. It's partitioned into a bright bedroom and a bathroom. Photo taken at E on floor plan.

page) there's a large living room with a fireplace and a small kitchen with marine appliances (top photo, this page). The second floor contains the bedroom and the bathroom and is open on two sides to the floor below (bottom photo, this page). The third floor, at this time, remains a large roof deck with a 4-ft. perimeter wall. It has been structurally engineered and designed to be roofed over and completed in the future.

Saving a bundle—I haven't added up all the receipts to determine the exact cost for the house, but for materials alone I spent close to $30,000. This house could be built for a lot less. I occasionally purchased costly materials, such as the copper roof over the stairwell section, the quarry floor tiles and the redwood siding.

On the other hand, I did a lot of shopping around and discovered that looking for a good deal is worth the time. For example, I found 6-in. by 14-in. by 20-ft. beams for the carport in the "boneyard" section of the lumberyard for $9 each. Estimates for welding the steel corner pipes ran from $100 per pipe to $200 per pipe. We used 12 pipes in the house framing and six in the carport, so shopping around saved us $1,800.

People loved looking at my always-handy photo album and were quick to give me advice on all sorts of things, including how to find things cheaply. I hung out at places like Cleveland Wrecking, a local junkyard that specializes in building-demolition leftovers, and I read the *Recycler* newspaper daily. Once I even found a solid-pine dresser lying in a ditch alongside the road. I cleaned the dresser, painted it and built it into the bedroom wall.

It's no secret that paid labor is expensive. Contractors were always stopping by, wanting to bid out one job or another. (They got my name and address from a local listing of new building permits.) We received three foundation bids, all at around $80,000; our cost was $6,000, including the purchase of a jackhammer. Someone wanted $3,800 to install a fire-sprinkler system; we installed ours in six hours, spending $350 on materials. The 200-amp electrical-system bids were around $3,200; we did the entire thing ourselves for $389. The moral is if you're on a tight budget, do the job yourself.

I should tell you, though, that building your own house has much in common—good and bad—with sailing a small, tender sailboat across thousands of miles of seas. You live life in the extremes, from fear to exhilaration, but after you've made it through this adventure, you're home in a safe harbor. □

Kathleen Kenny lives and writes in Topanga, Calif. Photos by the author except where noted.

Photos this page: Charles Miller

Building Small and Tall

From its foundation made with pallets and old tires to the rooftop deck 35 ft. in the air, this house makes the most of a minimum space

by Chris Prokosch and Shannon Green

As our tower house took shape, we heard a lot of interesting comments. The stucco contractor wanted to use the house for a deer stand, and the local building official joked that it was probably the first high rise in Floyd County. The old-timer who did the roofing said, "I couldn't live in this place; my wife would corner me up here!" But for us, a tall house made sense.

Our limited budget and our desire to minimize the disturbance to the wooded site we owned suggested a small footprint for the house we wanted to build. But in order to create enough living space, we needed three stories (top photo, facing page). The concept of building small and tall was the starting point for design as well as a benchmark for decisions during the project.

We determined that three stories would be tall enough to reach cool summer breezes and to give us a view over the treetops to surrounding ridges. At the same time we didn't want a house that blended in and disappeared meekly into its environment. Instead, we designed this house to stand in bold contrast to its surroundings. We envisioned the tower as sharp-edged and self-con-tained, with the tall, white walls of the tower forming a backdrop for the woods.

Our original plans called for a 20-ft. by 20-ft. three-story building. However, a quick study model revealed that this house would look more like a squat box than a tower.

To bring out the building's slender appearance, we raised our ceilings to 10 ft. and extended the walls above the level of the rooftop deck to form parapets. We shrank the floor area to 18 ft. by 18 ft., which gave us the smallest area we believed was livable. We also broke up the corners

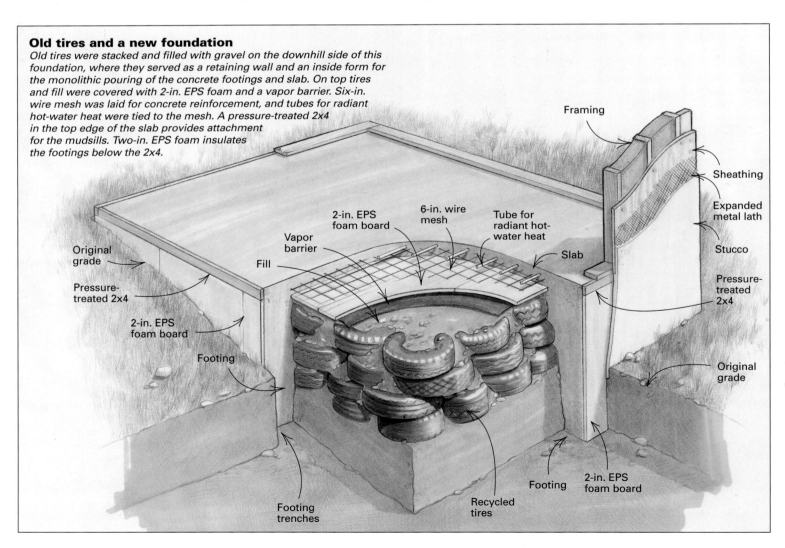

Old tires and a new foundation

Old tires were stacked and filled with gravel on the downhill side of this foundation, where they served as a retaining wall and an inside form for the monolithic pouring of the concrete footings and slab. On top tires and fill were covered with 2-in. EPS foam and a vapor barrier. Six-in. wire mesh was laid for concrete reinforcement, and tubes for radiant hot-water heat were tied to the mesh. A pressure-treated 2x4 in the top edge of the slab provides attachment for the mudsills. Two-in. EPS foam insulates the footings below the 2x4.

Framing

Sheathing

Expanded metal lath

Stucco

Pressure-treated 2x4

Original grade

2-in. EPS foam board

6-in. wire mesh

Tube for radiant hot-water heat

Slab

Vapor barrier

Original grade

Fill

Pressure-treated 2x4

2-in. EPS foam board

Footing

Footing

2-in. EPS foam board

Footing trenches

Recycled tires

Drawings: Bob La Pointe

Living on different levels. By stacking up the three levels of living spaces on a minimal footprint, this house required little clearing of the surrounding woods, which provide cool summer breezes. The house's angular shapes and clean white walls stand in stark contrast to the pastoral environment. Photo taken at A on floor plan.

Used pallets make cheap, sturdy forms. Pallets were splined together with scrap 2x4s and braced laterally for pouring the concrete. A pressure-treated 2x4 was tacked to the inside of the pallets at finished-floor level for a screed guide, and foam board kept the concrete from oozing between the pallet slats. Photo taken at B on floor plan.

Top photo: Sandy Sorlien. Bottom photo: Chris Prokosch.

More Small Houses 51

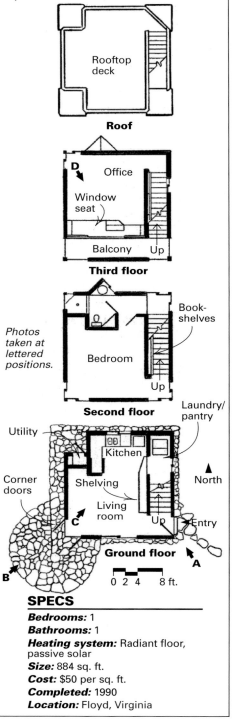

Living in layers

This house fits on a tiny 18-ft. by 18-ft. footprint, but it has four levels extending up over 35 ft. into the air.

Rooftop deck

Roof

D — Office
Window seat
Balcony — Up

Third floor

Photos taken at lettered positions.

Book-shelves
Bedroom
Up

Second floor

Laundry/pantry
Utility
Kitchen
Corner doors
Shelving
North
Living room
Up — Entry
C
B
A

Ground floor

0 2 4   8 ft.

SPECS

Bedrooms: 1
Bathrooms: 1
Heating system: Radiant floor, passive solar
Size: 884 sq. ft.
Cost: $50 per sq. ft.
Completed: 1990
Location: Floyd, Virginia

Making the most of limited space. The first floor of this house is the most social and the most active of all of the levels. The kitchen is tight but comfortable, and the laundry/pantry area is tucked conveniently under the stairs. Bookshelves hang from the beams to save floor space, and there is even a niche for the upright bass. Photo taken at C on floor plan.

of the house with doors, windows, glass block and a balcony. By drawing attention to the central 10-ft. portion of the wall that extends 35 ft. from the ground to the rooftop parapets, we enhanced the tall and narrow look of the house. After building another model and working with sections and floor plans, we were finally satisfied with the design and ready to begin building.

Recycled tires work as a hidden retaining wall and concrete form—We poured a monolithic slab and footing to get out of the ground

quickly and inexpensively. The slab also provides the thermal mass for our radiant-floor heating system. Because our site slopes to the west, we needed to add fill on the downhill side before pouring. The situation called for a temporary retaining wall that would double as the inside form for part of the footing that was above grade. We were getting rid of dozens of old tires that had found a home in a barn on our property, so we filled them with soil and gravel, and used them for our retaining wall (drawing p. 50). We topped off the fill with a vapor barrier, a layer of

EPS insulation and 6x6 wire mesh, with tubing for the hot-water radiant-heat system tied on top.

For our outside formwork we used hardwood pallets that a local industry was tossing out. We splined them together with 2x4 scraps and braced them laterally (bottom photo, p. 51). A pressure-treated 2x4 was tacked along the inside of the pallets at the height of the finished floor as a screed guide for pouring the slab. We lined the forms below the 2x4 with 2-in. EPS foam panels. After the forms were stripped, the 2x4 was left embedded in the concrete as a nailer for the

A seat, a cabinet, a stairway and a view. The multifunctional built-in along the south wall of the office makes the most of a confined space, serving as a window seat and a drawing cabinet with steps leading up to the balcony. The view through the trees makes the room feel more spacious. Wire screening required by code was added to all of the outside railings after these photos were taken. Photo taken at D on floor plan.

wall plates and door thresholds. The EPS panels bonded permanently to the footing when all of its nooks and crannies filled with concrete. Our inexpensive forms turned out to be remarkably sturdy and easy to strip, plus they gave the job site a bit of that OK Corral look.

Sweat equity pays dividends—We tried to keep within our budget by doing most of the work ourselves, with occasional help from friends and neighbors. To keep everyone's backs intact, we hired a crane to lift the beams and flooring materials to the third floor.

Besides the crane the only other things we subbed out were the excavation, the finish stucco and the metal roofing. The framing was fairly straightforward except for the added wind bracing and corner window headers (more on these later). Six-by-eight oak beams were used to carry the 2x6 tongue-and-groove yellow-pine flooring. We balloon-framed the third-floor walls and parapets, using 12-ft. 2x6s.

Stair stringers brace the outside walls—Building a tall structure in a windy area calls for lots of bracing. Builders in our area usually sheathe the corners of their walls with plywood and the rest with foam board. But because of the anticipated wind loads on the tower, we sheathed all of the exterior walls with plywood.

To allow for the open corners, vertical loads are transferred to the tall, central portions of the walls. The middle parts of the stairwell and west wall carry the floor beams and with them more than three-quarters of both the floor and roof loads. We designed built-in cantilevered corner-window headers to take care of the relatively small loads remaining.

We built these headers by letting in a layer of plywood on the inside of the framing at the corners of the house. The inner skin works with the exterior plywood sheathing to create a box beam

that is an integral part of the wall. For added peace of mind, we applied metal wind bracing diagonally to the corners.

The stairs stacked along the east wall also provide support. The outer 2x12 stringers function as large diagonal braces, and the inner stringer helps resist any twisting forces that might be applied by freak gusts of wind.

The structure was severely tested just two weeks after we moved in when Hurricane Hugo blew through with 90-mph gusts. We sat on the third floor and watched trees whipping around like seaweed in the surf. The house held steady, shivering slightly when two trees bounced off.

Exterior is low maintenance—We chose white stucco for virtually maintenance-free walls. But the day after Hurricane Hugo, we were mortified to find the pristine white-stucco walls plastered a sickly beige with Carolina silt. To our relief, it soon dried and fell off on its own accord. After five years the unpainted walls are still pure white and act like a movie screen for the tree silhouettes projected by the sun and moon.

The flat-seamed, soldered terne roof should outlast us with just an occasional coat of paint. We bolted the framing for our rooftop deck to the parapets, which eliminated roof penetrations, and we installed the decking with screws to allow access to the metal roof below. Handrails were fashioned of welded and painted steel pipe.

Each level has a different purpose—The interior of the house consists of three rooms and a rooftop deck stacked one above the other (drawing facing page). The first floor combines a comfortable kitchen and living room. We squeezed a laundry and pantry space underneath the stairs and suspended shelves for books, music and a stereo from the ceiling beams. A small niche shelters Chris' bass fiddle (photo facing page). We finished the concrete floor with epoxy paint

rated for nuclear-power plants. But the paint should have been rated for Nick, our 14-year-old hound who destroyed the finish in less than a week. Two out-swinging glass doors close perpendicular to each other to form the southwest corner of the first floor. These doors lead to a stone terrace shaded by two of the many large wild dogwoods native to the site.

The stairway to the second floor is paneled with V-groove tongue-and-groove basswood we found at a local lumber mill. The second level includes the bedroom and a bathroom with a tile and glass-block shower. We built a triangular bay nicknamed "the blip," which sticks out from the north wall of the bathroom. It houses the vanity with a small window flanked by a large mirror on the inside walls above the sink.

A second set of stairs to the third-floor office is directly above the first. We lined the walls of this stairway with oak bookshelves for our library. The office walls are paneled with basswood to provide a soft but durable surface for pinning up drawings. A window seat runs the length of the south wall beneath a 12-ft. sliding-glass door that opens onto a covered balcony (photo above). The window seat functions as a drawing cabinet, and built-in steps lead up to the level of the balcony. Outside, a third stairway connects the balcony to a secluded deck tucked inside the parapets at treetop level.

From ground floor to roof deck, the rooms in the house shift in character and function: from noisy to quiet, cool to warm (the reverse in winter), closed to open, and shady to bright. With most of the traffic and public functions on the first floor, the tower also becomes more private as one climbs farther upstairs. □

Designer/builders Chris Prokosch and Shannon Green are partners in DesignWorks Construction in Floyd, Virginia. Photos by Roe A. Osborn except where noted.

Sunspace House

Roll up the door to the solarium, and the center of this inexpensive, energy-efficient house becomes an outdoor living room

by David Hall

As much as any factor, the climate of a place influences the way the houses look. Here in the Pacific Northwest, for example, we pay particular attention to the roofs. Builders and architects have designed many a roof and awning to shelter passageways and sidewalks, and wide eaves to keep the frequent rains off the sides of the houses. And because this is a timber-rich landscape, the roofs usually are constructed out of wood. But the wide eaves (and the resulting deep rafter tails) end up stealing the light from the interior of the house.

As a result, daylight is a precious commodity in our houses. When I began designing a new home for Roger and Karen Adams, keeping the rain off the house while ensuring plentiful natural light inside was one of my priorities.

The bucks stop at $100,000—Providing plenty of daylight wasn't the only challenge. Karen and Roger had a $100,000 construction budget, period. Fortunately, we had our first design meeting before they had bought a homesite. The parcel they were considering had several obstacles, including sloping terrain and entangling ease-

Luminous eaves. The Pacific Northwestern climate can be counted on to deliver a steady diet of clouds and rain for much of the year. The translucent fiberglass eaves that border the roof keep rain from the house without plunging rooms into darkness. Purlins carry the weight of the eaves. Photo taken at A on floor plan.

ments, which would have caused an increase in the price of the house.

Roger and Karen passed on the first site, eventually settling on a long, narrow four-acre parcel on Camano Island in Washington's Puget Sound. The site is approached from the southwest, through a meadow that abuts a stand of second-growth conifers and hardwoods. To promote economy and to get as much sunlight as possible, we decided to place the house in the meadow at the forest's edge (photo facing page). The meadow occupies the flattest portion of the parcel, and it's also fairly close to the road. This kept the sitework to a minimum and the driveway within reason.

To meet a tight budget, the building's footprint and its assembly details had to be simple. To this end, I devised a rectangular floor plan of 1,150 sq. ft. I stretched it out, orienting the long side of the 20-ft. by 56-ft. plan toward the southwest (floor plan below). The layout follows a 4-ft. sq. grid. This modular theme was repeated in the floors, walls, ceilings and windows.

The plan centers around the sunspace, which lets in daylight through corrugated fiberglass roof

SPECS

Bedrooms: 1
Bathrooms: 1½
Heating system: Passive solar with propane-fired radiant heat and woodstove backup
Size: 1,150 sq. ft.
Cost: $87 per sq. ft.
Completed: 1993
Location: Camano Island, Washington

Photos taken at lettered positions.

North

0 2 4 8 ft.

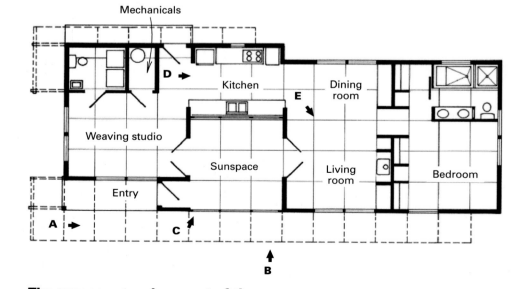

The sunspace touches most of the rooms. *Interior windows and French doors in rooms that embrace the sunroom let daylight in the house.*

Photo: David Hall. Drawing: Jeff Bellantuono

Open to the meadow. The segmented window wall of the sunspace can be retracted, creating a quasi-front porch covered with translucent corrugated fiberglass. Corrugated metal roofing continues the texture across the rest of the house. Photo taken at B on floor plan.

Photo: David Hall

panels (photo left). On clear winter days the room heats up enough just from the sun to make it a comfortable place to sit and read. The space can be opened to the outdoors by lifting the handle on the glazed overhead garage door. Open to the meadow on a warm day, the sunspace becomes the modern equivalent of the traditional front porch.

Flanking the sunspace are the living room and Karen's weaving studio. Both rooms borrow light and space from the sunroom through double French doors. The kitchen shares the third interior wall of the sunroom. A 6-ft. by 12-ft. fixed window, made from a glazed garage door, allows light from the sunroom into the kitchen (photo below). Not only does the glazed garage door carry on the look of the operable door on the exterior wall, but it also made sense economically. At $625 for the cost of the three glazed sections, the window came to $8.70 per sq. ft. A comparable custom window would have cost Karen and Roger at least $1,500.

The galley-style kitchen serves as a passageway to the back door and weaving studio. We used open shelves and drawers without traditional doors and fronts for economy and efficiency.

The living room and dining room are essentially one space with shared views of meadow and

The sunspace collects and distributes the sun's warmth. An insulated concrete slab, tinted rusty red, serves as the finished floor throughout the house. Circular, wall-mounted fans near the sunspace's ceiling convey heated air to the studio and living room by way of ducts concealed in the walls. The windows at the top can be opened to keep the room from overheating. Photo taken at C on floor plan.

The kitchen is in the middle. A galley-style kitchen overlooks the sunspace, which lets abundant light into the rest of the house. The glass wall that separates the two is composed of three sections of a segmented, glazed garage door. Traditional cabinet doors and drawer fronts were omitted purposefully to emphasize the utilitarian nature of the house. Photo taken at D on floor plan.

forest. These rooms are open to the kitchen, but they are separated from the bedroom and bath by cabinet partitions that serve as closet space on the bedroom and bath side. Concrete floors and sloped ceilings continue uninterrupted from room to room.

Heating the house—Because it acts as a buffer against the weather, the sunroom contributes to the overall energy efficiency of the house by providing protection from the harsh changes in temperature and wind. Thermostatically controlled fans near the sunspace ceiling direct the hot air that collects in the sunspace to the weaving studio and the living room by way of ductwork hidden in the walls.

The sunspace roof continues past the ridge, which makes a space for clerestory windows that let in light. Perhaps more importantly, the clerestory windows can be opened to vent the sunspace when it gets too hot to be comfortable.

In addition to the heated air from the sunspace, the solar gain through the south-facing windows falling on the insulated concrete floor further tempers the heated portions of the house. Between the solar gain and the hot air from the sunspace, the house requires no backup heating for all but a few months of the year. When it does

get cold, Roger and Karen can fire up the baseboard heaters or stoke the woodstove (photo below). The stove's location in the living room provides even heat throughout the house. And with an almost unlimited supply of alder in their backyard forest, Roger and Karen have yet to rely on the baseboard heat.

Translucent eaves, plywood walls—The eaves extend several feet beyond the walls of the house, but instead of being made of shingles, sheathing and rafters, these eaves are a lattice of galvanized steel tubes and 2x4 purlins covered with translucent fiberglass panels (photo p. 54). These fiberglass panels tuck under the corrugated-metal roofing. The overall appearance is light and airy. And by providing a galvanized steel frame for the translucent eaves, the problem of exposed wooden rafters rotting in our wet climate was eliminated.

We used 4x8 sheets of MDO plywood, which has a smooth, resin-impregnated skin, as both the sheathing and the siding on the house. Satin exterior-grade varnish protects the plywood, and cedar battens cover the vertical seams between the sheets.

Concrete floors are an opportunity to use the structure as the finish, which can keep overall

costs down. We dressed up the floors by adding a red oxide pigment to the concrete prior to placing the slab. Originally we'd imagined a smooth, hand-troweled finish. But the concrete didn't behave as predicted. A stubborn cold snap kept the concrete from setting up even though the workers tried troweling it after dark, illuminated by truck headlights. Builders Gerry and John Robbins weren't satisfied with the finished surface, so they used floor grinders to level out the slab, which revealed the colors of both the aggregate and the pigment. The result, finished with a clear acrylic sealer, is better than we'd originally hoped for.

For Roger and Karen, living the simple life in a simple house has required some adjustments. With limited living and storage space, hard decisions concerning furniture, books and other items collected over the years had to be made. A large garage sale helped to trim their possessions. But when funds permit, this homestead will start to grow again. Karen and Roger's additional plans call for a detached carport with storage space and a shop. □

Architect David Hall is a partner in the Henry Klein Partnership in Mount Vernon, Washington. Photos by Charles Miller except where noted.

Bringing down the ridge beam. A 4x12 ridge beam supports the rafters, but instead of concealing it in the roof, the architect lowered the beam to reveal the structure. The weight of the roof is conveyed to the beam by 2x4 posts, which are sandwiched by triangular particleboard gussets. Here in the living room, a woodstove provides backup heat in the winter. Photo taken at E on floor plan.

Small House, Simple Details

The right details simplified construction, lowered costs and led to an elegant house that's compatible with its neighbors

by Martha B. Finney

The mail boat to this island in Maine's Penobscot Bay pushes past a picturesque assembly of rambling houses, fish-salting shacks and simple capes, all dominated by a church that has stood as a beacon to sailors for more than 100 years. My brother Garrett and I were asked to design a simple three-bedroom house for a site immediately adjacent to this church; both the house and the church sit high on the hill in view of all who pass by. Our clients' main concern was that the house fit in and that it look from the outside as though it had been there for a hundred years. They also wanted the house to have its own character, yet not cost a fortune.

Neighboring houses yield forms and details—We began by photographing surrounding buildings to create a record of existing detail and form. The photographs set some guidelines. The majority of buildings on the island are of one or two stories and sit on stone foundations or wood

piers covered with lattice skirts. They have 4-in. clapboard siding, double-hung windows and steep gable roofs. Most have single gables, and some have shed additions. Their finishes vary from the black-brown of weathered cedar to stains and paints of all colors. Window trim, soffits, rafter tails, fascia and corner boards are predominantly white. With these elements established, we had to design a house that would melt into this context without disappearing.

The church steeple rises high above the trees. But the church itself is rather modest, and we were concerned the house would overpower it. We broke the house into a series of volumes to accomplish two things: The design would suggest that the house had grown over time, mimicking the add-on essence of its neighbors; and from the road and the water, the house would appear smaller than it actually is (1,588 sq. ft.) and, therefore, wouldn't compete in scale with the church (photo above).

The house eventually was broken into two gable-roofed sections that are connected by a lower, broken gable and extended in the rear by a single-story shed (photo facing page). We used the prevailing 12-in-12 pitch on the gables and a shallower 6-in-12 pitch on the sheds. The stairs are enclosed in a two-story tower capped off by another shed roof (right photo, p. 61). Framing the series of roofs we designed required a lot of patience and skill from the builders.

Most of the windows on the island are flat-trimmed and have true divided lites. Keeping in mind that windows affect the character of a house but that true divided lites are expensive, we used standard-size, undivided, double-hung windows and factory-milled brick mold (window trim) throughout.

Rafter tails at the eaves soften yet animate the line of the roofs. The wide, white corner boards accentuate the height of the gable ends and separate the house ever so slightly from its squatter

neighbors while marking a series of strong verticals that help unify the house.

Determining the clients' needs—For most of the year, our clients live in a spacious and airy Manhattan apartment that has distant views of the Hudson River. In the summer they move to Maine and had been living in a former salting shack (dubbed "The Cave" for its dark interiors and 6-ft. ceilings) built on pilings in Penobscot Bay. The Cave (photo facing page) has magnificent views and stacked, wraparound porches and is just down the hill from the site for the new house. The clients wanted my brother and me to give the best of both Manhattan and Maine.

Early in the design process, it became clear that the interior did not need the tight rein we were holding on the exterior. As long as the program was laid out with an eye to efficiency and as long as our clients were satisfied, the space was ours to shape.

Sun and view influence plan—On our first visit to the site, we struggled through a field of barberry bushes to reach a tree we could climb. The scratches were worth it. With every foot of elevation, the views expanded.

The northern views were the ones our clients felt most strongly about—views they didn't get from The Cave just down the hill. To capture these views we had to be as high on the hill as possible, and this location put us against the road to the church, which runs through the top of the site. For privacy, we tucked the house into the stand of pine trees that separate the site from the church to the west. For light, we took advantage of the opening the church road gave to the south and the clearing that opened to north and east.

This design allowed us to keep the house a room or a room-and-a-corridor wide so that every room but the bathrooms has at least two exposures. We were able to light time-specific activities in every room. Our clients and their guests

may eat dinner with the sunset to the west while catching glimpses of the channel. After shifting the deck all around the house on the first floor, we put it on the second floor so our clients could enjoy reading and sunning in relative privacy.

Breaking with tradition—In a traditional cape, you enter the living room or dining room, the stair is visible from the front door, the fireplace is in the middle of the house, and the bedrooms are in the loft space above. So it is in this house, although we tinkered a bit with tradition. We decided to focus our design around the two vertical elements of the house, the stair and the fireplace.

As in the traditional cape, we set the fireplace between the living room and the dining room. We chose, however, to make the fireplace the only division between these two spaces (photo p. 60). Sight lines stretch beyond their usual boundaries; all four corners of the living room/dining room are visible from the front

door. Light and air are free to circulate, but the one space suggests separate rooms.

The hearth opens into the living room. Two almost clerestory windows flank the chimney on the north wall, marking off the two sides of the great room. Windows in the main areas of the room are dropped down to ensure views for people sitting down and to give the room height.

The stair has a tower all its own, which becomes a link between floors and connects the main volume of the house to the sheds beyond. By opening the stair to the living room, we borrowed light from the second floor, which gives the great room direct light when the sun is out.

On the first floor, the stair divides the leisure spaces of the great room from the working spaces of the kitchen and office beyond. To open

everything as much as is practicable, the kitchen is connected literally and visually to the dining room with a pass-through opening in the pantry (bottom left photo, facing page).

On the second floor we added clerestory windows to light the stair and second-floor hall (top left photo, facing page). The windows are tucked into a break in the gable. Inside, the hall is filled with indirect light that adds height without taking away from the view at the end of the hall. Outside, the broken roofline acts both as a connection and a break in the volumes to create that add-on feeling.

The character of the stair and the fireplace is revealed on the deceptively traditional exterior. The straight run of the chimney is interrupted just below its cap by brickwork that steps out and

back in. The 3-in. clapboard exposure on the stair tower makes it stand out subtly from the 4-in. exposure used on the rest of the house.

Asymmetry is more interesting—In addition to breaking away from the traditional plan, my brother and I used asymmetry to lend character to the house. For instance, in the middle of the great room, the fireplace first appears to be formed by a simple arch that springs from two granite stones. On closer inspection its asymmetries are revealed. Each corner of the fireplace sits on a block of granite, and each block has a different shape with a different finish and sits on a different plane. The asymmetrical detail of the fireplace is carried out through the roof, where the chimney bows out and then backs in. We

Clean lines and good light. In the top photo, natural light enters the upstairs hallway from clerestory windows set into a break in the gable. Photo taken at D on floor plan. Clean lines and simple baseboard and baluster trim run throughout the house, as in the baseboard corner design (photo above), which simplified trim installation and adds a custom touch.

Nothing too elaborate. The simple kitchen layout goes well with the unimposing design and details of this island getaway. Photo taken at E on floor plan.

Tinkering with tradition. *Composed of two gable sections connected by a lower, broken gable (photo below taken at F on floor plan) and extended in the rear by a single-story shed, this three-bedroom house incorporates traditional features from surrounding architecture while maintaining its own identity in elements such as the second-floor sunroom and deck and dining room/living room separated by a freestanding stone-and-brick fireplace.*

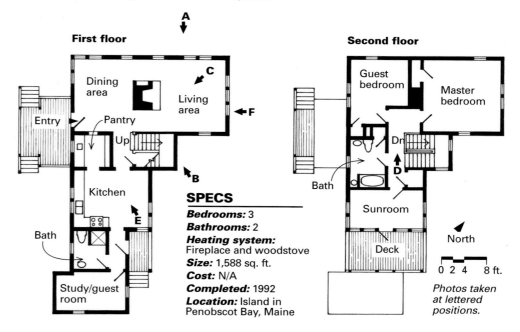

First floor

Dining area

Entry — Pantry

Living area — F

Up

Kitchen

Bath

B

E

Study/guest room

SPECS

Bedrooms: 3
Bathrooms: 2
Heating system: Fireplace and woodstove
Size: 1,588 sq. ft.
Cost: N/A
Completed: 1992
Location: Island in Penobscot Bay, Maine

Second floor

Guest bedroom

Master bedroom

Bath

Dr

D

Sunroom

Deck

North

0 2 4 8 ft.

Photos taken at lettered positions.

treated the windows and the exterior in a similar fashion. Their asymmetries draw you in and pull you around from one side of the building to the next. By the end of a trip around the house, its character is clear. It's difficult to put a finger on the center of any one side of the house. Volumes and windows work together to create the illusion of symmetry while dancing an asymmetrical jig.

Animating the simple trim—Respect for the architecture of the island, constraints of the site and cost concerns required that design details be kept simple. Working with the idea that if you look more closely you will see more, we attempted to animate that simplicity.

The railing for the stair is made of 1x1 and 1x4 stock. The solid south wall of the living room

drops off into a vertical screen of 1x1 along the stair. The railing itself, which runs just inside the screen, is composed of 1x1 balusters, a pair of 1x4 rails and a 1x4 on top.

The baseboard is 1x6 stock on the first floor and 1x4 on the second, and it is animated at each corner by a peaked tower of 1x1 stock (center left photo, above). This corner detail makes baseboard installation quicker and easier because it eliminates mitered or coped joints. On the first floor, we further dressed the trim with a standard section of beaded molding. This same section is used as crown molding throughout the house. Quarter-round shoe molding finishes it all against the painted pine flooring.

The windows and the doors are flat cased with 1x4 stock on the verticals and 5/4-in. by 6-in.

stock at the head. This construction design leaves a ¼-in. reveal that lends a delicate but clear shadowline.

Finally, we chose finishes that would age with grace. The interior walls are painted a flat China white; the trim is glossy. The pine floors are finished with deck paint, the first floor in forest green, the second floor in sea green, with the shift at the top of the stair. The exterior is stained a deep Cabot's blue, which will fade but not peel. The windows have a white factory-applied finish. The corner boards, fascia and rafter tails are stained white. □

Martha B. Finney is an architect who divides her time between Georgetown, Maine, and Philadelphia, Pennsylvania. Photos by Steve Culpepper.

Drawing: Jeff Bellantuono

A Town House
Opens up in Philadelphia

Larger windows and a new third floor transform an inner-city row house

by Tony Atkin

After buying his new house, Tom Pederson came to us with two simple requests: He wanted more space and more natural light. Not a terribly tall order, on the face of it, until you consider that the house was a tiny (11 ft. wide, 30 ft. long) two-story row house in central Philadelphia (photo facing page). Our challenge was to create flexible, open living space, to improve circulation in plan and section, and to capture plenty of natural light within the existing building. Because the house is located in a historic district, we needed to accomplish all this without substantially altering the street facade. Our approach was to open the interior space and then to break out of the existing envelope by adding a third floor (photo top right) and a small addition on the back.

The problems of limited space and light—

Built in 1752, the existing house was wedged into a small, narrow street—the garbage truck's wheels rub the curb on both sides of the street. The dark, cramped interior of the existing house was chopped up by partition walls, which made a small footprint feel still smaller. The available daylight was severely limited as well. In front, houses on the opposite side of the street are only 12 ft. away; to the rear, the backs of buildings on the next block are 18 ft. away. The house's windows admitted only a minimum amount of light. The living room and the dining room/kitchen were on the first floor, with two small bedrooms and a bathroom on the second level. Typical of row houses, the kitchen—at the back of the house—was dark and gloomy.

Designing compact additions that capture more natural light—

The ability to add to the existing house was restricted both by cost considerations and by Philadelphia zoning ordinances, so we planned to make the most of every square foot. We also envisioned both additions as collectors of much-needed natural light, in addition to providing more usable space. After researching the zoning requirements, we determined the maximum buildable area and height requirements for the site and designed a new third-floor bedroom suite with a terrace (photos right) and an 8-ft. by 9-ft. three-story wing on the back side.

On the third floor, we maximized the glass in the north and south walls because no openings were permitted by code in the other two, which are firewalls separating the row house from those on each side. We installed oversize wood double-hung windows that flood the bedroom

A third-floor addition gives the house extra room, light and a skyline view. The author designed this third-story addition to step back from street sight lines in compliance with historic-district code and to give the owner a small deck. Photo taken at B on floor plan.

Large third-floor windows help to light the lower floors. An open stairwell channels sunlight from the top floor to the rest of the house. Sliding doors hidden behind the closet at left provide privacy for the bedroom. Photo taken at C on floor plan.

Rumford fireplace adds warmth to a cozy library. The architects chose to use a Rumford-inspired fireplace in the library because the fireplace's shallow profile takes up little space and throws lots of heat. Photo taken at D on floor plan.

0   2   4   8 ft.

▲
North

Modest additions and an open stair improve the circulation of a row house. *To maximize the amount of space, the architects eliminated unnecessary partitions and added an unobtrusive third-floor addition that conformed to historic-district codes. Windows in a small addition at the rear of the house bring much-needed light to the interior.*

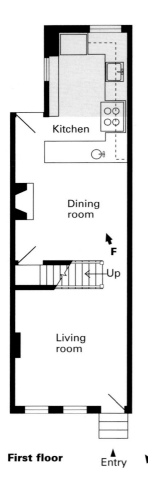

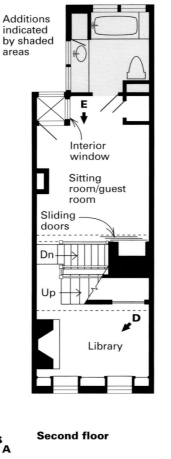

Additions indicated by shaded areas

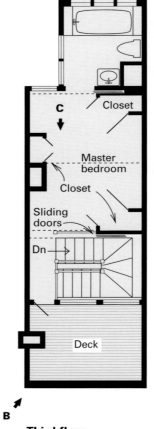

First floor   Entry ▲ ↖ A

Second floor

Third floor

SPECS

Bedrooms: 1
Bathrooms: 2
Heating system: Gas-fired hot air
Size: 1,555 sq. ft., including basement
Cost: $152 per sq. ft.
Completed: 1995
Location: Philadelphia, Pennsylvania

Photos taken at lettered positions.

Drawings: Scott Bricher

Sliding doors of sandblasted glass and fir serve as optional privacy screens. Traffic from the open stairway and library beyond can be blocked off from the second-floor sitting room, which can double as a guest room. Photo taken at E on floor plan.

suite with natural light and offer views in both directions. We used stock sizes of Marvin Magnum-grade windows (Marvin Windows and Doors, Warroad, MN 56763; 800-346-5128) in the front because their style was approved by the Philadelphia Historic Commission. We opened the ceiling to the gable roof and separated the roof from the north and south walls with clerestory windows at the eaves. We also designed an operable transom window to maximize light and to enhance air circulation. The light entering on this level also enables the stair to act as a lightwell, bringing natural light to the center of the house.

To bring much-needed light to the kitchen and dining area, we designed the smaller addition at the back of the house. The addition steps back at the northwest corner, creating a notched-out corner that is mostly glass, with six Kolbe & Kolbe double-hung wood windows joined together vertically from the first floor to the third (floor plans, p. 64).

Reinventing the character of the existing space—To start with, we decided that the living and kitchen/dining rooms should remain on the first floor. A new library, a bathroom and a sitting room that could double as a guest room would occupy the second level, leaving the master suite secluded on the third floor.

As we developed the building plan, we attempted to suggest rather than to define the living spaces. We removed all existing interior partitions—one of the few advantages of a space that's only 11 ft. wide—and limited our use of new partitions as much as possible. The first floor is free of partition walls and open front to back; the kitchen is separated from the dining area by a 36-in. high cabinet with a marble countertop (photo below). Because the kitchen is open to the living and dining areas, we worked with materials and colors that were warm and durable, yet handsome enough to complement the formal spaces. The cabinetry is natural cherry; the countertops are Tennessee pink marble.

On the second and third levels, we enclosed each bathroom with walls topped with operable transom windows. These oversize windows allow exterior light and air into the house while permitting privacy in the bathroom.

The existing stair from the first floor to the second floor had been built against a partition wall and created a visual barrier between the front and rear of the house. We removed the wall and rebuilt the stair in the same location, extending it up to the new third floor. By leaving the stair open on all levels, we created easy circulation flow vertically and horizontally, and invited views from one level to another. On each floor, the stair provides a visual delineation between spaces without actually separating them from one another.

Sliding shojilike doors of Douglas fir with sandblasted glass can separate the library from the sitting room and can give privacy to the second floor (photo p. 65). On the third floor, sliding wood screens with operable shutters work similarly to close the bedroom suite from the stair. Both sets of sliding doors used tandem roller hardware by Häfele (3901 Cheyenne Drive, Archdale, NC 27263; 800-423-3531).

Rumford fireplace is a good choice for a small library—Creative use of existing space included space-saving elements such as bookcases and storage cabinets built into the stair, two-sided corner closets in the bedroom and the incorporation of a Rumford fireplace in the library (photo p. 64). Rumford fireplaces, based on a 200-year old design originated in England by Count Rumford, are characterized by a relatively tall, shallow, straight-backed firebox with a small, rounded chimney breast. Rumfords are energy-efficient space savers and burn cleaner than traditional fireplaces, making them an ideal design for urban residential situations. After investigating Rumford-design techniques, we came up with our own version, incorporating liner components manufactured by Superior Clay Products (P. O. Box 352, Uhrichsville, OH 44683; 614-922-4122). The fireplace, detailed with painted-wood mantel and handmade tile, lends character and warmth to the room without sacrificing valuable space. □

Small 9-ft. by 8-ft. addition at the rear of the house creates a brighter kitchen space. A three-story notch above the rear door contains windows that illuminate the cherry cabinets and marble countertops of the new kitchen. Photo taken at F on floor plan.

Tony Atkin is a partner in the firm Atkin, Olshin, Lawson-Bell & Associates in Philadelphia, Pennsylvania. The project architects were John Andrews and David Bae. The builder was Hanson General Contracting of Philadelphia. Photos by Charles Bickford.

A Mountain Retreat

A designer/builder blends curved walls and windows with traditional New England shapes and materials

by Lee Stevens

The curved wall provides eastern views and southern exposure. This home's modern look is tempered with vertical siding, metal roofing with a cupola and arched windows with muntin bars, all of which create connections with New England tradition. The metal roofs, aluminum window frames and steel deck rails are painted red to contrast with the weathered gray, rough wood. Photo taken at A on floor plan.

Anyone who's been commissioned to design and build a house dreams of ideal clients, people with the least conceptions of what a house should look like, willing to focus on the functions the house serves and not fixated on details. Hank and M. J. Powell are as close as I've come to ideal clients. They're receptive to new ideas, but they consider how the idea will affect the big picture. Having worked for the Powells in the past, I was thrilled when they asked me to design and build a vacation home for them in the heart of New Hampshire's White Mountains (photo above). The site was spectacular, and my bread and butter has been designing and building additions and renovations for old houses. Almost universally, my clients have wanted innovative floor plans within exteriors that respected the conservative context of house and neighborhood. The Powells also wanted a contemporary, open floor plan in a house that looked like it belonged in New England.

After analyzing the site, however, I realized that a traditional building form, a barn or a colonial, was well-nigh impossible. The best views were to the east, yet the southern exposure was also good. The form that contained an open plan, offered views to the east and provided a southern exposure was hardly traditional: a semicircle.

Traditional tastes with untraditional requirements—In addition to an open floor plan, the Powells wanted an informal, one-room living space, big enough for a ski crowd but cozy and comfortable for two on quiet weekends. Sleeping quarters were to include a loft for a general sack-out area and a private bedroom. They also wanted a garage, several bathrooms and an entry with ski and boot racks. Rough-sawn post-and-beam construction, with a board finish throughout, was the look Hank wanted for a low-maintenance cabin atmosphere. All of this had to be wrapped within a structure that expressed a traditional New England heritage and the conservative context of the neighborhood.

We first discussed how to build a cabin on this particular site. First, the lot is high on a ridge. A small amount of level ground on the property is bounded on the west by the access road and on the east by a slope that drops sharply into the Pemigewasset River valley. The valley view dominates the entire eastern side of the lot from north to south, and I wanted to have this view.

Unfortunately, the spectacular views also meant that the site was exposed to north winds

Segmented wall, roof deck and metal fasteners simplify post-and-beam construction. The foundation is a pedestal, and the curved portion cantilevers over the foundation. It's not really a curve; the wall is made of segments that are sized to match the rough openings for Pella windows and doors. Placing a roof deck over the circular eastern elevation also simplified the roof framing. And it's not a traditional post and beam, as evidenced by the use of joist hangers instead of mortise-and-tenon joinery. Photo taken at B on floor plan.

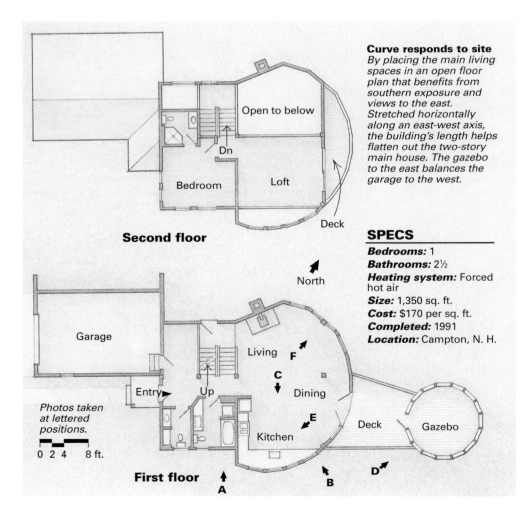

Curve responds to site
By placing the main living spaces in an open floor plan that benefits from southern exposure and views to the east. Stretched horizontally along an east-west axis, the building's length helps flatten out the two-story main house. The gazebo to the east balances the garage to the west.

Second floor

Open to below

Dn

Bedroom   Loft

Deck

Garage

North

Living   F

C

Entry ▶   Up   Dining

E

Kitchen   Deck   Gazebo

Photos taken at lettered positions.

0 2 4   8 ft.

First floor

A   B   D

SPECS

Bedrooms: 1
Bathrooms: 2½
Heating system: Forced hot air
Size: 1,350 sq. ft.
Cost: $170 per sq. ft.
Completed: 1991
Location: Campton, N. H.

that predominate in winter and to tough storms from the northeast. Although the site has excellent southern exposure, exploiting it by placing the long side of the house along the east-west axis meant the house's orientation would be perpendicular to the best views. Conversely, orienting the long side of the house along the north-south axis would mean the shorter side would face southward, minimizing solar gain. And passive solar gain is important in warming a house in winter.

Curved wall provides views and southern exposure—Knowing the site's many features and obstructions, I roughed out the basic floor plan, arranging the main living areas to take full advantage of the panoramic view and to maximize the southern exposure. I gave the kitchen the southern side to make it the lightest and brightest area in the morning. The living area took the northeast corner to focus on the most majestic feature of the valley view, Franconia Notch. The dining area looks out across the Pemigewasset valley to the east. Because the driveway is on the western side of the lot, I put the garage and the entry on this side of the house.

Wrapping all of these elements in a cohesive package seemed nearly impossible until I hit on the notion of superimposing a large semicircle on one end of a rectangular footprint (drawing left). The semicircle concentrates views on the eastern side and encompasses the living, dining and kitchen areas. The western, rectangular portion provides room for the remaining spaces.

Framing a true curve would have been a nightmare—I quickly rejected using a true curve for the semicircular wall. Not only would a true curve make for a post-and-beam nightmare, but fitting windows and doors would be a problem, too. Instead, I drew a circle, then I laid out the walls as chords of that circle. The length of the chords was based on the rough-opening dimensions of Pella French doors and similarly sized Pella double-hung windows. I chose these windows because their aluminum-clad frames would stand up to the severe weather with little or no maintenance.

The semicircular wall was relatively easy to build using post-and-beam framing. The posts at the corners of the wall segments bear on 4x10 floor joists that cantilever over a rectangular, poured-concrete foundation (photo above left). I adjusted the centerline spacing of the floor joists to coincide with the posts. Laying out the floor joists conventionally on 16-in. centers would have required that the posts be set on headers spanning between the floor joists.

Although post-and-beam construction typically uses mortise-and-tenon joinery, I chose instead to use several types of metal connectors and fasteners. These connectors made it faster and easier to build a complex shape with irregular spacing, many compound angles and a hip roof.

Windows and outbuildings achieve balance and symmetry—The greatest challenge in designing this home was to impart a sense of tradi-

Drawing: Vince Babak

tional architecture. Symmetry and balance are the hallmarks of a center-entrance colonial, but I used a subtler, less rigidly traditional form of balance for this vacation home.

An example of this approach is found in the treatment of the southern elevation (photo p. 67). Although it is not the entrance side, it is the primary elevation because it's the most visible and open to the sun. I carefully worked with the building's shape, its rooflines and its window locations until I got the gut feeling that the building was balanced. The squared west end of the elevation balances off the rounded east end because they are roughly equal in mass, and the straight rooflines of the west end lend the house a more conventional definition.

I emphasized the curved roofline by following it with four tall arch-top windows. In addition to establishing a traditional design heritage (the arch is one of the oldest building forms), the windows reinforce the semicircular design theme and soften the overall appearance of the house.

I then created a counterpoint to the arch-top windows by using four different-size double-hung windows to the left of the arch-top windows. Placing the longer windows at opposite corners, I arranged all four units around an imaginary cross axis. This window configuration subtly mirrors the four arch-top windows. Finally, the garage on the west end balances the gazebo (sidebar p.70) on the east end; together, they stretch the facade and soften the vertical aspect of the two-story section of the house.

Varying ceiling planes adds variety to an open plan—An explicit goal in this project was to have distinct areas within the overall living space and not just one big room. Each part of the space responds to different external views and light conditions and creates an internal environment appropriate to the activity there. For example, in the living area there's a huge semicircular window focusing on the stunning view to the north (bottom photo, p. 71). The shape of the window, inspired by the house's floor plan, gives a sense of enclosure and snugness. A large, square window might have felt open and cold, especially in winter.

Although the living-area window provides a view to the north, the space is laid out so that furniture focuses inward for relaxed gatherings. The cathedral ceiling increases the feeling of size and openness, but the steep roof pitch keeps the eaves low on the north side for a more human scale. The low roofline also deflects north winds and provides extra insulation because a roof section is thicker than a wall section.

A loft over the dining area results in a low ceiling and a more intimate feeling when diners are seated at the table (photo right). From the dining room, three French doors open onto a deck and provide an eastward view across the valley. Summer sunrises are a real treat from this vantage point.

Upstairs, tucked beneath an open roof frame, there are a bedroom, a bathroom and the loft. A stack of mattresses makes the loft the overflow sleeping space when a crowd shows up. From the loft, a large gliding door opens onto a little

Individualized spaces. The loft over the dining area gives it an intimate feeling within the open floor plan's cathedral ceiling. The loft bisects the tall arched windows, which are only fully visible at the kitchen counter. Photo taken at C on floor plan.

Photo this page: Rich Ziegner

A Steel Gazebo Doesn't Block the View

Early in the design process, the Powells requested a screened outdoor space that wouldn't shade the house or obstruct the views. A gazebo, rather than an attached porch, could provide the screened area, and framing it with steel would allow for the use of smaller structural members and clearer views. When you're in this gazebo, you feel like you're floating in the landscape (top photo below).

The structure is anchored to an octagonal block of concrete 4 ft. by 4 ft. by 4 ft. high, tied with steel dowels to an 8-ft. by 8-ft. by 12-in. thick, steel-reinforced concrete pad, or footing.

The gazebo and the deck it's attached to are supported by four 8-in. by 6-in. by $\frac{5}{16}$-in. thick steel columns. Large L-shaped plates welded at the base of each column fit over anchor bolts projecting from the top and sides of the concrete base.

On top of the columns, there are four steel beams arranged in a square. Steel outriggers project radially from the beams, giving the gazebo its 16-sided shape. Sixteen steel wall posts are welded to the ends of the outriggers (photo bottom left). Because the posts are so small— only 2 in. by 2 in.—they keep the structure to an absolute minimum visually.

Hanging the steel was slow and involved. We spent an 11-hour day setting the main steel with a crane, and that was only for 12 pieces. It took two more long days to install the wall posts, center rails and roof ties.

Marrying wood and steel— Though most of the gazebo is steel, the roof and the floor are pressure-treated fir and pine. Clip angles welded to the steel have holes so that the wood framework can be bolted to the steel. For example, pressure-treated 4x4s are bolted to angles on top of and underneath the steel outriggers (photo bottom right), creating a double band that supports the rough-sawn pine skirting.

The fascia boards, actually header beams, are bolted to top wing plates welded on the wall posts. From there, the 3x8 rough-sawn rafters and 2x8 tongue-and-groove roof decking are put together in a normal fashion.

Both the walls and the floor are screened. I stapled fiberglass insect screen over the 4x4 floor joists before screwing down the 5/4x6 pressure-treated southern yellow pine decking.

At the tops of the wall posts, two pairs of steel tubes at right angles to each other act as ties that keep the rafters from pushing the posts outward. The ties also serve as the support for an octagonal light fixture, which was created from rough-sawn pine and scrap roof-flashing metal.—*L. S.*

Steel posts support the roof without obstructing the view. Resting on splayed steel columns, this 16-sided gazebo provides screened outdoor space that doesn't shade the house. Photo taken at D on floor plan.

Tied to the house for more stability. Two steel beams connected to the house will support a deck. In the gazebo, wall posts are welded to outriggers, and two pairs of ties will prevent the roof from spreading the posts. The plates at the tops of the posts will carry the roof headers.

Wood is bolted to welded-on plates and clip angles. Here, the 4x4 banding provides backing for the skirt. The floor joists will be attached to the angles on top of the beams. Because the deck boards will butt into a 6-in. border, an additional inner band was necessary for fastening the flooring.

crescent of deck space. Aside from being a great place to hang out in the summer, this second-floor deck cuts off the semicircular wall.

The south-facing kitchen has the largest expanse of glass (photo right). However, the windows' considerable height is only apparent from the kitchen because the loft spans across the windows, bisecting the view in every area except right at the kitchen countertop.

Window muntins enhance a traditional look—Although they offer nice views, big panes of glass appear as vacant, staring cutouts from the exterior. Because the kitchen windows are so large, I decided to use muntin bars. Muntins divide the large expanses into small panes, recalling traditional New England architecture. However, orderly alignment of the muntins, as found in a traditional design, was impossible because each arched window in the kitchen is a different height to follow the rising eaves.

So instead of aligning the muntins, I kept the same number of panes in each window by increasing the spacing between muntins. I did the same with the bed and bath windows on the southern elevation, which are also different heights. The muntins create small panes of glass that are roughly the same size. To keep the pane sizes consistent, the bars for every window in the house, including the doors, were custom built.

As the project developed, I realized one disadvantage of the Pella units we chose: The windows' narrow frames, with no casing, have a Spartan, modern look, not at all emphasizing a traditional heritage. To solve the problem, I painted the frames—but not the sashes—barn red to match the roof panels. The narrow red frames highlight the window shapes without appearing too heavy or overbearing, and thus serve the purpose that a traditional wide casing would.

Red metal roof lends a barnlike quality—The most arresting feature of the exterior is the bright red roof. The color reminds me of a barn; the metalwork on the house is painted to match. Ribbed metal roofing, which is commonly used for barns and outbuildings, provides another reference to traditional barns. I chose this particular roofing, Ameri-Drain (American Building Components Co., 1212 E. Dominic St., Rome, N. Y. 13440; 800-544-2651), because its 6-in. rib spacing was the same as the spacing of the balusters on the metal railings and was close to the width of the vertical-board siding.

The roof pitch was originally selected to shed snow. The pitch also leaves adequate headroom for both the loft and the living area below. The steep pitch—9-in-12—conforms to the look of traditional New England farmhouses.

Late in the design stage, I added the hips on the main house. The hips are not traditional but are important because they result in an outline that ties in with the arches and the curved plan form. The hips also put a shorter wall at the entry side. A cupola capping off the roof adds summer ventilation and another traditional touch. □

Lee Stevens is a designer/builder in Nederland, Colo. Photos by the author except where noted.

Photos this page: Rich Ziegner

Large kitchen is equipped to handle a hungry ski crowd. On the south side of the curved first floor, the kitchen is a bright area. The open shelves and cabinets reinforce the house's casual atmosphere and make it easier for guests to find things. Photo taken at E on floor plan.

Custom windows view the northeast. In the living area, a dramatic curved window picks up on the home's curve theme. But the window's shape also creates a sense of snug shelter as it mimics the arch of a cave opening. Photo taken at F on floor plan.

Compact elegance. Dramatic exterior elements enhance the simple form of this New England saltbox. A strict limit on the size of the house resolved the common dilemma of producing an appealing design on a small budget. Photo taken at A on floor plan.

Shingle Style Meets Saltbox

With a tower, angled bays, multiple decks and a covered porch, it's hard to believe that this rural Rhode Island home is under 1,000 sq. ft.

by William L. Burgin

Susan and Paul are my idea of forward-thinking clients. While still engaged, they spent a large part of their savings on a 10-acre parcel of land in southern Rhode Island. They came to my office with a request to design a small, budget-conscious and appealing home for them to move into as newlyweds.

The house was to be sited to allow for a much larger family home to be built in the future. The cottage then would become a guest house. Susan, a full-time accountant, and Paul, a merchant marine who alternated four months at home and four months at sea, were to act as general contractors, supplying as much sweat equity as their schedules permitted.

Adding sugar to a saltbox—I wanted the house to have the feel of a typical New England saltbox, with one side of the roof extending farther down than the other (photo facing page). However, I broke up the roof planes and wall planes with bays and asymmetrical, angular features. These elements, combined with a hip-roofed tower and curved-porch details, give the exterior of the house a sculptural quality emblematic of the shingle-style architecture typi-

cally found in the northeastern part of the country. Unlike the usual large, rambling houses often associated with the shingle style, however, the house Susan and Paul wanted would be less than 1,000 sq. ft.

We kept the house 18 ft. wide to reduce framing spans, thereby keeping partitions to a minimum. The only interruption of the downstairs space is a nook in the kitchen that hides the refrigerator (floor plans, p. 74). A section of countertop stretches between the nook and the outside wall, forming one leg of a U-shaped kitchen (bottom photo, p. 75). From here, the cook can

SPECS

Bedrooms: 2
Bathrooms: 1½
Heating system: Electric baseboard
Size: 935 sq. ft.
Cost: $128 per sq. ft.
Completed: 1991
Location: Charlestown, Rhode Island

Photos taken at lettered positions.

0 2 4   8 ft.

◀ North

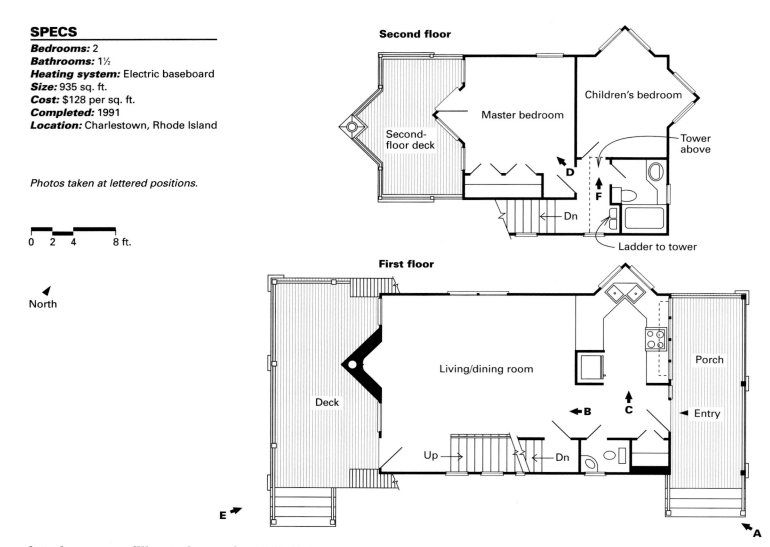

Interior spaces fill exterior angles. *With this house designed to become one day a guest cottage for a larger house, interesting features such as angled bays, dormers and bump-outs give the exterior a larger appearance. Fitting the interior layout to these features makes for interesting spaces inside.*

survey the nearby dining room and the living-room fireplace (top photo, facing page).

Exterior angles shape interior spaces—The countertop around the kitchen sink projects into a two-story sidewall bay, creating a sink alcove that helps to disguise the small galley nature of the kitchen without adding a lot of extra floor space. The angled bay also offers useful, entertaining interior features in the children's bedroom on the second floor. One corner of the room fills the bay over the kitchen sink (bottom photo, p. 77). The other corner of the angled wall juts out into a playful right-angle dormer, again creating a room that feels much larger than it really is.

On the exterior of the house, the angled bay and the dormer that form the wall of the children's bedroom are sided with medium-density

overlay plywood painted to match the trim of the house. This treatment hints at the interior spaces in the shingle-style tradition. It also intensifies the sculptural effect of the house by unifying the two separate elements and making them appear joined like a giant cube that slices through the shingled exterior.

The entire west end of the house appears to be a large stepped dormer. The rooflines on the north and south sides of the house run uninterrupted from the roof peak to the first-floor deck, wrapping around the master bedroom on the second floor and the living room on the first floor to help create the saltbox appearance (top photo, p. 77). The short side of the saltbox roof covers a porch that greets visitors through its curve-topped entryway.

French doors mounted in an angled bay in the master bedroom open onto a deck above the

living room (photo p. 76). On the first floor, another angled bay at the end of the living room houses a metal fireplace insert. Using a fireplace insert allowed us to stretch a band of windows above the fireplace across the living room. Acknowledging the honesty and economy of the metal flue, we left it exposed above the handrailing of the second-floor deck as an attractive alternative to a traditional masonry chimney.

Finding the view above the trees—Most of New England is so forested that many landowners never know what their views might be until they cut down trees and clear land. To give Susan and Paul an idea of what their distant views would look like, I fastened a camera to the top of a 25-ft. tall telescoping surveyor's rod and snapped dramatic panoramas of potential views that would be possible from their house.

Drawings this page: Mark Hannon

With this periscope I not only positioned the house for the best possible views, but I also persuaded Susan and Paul to create a treetop room to give them winter glimpses of the Rhode Island coastline. With its hip roof, the square tower unifies the complicated roof planes of the house, creating the high point both literally and figuratively (top photo, p. 77). The room provides a pleasant getaway.

To stay within Susan and Paul's budget, I produced only a rudimentary set of working drawings and limited my supervision during construction. When I prepared to visit the site after a substantial part of the construction had been completed, I had visions of a mutated design that would be a mere figment of the original plan. I figured that the design probably would be modified by cost overruns as well as the advice of well-meaning friends, and tradesmen no

A small space with a big look. The narrow width of this house meant that it could be built without interior partitions that make spaces feel more confined. A zero-clearance fireplace allows a band of windows to stretch the entire width of the room. Photo taken at B on floor plan.

An angled bay extends the kitchen. The kitchen sink fits nicely into the first floor of a two-story bay, expanding the kitchen without adding floor space. A band of under-counter windows provides natural light for kitchen workspaces. Photo taken at C on floor plan.

A French door leads to a private deck. Mounting the panels of the French door at right angles creates a bay on a bias opening onto a secluded deck off the master bedroom. Photo taken at D on floor plan.

doubt would have retailored the project to suit their needs and abilities. But my worries were unfounded. Although I had heard almost nothing from Susan and Paul during their three-year building process, I was pleasantly surprised to find the house finished almost as I had drawn it.

Susan and Paul had had the wisdom to hire Nelson Brothers Construction, one of the best and most creative crews in the area. Their superb craftsmanship showed in their execution of difficult exterior details such as curved brackets on the front porch, curved handrails and myriad intersecting rooflines. When I expressed my surprise, Paul told me that every temptation to "improve" the design had been met with the age-old mariners' call to "stay the course." □

William L. Burgin is an architect who lives and works in Newport, Rhode Island. Photos by Warren Jagger, except where noted.

A strong roofline recalls a saltbox. On the backside of the house (photo above), the roof swoops low, embracing decks on both floors. Photo taken at E on floor plan.

Playful room at the top of the bay. The upper part of the bay that houses the kitchen sink turns into an alcove in the children's bedroom (photo right). The other side of wall ends in a right-angle dormer above the porch. Photo taken at F on floor plan.

A Small House of Concrete Block

Manipulation of scale and space makes the most of a small floor plan

by Kelly Davis

If you were dreaming about building a new house, concrete block might not be your first choice for the primary building material. But then you're not Wayne and Donna Johnson. They own a company near Le Sueur, Minnesota, that supplies aggregate to local ready-mix and concrete-block companies. By choosing concrete block for their house, the Johnsons got a chance to showcase the flexibility and texture of a material that isn't the usual choice for houses in their part of the country.

I didn't need any convincing. When detailed with some sensitivity and finesse, concrete block can be elevated to a much higher aesthetic

plateau than it's usually credited with. While the Johnsons wanted a sense of boldness in the design, they didn't want the concrete to become severe. Nor did the Johnsons want a large house, and that meant their building project posed one of the greatest challenges in house design: Manipulating scale and space so that a structure feels larger than its actual dimensions would suggest. Small houses, though, have some advantages over bigger houses. Reducing the square footage of the house allowed the Johnsons to devote more of their building budget to architectural details, and a smaller house would be easier to heat, to cool and to maintain.

Making block work warm and attractive— Concrete block is the dominant material for interior and exterior walls (photo, above), and the block is exposed both outside and inside the house. Walls are actually a sandwich made of two layers of 6-in. wide concrete block with loose-fill vermiculite insulation in the block cores and a continuous layer of 2-in. isocyanurate foam insulation between (drawing, facing page).

Masonry ties set in the mortar joints every other course tie the two block walls together, and the walls are reinforced with No. 4 rebar set vertically every 4 ft. The R-value of the block walls is about 22, close to a 2x6 stud wall. To create an in-

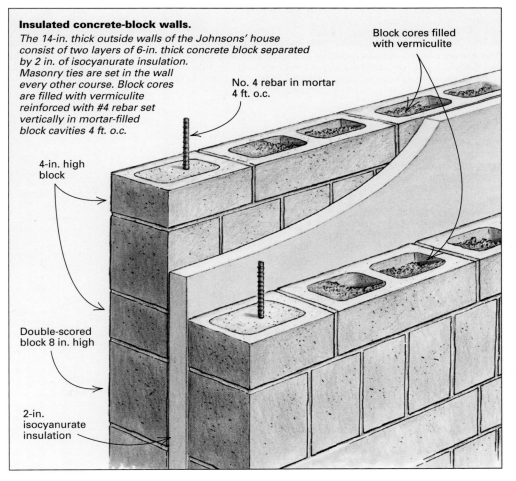

Sandblast the walls for added texture. Concrete-block walls, made more interesting by alternating 4-in. and 8-in. courses, also were sandblasted to expose the aggregate and enrich the color. Photo taken at A on floor plan.

Insulated concrete-block walls.
The 14-in. thick outside walls of the Johnsons' house consist of two layers of 6-in. thick concrete block separated by 2 in. of isocyanurate insulation. Masonry ties are set in the wall every other course. Block cores are filled with vermiculite reinforced with #4 rebar set vertically in mortar-filled block cavities 4 ft. o.c.

Block cores filled with vermiculite

No. 4 rebar in mortar 4 ft. o.c.

4-in. high block

Double-scored block 8 in. high

2-in. isocyanurate insulation

teresting pattern, I specified 4-in. and 8-in. high concrete block 16-in. long laid in alternating courses, with the 8-in. high block double-scored (a molded pattern that makes each block look as if it had two vertical mortar joints). After the block was laid up, it was sandblasted, a process that took just a couple of hours but transformed the material aesthetically. Sandblasting removes the chalky layer of surface lime from the blocks, exposing the aggregate and permanently enriching the color. Block walls are finished with two coats of clear silicone sealer.

Exterior walls on the west side of the house (photo, p. 80) are wood-framed to contrast with the concrete block. Two widths of saw-textured redwood bevel siding echo the wide and narrow concrete-block courses.

Wood to give the house warmth—Concrete also was the choice for floors in corridors and high-traffic areas inside the house, including the entry, bathrooms, kitchen, workroom and porch. The exposed-aggregate floors continue outside to form terraces.

Inside, a series of 1x4 redwood strips were set on edge in the floor before the concrete was poured. They divide the floor into 4-ft. modules on which the house was designed. The gridwork helps establish a subtle sense of rhythm and order within the building, and it is somewhat reminiscent of the pattern of tatami mats, the basic building module of traditional Japanese houses. These redwood dividers also have a practical benefit by acting as control joints to reduce cracking in the concrete.

Considering the northern climate, where winter days are short and cold, I wanted to balance the severity of the concrete-block walls and poured-concrete floors. So I used birch and redwood extensively in trim, cabinetry and siding and also used maple strip flooring in the living/dining areas. Interior spaces exude warmth and light, es-

Drawings: Dan Thornton

The living room extends outside. Choosing a natural clearing on the heavily wooded Minnesota site helped preserve oak trees while retaining walls and terraces on the west side of the house make the transition from inside to outside a smooth one. Photo taken at B on floor plan.

pecially during winter months when trees have lost their leaves and no longer shade the house. Carpeted floors in the bedrooms, neutral-colored gypsum-board walls and ceilings with redwood battens complete the palette of materials.

In the kitchen, a redwood light deck suspended from the ceiling illuminates the work area (top photo, facing page). The color of the redwood adds warmth to the room while the expansive fixture defines the area without adding walls. The light deck interrupts an expanse of relatively high ceiling to reintroduce human scale to the area. Keyed in at the same height as the light deck is a series of redwood valances that conceal window coverings and indirect lighting and establish horizontal lines that help tie the house together visually.

Creating an illusion of space—In my attempt to expand the sense of space within the house, I experimented with a variety of techniques. First, and probably most important, was to establish long sight lines through the building and to minimize the number of dead-end corners that would stop the flow of space visually (floor plan, left). I also played with a variety of ceiling heights to affect spatial perception. And finally, lighting, color, continuity of line and detail and even proportions of furniture were studied carefully for the effect they had on interior spaces. No one of these elements has particular significance by itself. But taken collectively, the techniques make the house feel right despite its small size.

For example, you enter the house beneath a low, flat ceiling, and you move down a corridor lined with bookshelves and storage cabinets that stretch to the far end of the house (bottom right photo, facing page). The view continues through a piece of floor-to-ceiling insulated glass to a planter at the end of a concrete-block spline. The distance is more than 80 ft. Redwood box lights along the corridor 7 ft. above the floor lower the apparent ceiling height.

While the entry is protective and almost cave-like, the heart of the house is lofty and bathed in natural light. Making up nearly half the building's square footage, this living/dining/kitchen space was from the beginning the Johnsons' top priority. Glass on three sides, including a line of east-facing clerestory windows above, allows direct sunlight throughout the day. Visible from all parts of the main living area is a fireplace of sandblasted concrete block (bottom left photo, facing page). The kitchen is open and integrated with the rest of this space, making it appear larger than three separate rooms.

This main living area, with its high ceilings, feels open. To provide a more intimate atmosphere for dining and conversation, however, the sloping ceiling in the dining area descends to 6 ft. 6 in. at the west exterior wall. Altering ceiling heights in this way helps divide the room into separate areas without walls.

Energy detailing in the roof—A propane gas-fired, forced-air furnace heats the house. Natural ventilation, aided by remote-control operation of the clerestory windows, is so effective that air conditioning is needed only on the stillest of

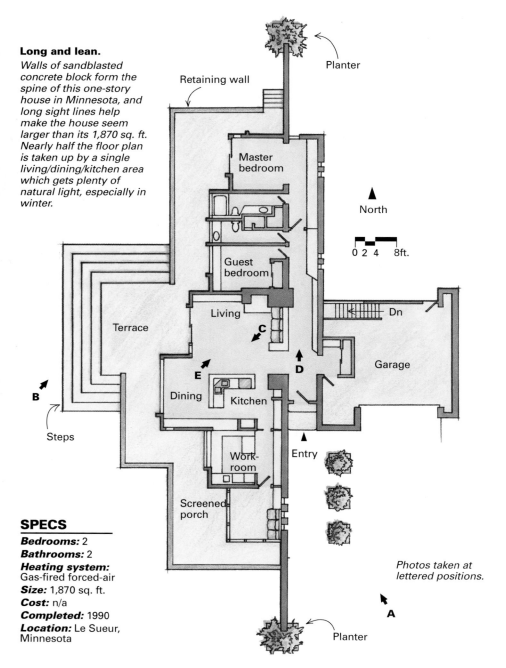

Long and lean.
Walls of sandblasted concrete block form the spine of this one-story house in Minnesota, and long sight lines help make the house seem larger than its 1,870 sq. ft. Nearly half the floor plan is taken up by a single living/dining/kitchen area which gets plenty of natural light, especially in winter.

Planter

Retaining wall

Master bedroom

North

0 2 4 8ft.

Guest bedroom

Living

Terrace

C

E

D

Dn

Garage

B

Steps

Dining

Kitchen

Work-room

Entry

Screened porch

SPECS

Bedrooms: 2
Bathrooms: 2
Heating system:
Gas-fired forced-air
Size: 1,870 sq. ft.
Cost: n/a
Completed: 1990
Location: Le Sueur, Minnesota

Photos taken at lettered positions.

A

Planter

Ceiling heights define areas in a big room. High ceilings over the main living area slope down to a more intimate 6-ft. 6-in. over the dining room table in the far right corner. A redwood light deck over the kitchen helps define that space without walls. Photo taken at C on floor plan.

summer days. An air-to-air heat exchanger boosts air quality during winter in the tightly built house.

Much of the energy performance of the house can be attributed to the roof design, created and patented by Joe Forrest, a contractor I've worked with on many occasions (Joe Forrest Construction Co., P. O. Box 154, Somerset, Wis. 54025; 715-247-3273). Rafters are 12-in. deep wood I-joists sheathed with ¾-in. fiberboard. The entire rafter cavity is filled with fiberglass insulation. Above each rafter, on top of the breathable fiberboard sheathing, is a ¾-in. by 1½-in. sleeper, creating 1½-in. deep channels that ventilate the roof. Tapered sleepers on the flat roof areas, cut from 2x4s, provide drainage. Over the sleepers is a layer of ⅝-in. plywood sheathing, followed by wood shingles or membrane roofing. Where the roof and diagonal concrete-block walls intersect, I used ridge vent from Cor-A-Vent (P. O. Box 428, Mishawaka, Ind. 46546-0428; 800-837-8368) to avoid dead-end ventilation spaces . On ceilings inside, a 1-in. layer of foil-covered foam insulation and a 4-mil continuous air/vapor barrier are installed above the gypsum-board ceilings. □

Kelly Davis is an architect with Mulfinger, Susanka & Mahady in Minneapolis, Minnesota. Photos by Karen Melvin.

A long view in a small house. Lined with bookshelves and cabinets, a low-ceilinged hall (above) runs the length of the house. The long view makes the house seem bigger than it is, and the low ceiling provides contrast to the openness of the main living area. Photo taken at D on floor plan.

Wood adds visual warmth. Maple floors and redwood valences, along with birch cabinets and shelving (left), come together at the sandblasted fireplace wall. The wood tones add a balancing warmth to the visually chilly concrete surfaces. Photo taken at E on floor plan.

A Redwood Remodel

Meticulous trim carpentry adorns a Craftsman-style cabin with cathedral ceilings and a trellised deck

by Julie Erreca & Pierre Bourriague

Redwood inside and out. Paneled in redwood, this high-ceilinged room looks out on a grove of redwood trees in the backyard. The 8-ft. tall French doors and the transom window above them emphasize the lofty feeling of the room and let in daylight to balance the rich, dark paneling. Photo taken at A on floor plan.

The earthquake that stopped the 1989 World Series started a lot of building projects in our neighborhood. We live in the redwood-forested hills just north of Santa Cruz, California, near the epicenter of the Loma Prieta earthquake. Fran Lapides and Bill Jurgens live down the road from us in the town of Felton.

Compared with what happened to many of the nearby houses, the damage to Bill and Fran's place was minimal. Their house remained intact, but the brick chimney came apart during the quake and fell off the side of their house. Bill and Fran wanted their fireplace restored and the house patched up. Because we are a design/build team, we were called in before any plans had been finalized to discuss the scope of the project.

Time for an upgrade—In the 1930's and 40's, Felton was a vacation community of summer homes for folks from San Francisco and San Jose. Bill and Fran's house was typical of the cottages built then. It was small—about 800 sq. ft.— and it had simple batten doors, minimal windows and pine paneling everywhere. The bill of sale, which we eventually found in one of the walls, revealed that the cabin originally had been sold for $1,850.

As we talked with Bill and Fran about their plans for the house, we quickly learned that the couple planned to live in it for the rest of their lives and that enlarging the house would suit them just fine. They also wanted to add an outdoor space where they could enjoy warm summer evenings. The chimney repair soon grew into a full-scale makeover that doubled the size of the house. Our mandate from Bill and Fran was to expand the house and to enrich the finishes, such as the trim, counters, cabinets and floor, yet retain the sense of the house as a cabin. We

Form follows foundation.
In doubling the size of this house, the designers placed new structure atop and beside the old foundation. At the southeast corner, a generous deck expands the living space at the apex of the private and public portions of the house.

Photos taken at lettered positions.

SPECS
Bedrooms: 2, plus a study
Bathrooms: 2
Heating system: Forced hot air
Size: 1,600 sq. ft.
Cost: $125 per sq. ft.
Completed: 1992
Location: Felton, California

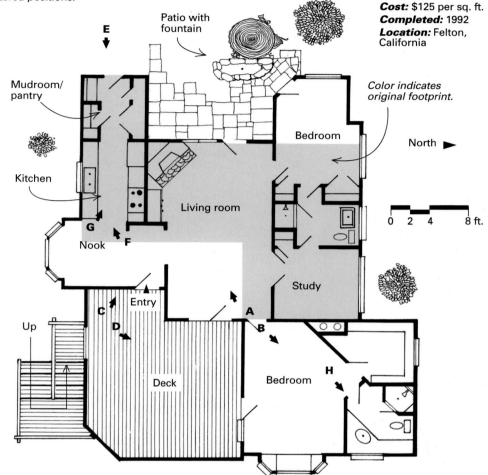

A family of gables.
Under a single gable roof, the rooms of this house are topped with cathedral ceilings of varying heights. The result is a collection of rooms with individual personalities, and building them under a single roof simplified weatherproofing the house.

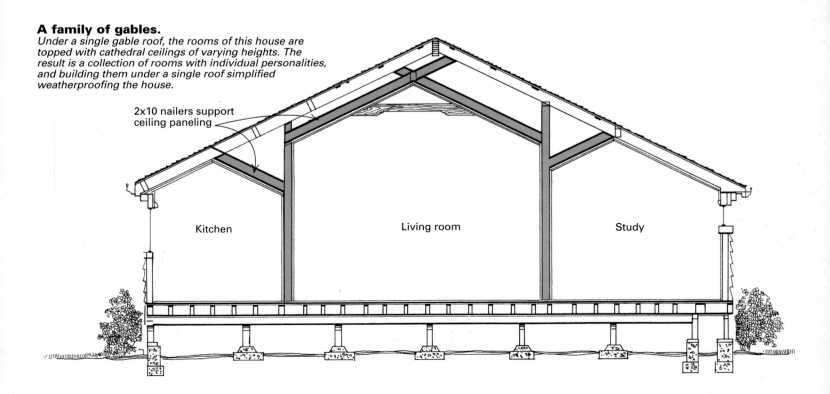

Drawings: Andre Junget

Unpredictable ceilings add visual interest. The off-center ridge and collar beams in this bedroom direct the eye around a play of light and shadow. Turned at a 45° angle, the view from the bed is directed at the bay window and the French doors onto the deck. Photo taken at B on floor plan.

also wanted the house to embody the spirit of the Craftsman tradition, which Gustav Stickley spelled out in a description of a home in *The Craftsman* magazine: "For the spirit of the home is there—the brooding quiet, the sheltering friendliness that comes with simple walls and solid woodwork, pleasant windows that gather air and sunlight, and furnishings that invite to sociability and rest." For us, that meant no drywall: All the walls and ceilings would be paneled in redwood.

New rooms on an old foundation—Bill and Fran's house is on a 10,000-sq. ft. lot that abuts the boundary of Henry Cowell State Park. The house is ringed by redwood trees, some of which are 150-ft. tall. The setback to the park boundary and the restrictions imposed by the local building department meant that an entirely new house could be only about 1,000 sq. ft. A quirk in the

code, however, allows an existing house to be expanded to as large as twice its original size. By retaining the old foundation, we were able to call the project a remodel and build an essentially new house that totals nearly 1,600 sq. ft. We added new spaces to the front and to the rear of the original footprint, carefully tucking new rooms into the spaces between the trees and the side-yard setbacks (floor plan, p. 83).

When a house is surrounded by trees that are more than 100-ft. tall, it needs a high ceiling and plenty of windows to keep it from feeling claustrophobic. And, of course, the dark paneling would make it doubly important to provide daylight at strategic places throughout the house. So at the beginning of the design stage, we made it a priority to give each room a lofty feel and at the same time to make the rooms feel distinctly different from one another.

How high should the ceiling be?—The plan we settled on places the living room at the center of the house. The ridge of this cathedral-ceilinged room is 14-ft. 6-in. high, but it could have been higher. As you can see in the section drawing (bottom drawing, p. 83), the living-room ceiling is well below the gable roof that spans the width of the house. The ceiling boards are affixed to 2x10 nailers on the same pitch as the 6-in-12 roof.

You might ask, "If you want a room to have a lofty feel, why not make it as high as possible?" We lowered the ceiling because if it had been any higher, the room would have lost its sense of intimacy (photo, p. 82). In our experience, if the ceiling gets much taller than 15 ft. or if the wall plate gets higher than 11 ft., the space starts to feel uncomfortable. The wall plate is 11-ft. high in this room, and the room is 17-ft. wide by 25-ft. long. Midway between the wall plate and the

Sculpted timbers surround the deck. To the right of the front door (photo, above), the entry spreads out to create a broad seating area under a trellis. The sturdy trellis structure is designed to support glass panels for yearlong deck use. Photo taken at D on floor plan.

Leaded glass marks the front door. Bordered by a combination trellis and railing, a staircase leads to the front door (photo, right). Where it meets the wall of the house, the horizontal line of the railing is continued as a wainscoting of vertical siding boards. Photo taken at C on floor plan.

The owners use the back door. Screened by a broad overhang, the back door leads to a combination mudroom and pantry (photo, far right). Photo taken at E on floor plan.

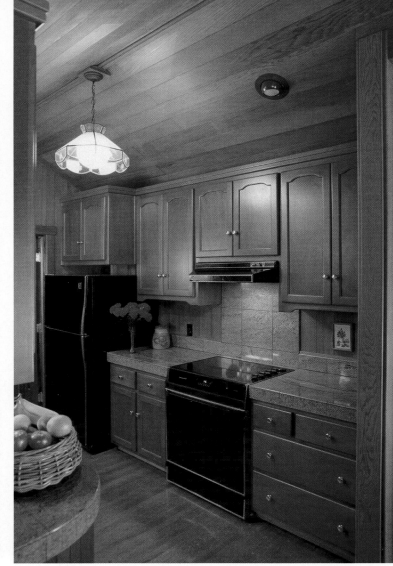

A French door leads to the pantry/mudroom. Counterspace is at a premium in a compact kitchen such as this one. So the authors kept most of the food-storage shelves out of the kitchen by placing the pantry in the mudroom at the back of the house. Photo taken at F on floor plan.

Related colors in the kitchen. Redwood is too soft for heavy-use areas such as kitchens, but durable mahogany used instead is nearly the same color. Floors are red oak, stained to match. Coral and black marble covers the counters and wall behind the cooktop. Photo taken at G on floor plan.

ridge, a row of 6x8 redwood timbers imparts a sense of sturdiness and structure to the room. The ends of the timbers are supported by sculpted corbels, and the edges of the timbers are softened with a ⅝-in. radius.

All the doors in the living room are 8-ft. tall by 32-in. wide. This is a particularly pleasing proportion for a four-panel door or a French door, and the doors aren't hard to come by. The Weather Shield doors we used on this job were a stock item at our local lumberyard (Weather Shield Manufacturing Inc., 1 Weather Shield Plaza, Medford, Wis. 54451; 800-222-2995). The extra height of an 8-ft. door dramatically alters the feeling of a room, and in this case the taller French doors at each end of the room let in more light than a standard-height French door. The transom windows over the French doors emphasize the height of the room, let in still more precious light and showcase the view of the redwoods in the backyard.

One end of the living room has a large table for big dinner parties. At the other end a river-rock fireplace by Michael Eckerman dominates the sit-down part of the room. Eckerman's work (see

FHB#82, pp. 88, 89) extends to the backyard, where a small fountain bubbles just outside the French doors. When the doors are open, the sound of falling water can be heard throughout the house. The fireplace design is a stylized horn of plenty, and the fountain includes a fireplace hearth so that people can sit and relax at the side of the waterfall.

Each room has its own cathedral ceiling— There's a Chinese saying that spirits get caught in the corners of shed-roof ceilings. That's probably okay if they're friendly spirits, but we avoid shed-roof ceilings anyway because the eye gets caught in their corners. We much prefer to put cathedral ceilings over a room; they direct the eye up the wall and then back down and around the details much in the way that people would view a painting.

It's not necessary for the ridge of a cathedral ceiling to be centered in the room. In fact, it can add interest to put it off-center, such as the ceiling in the new bedroom (left photo, p. 84). In this room, we further tweaked the typical layout by angling the wall behind the bed at 45° to point

the bed toward the view out the French doors onto the deck.

Enter at the deck—A switchback staircase leads to the front door of the house (bottom left photo, p. 85). The stair is bordered by a picket railing that grows into a trellis as it approaches the door. Where the railing intersects the wall of the house, a band of wainscoting topped with a water-table trim detail extends the horizontal line of the railing around the house.

The deck stretches out from the front door, filling in the roughly 20-ft. square notch in the footprint between the new bedroom wing and the outline of the original house (top photo, p. 85). The deck has several functions. Its sunny location and spaciousness provide the primary outside living area. The trellis off the bedroom was designed to support a glass roof so that the deck can be usable even during the rainy season.

The real entry—There's a good place to park cars right outside the back door, so the rear entry is the one Bill and Fran use most often. For shelter from the sometimes intense winter rainstorms, we extended the roof 48 in. past the wall to act as a canopy over the doorway (bottom right photo, p. 85). This portion of the roof is borne by 4x12 beams that have been detailed with the same stepped profile that shows up on the corbels in the living room and the beams over the deck. The 4x12s, which extend but a few feet into the wall, are supported by 4x8 knee braces.

Just inside the back door is a combination mudroom/pantry. Three closets provide space for supplies, and there is a flip-top bench for sitting to put on shoes and for storing them out of sight. Between the mudroom and the kitchen is another full French door to share the natural light and view between the rooms. For its compact size, the kitchen (photos, facing page) has plenty of counter space because the pantry provides most of the storage.

Colors and patterns—We are lucky enough to be in the heart of redwood country, where several mills are harvesting second-growth and third-growth timber. This wood doesn't have the tight grain pattern of the long-gone old-growth lumber, but it does have other attributes such as variegated colors and bold grain patterns. Fran's love of the wavy-grained redwood prompted the carpenters to select those boards to be used in prominent places, such as the wall under the skylight in the bathroom (photo, right).

All trim boards were routed with a rounded edge to soften their appearance. Also, the edges of boards that abut one another have been rounded over, which accents rather than hides the joints. In addition to trim elements, every beam, fascia and railing were treated this way by our trim carpenters, Craig Johnson, Jeff McGee and Pete Yarwood.

All the interior woodwork on the walls and ceilings is finished with Penetrol, an oil-based finish that has no coloration in it (Flood Co., 1212 Barlow Road, Hudson, Ohio 44236; 800-321-3444). Our painter, Peter Gillett, likes this finish because it's easy to apply, it brings out the richness of the wood and it is easy to clean.

Exterior woodwork (1x8 shiplap k.d. redwood), on the other hand, is finished with a product called Superdeck (Duckback Products Inc., P. O. Box 980, Chico, Calif. 95927; 916-343-3261). This finish has a tiny bit of color in it, which unifies the overall appearance of the siding. Duckback also makes stains that can be used to darken the sapwood that shows up in more and more redwood these days. Just hit the sapwood first with the stain, then go over the whole job with regular finish. Superdeck keeps the red in redwood, so if you want to prevent exterior redwood from turning gray, this product will do the job. It requires annual application.

We chose deep greens as the contrasting trim colors. Because green is the complement of red and the prevalent color of the nearby redwoods, it was tough to imagine any other trim color. Conveniently enough, the dark green Weather Shield windows and doors came prepainted.

When it came time to choose a countertop material for the bathroom, Bill and Fran's innumerable trips to scattered showrooms and dusty warehouses paid off. They found some rich

Skylights help a lot in a wood-paneled house. Bold patterns in dark wood don't mean much if you can't see them. Generous skylights in the bathroom ensure that this deeply figured redwood can be appreciated. Photo taken at H on floor plan.

green granite tiles with black swirls and cream-colored veins in them. We used this tile for the lavatory counter and for the stall shower.

We used coral-colored granite tiles in the kitchen for countertops and the wall behind the cooktop (photos, facing page). As we opened the boxes to inspect the color and pattern of the tiles, we were pleasantly surprised to discover that the tiles were cut from the same slab of granite. Each box was a puzzle in which all the pieces were the same size. So we spread out the tiles,

studied them, and put them back together on the wall and on the counters in the same order they were in when they were sliced out of the earth.

Granite tiles, incidentally, offer substantial savings over granite slabs. They cost on the order of $10 per sq. ft., which is a fraction of the price of a granite slab. □

Julie Erreca and Pierre Bourriague own and operate Bourriague Construction Design in Felton, California. Photos by Charles Miller.

Summer Cabin in the Land O' Lakes

Just three months from drawing board to final finish, this house
was built on an island where all of the materials
had to come over by barge

by Jonathan Rousham

Perched high on a rocky island. Up 70 ft. and back 100 ft. from the water's edge, this summer cottage looks like a tree house overlooking the lake. Accessible only by water, the island is easily reached via canoe.

The Trans-Canada Highway between Ottawa and Toronto passes through an area of rough granite hills and countless lakes known as the Land O' Lakes. The shores of these lakes are dotted with small seasonal cottages that serve as vacation homes for people from all over North America. Marla Isaacs and her husband, Larry Hirschhorn, had spent many summer vacations with their children renting cabins in this region. Wanting a place of their own, they purchased an island site on Bob's Lake in the fall of 1991.

In early June 1992 I got a message from Marla asking if I could design and build them a summer cottage. And did I think I could have the project completed by the end of the summer? Three days later, I was on a boat with Marla and Larry on our way to check out their island site.

June 14: A steep rock face means a building and design challenge—The site was located atop a granite slab that faced the shore, 70 ft. up and 100 ft. back from the water. After climbing the rock face and tramping through the brush that crowned the hill, we found the best location for a cottage to make the most of the lake view. After a brief discussion of what my clients were looking for in a summer cottage, I began to form the aesthetic and structural concepts in my head as I boarded the boat and headed back to the mainland.

Time and budget constraints dictated simplicity. The house was for summer use, so with no insulation required, wall and ceiling construction could be less complicated, with exposed framing and exterior sheathing providing the inside-wall finish as well. A light structure on concrete piers seemed appropriate, although it would need to weather Canadian winters.

Marla and Larry wanted a large, open interior with maximum views of the lake. My solution was to design a simple post-and-beam structure that would have lots of windows (floor plans, p. 90). A central clerestory section would be wrapped by a low-slope hipped steel roof with wide overhangs. As a summer retreat, the cottage would be informal and lighthearted, reminiscent of a childhood tree house (photo left).

Less than two weeks after the initial meeting, Marla and Larry reviewed my preliminary drawings and gave me the green light to finalize plans and to make arrangements to begin construction August 3.

Week 1: Drizzling rain, no crew and a barge full of lumber—On the morning of August 3, I arrived at Bob's Lake with tools and camping equipment and with a smattering of light rain on the windshield of my van. In the past five weeks, I'd completed the construction drawings, secured a crew and arranged for the necessary building permits and site approvals.

I slipped my canoe into the lake and paddled to the island, where I hoped to find my crew there with chainsaws sputtering, ready for a workout. Instead, the site was silent with no sign of man or machine, so I paddled to the other side of the lake to meet the clients. Marla and Larry hadn't arrived, and with materials for the cottage due to be delivered at noon, I paddled back to the marina to meet the truck.

I had a barge trucked in to transport all of the materials (except the windows and roofing) in one shot. By the time the barge arrived, I had paddled back and forth across the lake in the rain three times, searching in vain for clients and crew. The materials arrived on time, and feeling sorry for this sore and soggy crewless creature, everyone at the dock pitched in to transfer the two 5-ton truckloads of materials onto the barge, along with my tools and canoe. By 2 p. m., the sun was shining, and the barge was parked beside the island.

The next morning, I awoke in my tent to brilliant sunshine, and before I finished my coffee, the crew arrived and immediately began clearing the site. By noon the site was ready, and the crew split into two teams, the first one hauling material from the barge to the top of the hill.

Getting the materials up the granite face was an ordeal of strength and endurance. Even with the help of the tracked hauler that we rented, it took three crew members almost two whole days to move the house package to the site, including 85 bags of cement, the cement mixer, the water pump and all of our tools.

In the midst of this material migration, Ric, the crew leader, and I laid out and began to dig the 18 holes for the 18-in. dia. piers with the second crew. We found lovely yellow sand beneath the topsoil; unfortunately, that sand was full of rocks and boulders. With a power auger, an impact hammer, a pry bar and shovels, we struggled for three days to dig the holes. On a few of the holes, we mercifully reached bedrock, where we drilled and anchored the footings. But the rest had to be buried at least 4½ ft. to get below the frost line. By Friday of that first week, we had poured the piers and waved good-bye to the empty barge.

A seasonal cottage means simplified details. With no insulation in the walls or ceiling, the inside of the sheathing and the exposed framing lend a rustic feel to the cottage's light, open interior. Photo taken at A on floor plan.

Week 2: The post-and-beam grid takes shape—The following Monday, we donned our nail aprons and jumped to the task of building the post-and-beam frame. We were at least a day behind schedule and still hurting from the grueling work of the previous week.

The frame for the cottage consisted of eighteen 6x6 cedar posts arranged in a 32-ft. square grid pattern with a covered entrance porch jutting out on one side (drawing p. 90). Each post stood on one of the piers we'd dug and poured the week before. Near the base of each post, we notched in doubled 2x10 beams that were bolted to the posts through metal plates. These

beams tied the grid together front to back and supported the 2x8 floor joists, which joined the posts side to side. We cantilevered the beams from the front of the house to support the front deck. We also ran a doubled 2x10 beam notched and bolted to the tops of the posts around the perimeter of the cottage. A 2x6 top plate on top of the 2x10s added lateral stiffness.

We used 18-ft. posts for the 12-ft. by 22-ft. central section of the grid that rises 1½ stories. We started with the straightest 18-ft. 6x6 and laid it out for a story post. After marking the other posts, one team cut the notches while the other prepared the perimeter beams for assembly.

By the end of the second week, the frame was completed. With spirits buoyed by the fine weather, we had finished the floor framing, the exterior decking and the roof framing. The roof over the first floor wrapped around and butted into the central section, providing diagonal bracing that stiffened the structure considerably. Bracing also came from interior stair stringers, which were lag-bolted across a main support post and into the second-story floor beam.

Week 3: Delayed by the dock—As our third week began, it was apparent that construction of a landing at the water's edge with a floating

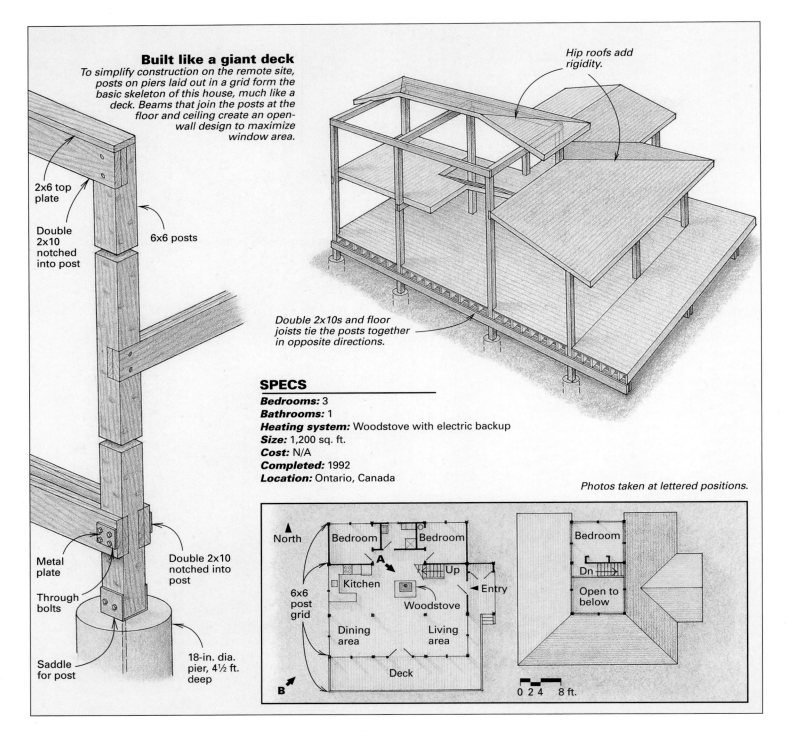

Built like a giant deck

To simplify construction on the remote site, posts on piers laid out in a grid form the basic skeleton of this house, much like a deck. Beams that join the posts at the floor and ceiling create an open-wall design to maximize window area.

Hip roofs add rigidity.

2x6 top plate

Double 2x10 notched into post

6x6 posts

Double 2x10s and floor joists tie the posts together in opposite directions.

Metal plate

Through bolts

Double 2x10 notched into post

Saddle for post

18-in. dia. pier, 4½ ft. deep

SPECS

Bedrooms: 3
Bathrooms: 1
Heating system: Woodstove with electric backup
Size: 1,200 sq. ft.
Cost: N/A
Completed: 1992
Location: Ontario, Canada

Photos taken at lettered positions.

North
Bedroom
Bedroom
A
6x6 post grid
Kitchen
Up
Entry
Woodstove
Dining area
Living area
B
Deck

Bedroom
Dn
Open to below

0 2 4   8 ft.

---

dock extending from it was now our top priority. We had to have an easy way to unload the windows and roofing material from the boat we were using to shuttle ourselves and our materials to and from the island.

The rock I had initially chosen as a landing was left alone to give swimmers a natural access to the water. The landing began beside this rock and was built into the nearby boulders with the end cantilevered over the water. A 16-ft. floating dock designed to be removable was attached to the landing with a dock hinge. The

finished dock seemed to anchor the cottage on the hill visually to the shore below. Unfortunately, it took the crew three days to complete the dock, much longer than I'd planned, which emphasized for the first time just how tight our schedule was becoming.

Back up the hill at the cottage, we built and installed the infill panels between the posts. Because no insulation was needed in the walls, the inside of the plywood sheathing became our interior finish (photo p. 89). We built all of our interior and exterior wall panels out of ⅝-in. fir

plywood glued and screwed to 2x2 cedar frames. These panels were then glued and screwed to the 6x6 posts. On the exterior we installed 1x2 cedar battens in a vertical pattern to cover the joints. For the roof we used ½-in. fir plywood on top of the 2x4 cedar rafters for the finished ceiling.

We sprayed the interior framing, paneling and ceiling with Sikkens clear sealer (Akzo Nobel, 1845 Maxwell St., P. O. Box 7062, Troy, Mich. 48007-7062; 800-833-7288 in the United States, or 800-663-6273 in Canada) before the windows

A steep climb from the driveway to the front door. Added after the house was completed, a long staircase makes the climb up the granite face easier. The builders didn't have that advantage when they were hauling materials to the top of the hill. Photo taken at B on floor plan.

and floors were installed. On Friday the 30-ga. galvanized-steel roofing arrived on the mainland, and two crew members spent the day ferrying it over and carrying it up the hill. With three weeks gone and a tremendous amount of work still left, we seemed to be hopelessly behind schedule, even with the five-day overrun period that I had secretly planned for.

Week 4: Windows, floors and the "Silver Cloud"—I arrived for the fourth week carrying the weight of our unattainable schedule as well as the windows that had been custom-made in my shop. The single-pane casement-style windows were made of cedar, and a third of the windows opened on brass hinges with cottage-style brass turn latches. By standardizing all of the windows, we also were able to precut all interior and exterior cedar trim in the shop.

Fabricating the windows in my own shop not only saved a lot of money, but also allowed them to be finished in time, which wouldn't have happened with the six-week to eight-week delivery time of a typical joinery shop. The windows were ferried to the island, and miraculously, only one pane of glass was broken in the transportation process.

With the windows and roofing on site, we were able to get back to more crowd-pleasing work. First, the galvanized steel roof went on, earning our project the nickname "Silver Cloud" from the clients' children. Next, the 5/4 tongue-and-groove pine flooring was installed. Then the win-

dows went into their appointed openings, fitting beautifully, much to my relief. The place seemed to look and feel more like a real house every day.

In a frenzy at the end of week four, we worked out all of the loose ends before Marla and Larry had to return to Philadelphia. Last-minute changes were detailed, along with hastily choosing and buying the kitchen cabinets and a woodstove. On the clients' last day at the lake, a severe-storm warning was issued for the region. By 10 a. m., the crew had secured the site and was heading back to the mainland with rain falling and the first peals of thunder sounding in the distance.

Week 5: Samaritans in a motorboat—The following Monday, I returned for what would be my last regular week on site. That Thursday I was beginning a project in Ottawa, and I'd be able to come back to the island only on weekends. Ric and his able crew took over the task of finishing the detail work on the cottage, and two weeks later, most of the work was completed.

On my weekend visits, I concentrated on cleaning up the site, removing leftover materials and delivering the clients' belongings from the mainland. I also had the unenviable chore of ferrying over the kitchen appliances, which I had brought from Ottawa.

On a lovely, sunny Saturday in September, we loaded the kitchen stove onto the boat. As we pulled up to the island dock, a pontoon boat

laden with Bob's Lake merrymakers drifted by. They watched my father, who had kindly offered to help me deliver these unwieldy objects, and me struggle to unload the stove with the hill to the cottage looming above us. Suddenly, three guys from the pontoon boat jumped in the water and swam over to give a hand. When we told them we had three more appliances on the mainland, they suggested that I ferry the appliances over while they carried them up the hill. An hour later, my father and I stood on the dock waving off the waterborne Samaritans and smiling up at the gleaming appliances waiting at the top of the hill.

On the last weekend in September, Ric and I met the clients for a final review of the project and to get them settled in for their first weekend at the cottage. As Marla and Larry carried groceries and supplies up to their new retreat, Ric and I lit a fire in the woodstove and installed last-minute electrical and plumbing fixtures. Marla and Larry were delighted with their island retreat (photo above), even with a list of items yet to finish. As I made my way to my canoe for the last time, I looked up in satisfaction at the house that 12 weeks before had not even been conceived of, and now was glowing like a warm lantern on the hilltop. □

Jonathan Rousham is a designer and builder now living in Montreal, Canada. He also supervises workshops at the McGill University School of Architecture. Photos by Roe A. Osborn.

A Small, Affordable House

A veteran builder reduces cost with a wood-post foundation, plywood siding and other surprising choices

by Bruce Caswell

Inexpensive doesn't have to mean ugly. At a cost of $45 per sq. ft., this house cost about 30% less than its north-Idaho neighbors. Plywood siding and a simple footprint helped keep the cost down, and cantilevered bays and blue trim keep the results from looking ordinary. Photo taken at A on floor plan.

A few years ago, a construction-site fall ended my career as a professional builder. With over 15 years of building experience, I decided to pursue my graduate degree in the new Wood Construction and Design program at the University of Idaho. This decision meant moving my family from Turner, Maine, to Moscow, Idaho, in the fall of 1993. The long trek was worth it, though, because this joint program between the colleges of Forestry and Architecture, under the direction of Dr. Tom Gorman, was to involve affordable-housing research.

For many years, I've believed that builders aren't taking sufficient advantage of innovative, cost-saving measures developed by researchers, manufacturers and other builders. People tend to be overly selective, assuming that one or two cost-saving strategies can provide significant savings. I think you need a comprehensive, systematic approach, one that uses cost-effective measures throughout the design and building process. At the same time, you must ensure that the resulting house is structurally sound and both energy-efficient and resource-efficient. But

there's no reason why an inexpensive house can't be a nice home.

In early 1994, I got the opportunity to prove my theory. The dean of the College of Forestry, John Hendee, and his wife, Fran, were in the market to build a low-cost house on their ranch near the small logging and farming community of Deary, which is in the panhandle of northern Idaho. I agreed to design and build the house as my master's degree thesis project, which would demonstrate several cost-effective ways of adding value to an affordable-house design while reducing

A simple floor plan is the most cost-effective

Only the cantilevered bays on each end keep this plan from being the most basic rectangle. This simple shape encloses the most space with the least amount of exterior wall. Note how the closets, bathroom and mudroom are lined up on the north side to buffer the rest of the house from the cold weather.

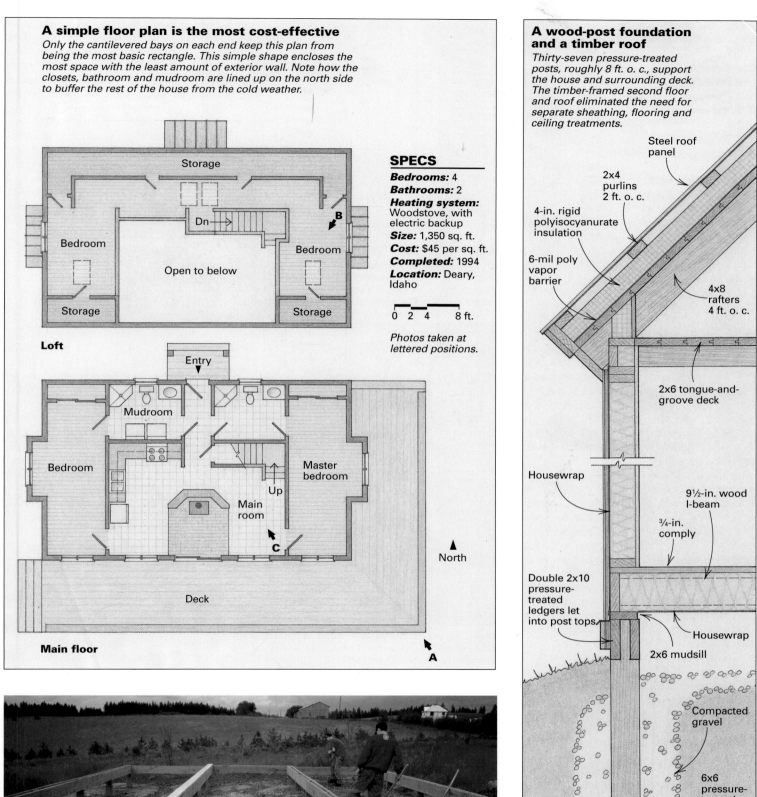

Loft

Storage

Bedroom

Dn

Open to below

Bedroom

Storage

Storage

B

SPECS

Bedrooms: 4
Bathrooms: 2
Heating system: Woodstove, with electric backup
Size: 1,350 sq. ft.
Cost: $45 per sq. ft.
Completed: 1994
Location: Deary, Idaho

0 2 4   8 ft.

Photos taken at lettered positions.

Entry

Mudroom

Bedroom

Master bedroom

Up

Main room

C

North

Deck

Main floor

A

Faster, cheaper and easier than concrete. Pressure-treated 4x6 posts, standing on precast footings and backfilled with gravel, take the place of a poured-concrete foundation. A post foundation not only costs less than concrete, but it also minimizes site disturbance.

A wood-post foundation and a timber roof

Thirty-seven pressure-treated posts, roughly 8 ft. o. c., support the house and surrounding deck. The timber-framed second floor and roof eliminated the need for separate sheathing, flooring and ceiling treatments.

Steel roof panel

2x4 purlins 2 ft. o. c.

4-in. rigid polyisocyanurate insulation

6-mil poly vapor barrier

4x8 rafters 4 ft. o. c.

2x6 tongue-and-groove deck

Housewrap

9½-in. wood I-beam

¾-in. comply

Double 2x10 pressure-treated ledgers let into post tops

Housewrap

2x6 mudsill

Compacted gravel

6x6 pressure-treated posts

8-in. by 24-in. dia. precast concrete footing, reinforced with #4 rebar

Photo this page: Bruce Caswell. Drawings: Vince Babak.

More Small Houses   93

the amount of energy and materials need to build a typical house.

Cantilevered bays break up the basic box—

If you're trying to keep costs down, you have to be realistic from the beginning, not start out with a design that is too big and then look for things to eliminate. Initially, I took the $55,000 budget and translated that to a workable footprint based on the typical $65 per sq. ft. cost of a modestly finished home in the general area. The rectangular shape I chose makes the most cost-effective use of space. It allows ample south-facing glass for direct solar gain and daylighting while using a minimum of window and door openings on the other three sides, which are most severely affected by adverse weather. Orienting the house due south not only improved its thermal performance but also made the deck spaces more comfortable.

The only problem with a rectangular house is that it can look too plain. As shown in the floor plan (left drawing, p. 93), the 960 sq. ft. of living space on the first floor is enhanced by a pair of 2-ft. by 8-ft. bays cantilevered off the east and west sides. These bays add interest to the flat gable-end elevations.

The compact layout of the first floor is supplemented by approximately 400 sq. ft. of open loft. With the loft, the house's total living area is nearly 1,400 sq. ft. A wraparound deck on the south and east sides (photo p. 92) creates extra seasonal living space and, along with a small, covered deck at the front entry, also helps to break up the house's boxy shape.

The small size and simple shape chosen for the design meant that the house had minimum exterior wall surfaces to build and minimum interior spaces to heat and to cool. The savings realized in these areas allowed for expenditures such as exposed timber framing in the loft floor and in the roof. By design, the framework in these areas serves as the finished floor and ceiling for the loft, and as the finished ceiling for the main roof. Besides having the visual appeal of exposed wood, this timber-and-plank system eliminates the need for floor coverings or ceiling finishes.

A post foundation costs less and reduces site disturbance—

This house stands on a wood-post foundation (photo p. 93). Pressure-treated 4x6 and 6x6 posts placed on concrete footings and surrounded by compacted gravel are linked by double pressure-treated 2x10s that support 2x6 sills and a wood I-joist floor system (right drawing, p. 93).

I had used a similar foundation style for years on agricultural buildings with excellent results. The cost of the post foundation was less than half of the estimated cost of poured concrete, which translated into over $3,000 in savings on just the cost of foundation materials. In addition, heavy-equipment costs and site disturbances

Four in. of rigid insulation warms the roof. The tongue-and-groove 2x6 roof decking was covered with a 6-mil polyethylene vapor barrier before the rigid insulation went down. Two-by-four purlins, 2 ft. o. c., run atop the insulation and serve as a nail base for the metal roofing.

Sleeping under the roof. Upstairs in the loft, the bedrooms are separated from the two-story main living space only by half-walls. This informal arrangement is fine for occasional guests and could be altered for more privacy should the need arise. Photo taken at B on floor plan.

were minimized. Natural drainage patterns were maintained, and landscaping costs were substantially reduced. Estimating conservatively, all of this work saved up to another $3,000 to $5,000.

The difficulty and expense of getting a concrete truck to our isolated job site was another reason for using wood posts. To gain access to the property by the shortest route, we would have had to rebuild a timber bridge to carry the additional weight of a concrete truck. With the post foundation, the concrete footings were precast at the concrete plant and delivered to the site on a much lighter lumber-delivery truck.

The footings were formed using 8-in. lengths of 24-in. dia. Sonotube. At the site, a series of holes was augered very quickly with a commercial truck-mounted auger. The holes were bored out

to a depth of 5 ft., where solid, undisturbed soil created excellent bearing for precast footings. Once the footings were firmly set at the base of the holes, the pressure-treated posts were set on the footings and simply surrounded with gravel fill, which provided enough pressure on the posts to prevent uplift.

The area created by the post frame system is a vented crawl-space, and because the floor joists are far enough from grade, they did not have to be pressure-treated. The floor system is fully insulated, with the insulation held in place by housewrap stapled under the joists. This fabric effectively prevents ground moisture from reducing the R-value of the fiberglass insulation yet allows any trapped moisture to migrate out.

We had to have the foundation plan professionally engineered before the local building inspector would approve this unconventional foundation. But since then, the inspector has become an ardent promoter of wood-post foundations.

Some people may question the longevity of a pressure-treated post foundation. But I firmly believe that the combination of the dry climate in northern Idaho and the overall positive drainage pattern of the site will allow this system to perform indefinitely. The biggest potential problem with this system occurs on grade and would make repair work easily identifiable and reasonably simple to remedy should the need arise. In areas of high humidity or poor drainage or persistently wet conditions, concrete piers would be more cost-effective.

The savings generated to this point allowed us to invest in high-quality windows and doors. Right out of the box, good windows and doors add to the thermal comfort and performance of the house. And in the long run, they lower maintenance costs and reduce energy demands. Trade-offs are inevitable in any construction job, and the lines are often blurred between choices. But when it comes to windows and doors, it's a good rule of thumb to find a way to upgrade these items during the beginning of the construction process.

Thinner studs work just fine—

I teamed up with a local sawmill and the university to develop a building product that would use resources more efficiently. We came up with reduced-thickness studs measuring 1¼ in. by 3½ in. and 1¼ in. by 5½ in. These studs cost us about 10% less but retain about 80% of the design value of standard 1½-in. studs. The Uniform Building Code (UBC) dictates a minimum stud thickness of 1½ in., but local building jurisdictions in Idaho have made exceptions for the use of this new product.

Thinner studs are more than adequate for many residential applications. They meet the grade standards of the Western Wood Products Association for stress-rated boards and offer adequate nailing surface for drywall and for exterior sheathing as long as they are manufactured with no edge wain. I didn't use these thinner studs for the main walls across the front and back, which bear the roof loads, but for the gable walls and for the interior partitions, these thinner studs worked fine.

Plywood siding serves as sheathing—
Another place where we eliminated redundancy was on the wall sheathing. Because we used structural T-111 plywood as the siding, no sheathing was necessary. Plywood sidings come in a variety of profiles, but some are definitely better looking than others. We chose a 1-ft. o. c., reverse board-and-batten panel because it gives the appearance of high-quality wide boards.

The use of plywood siding also allowed us to install and stain the siding while the walls were lying flat on the deck, which is much more efficient than working from ladders. Once the walls were framed, we covered them with housewrap directly over the studs before we applied the siding. Because plywood tends to warp at the edges, we were careful to stain the edges as we went along and to nail them carefully. Along all horizontal edges, including above and below rough openings, we nailed the plywood on the thick edge adjacent to either side of all thinner grooves. With the siding securely nailed, we gave it a good coat of stain before we raised the walls.

A common complaint with plywood siding is its plainness. To deal with this aesthetic problem, we applied simple trim boards to create visual interest. When painted a contrasting color to match the metal roofing, in this case Tahoe blue, the trim breaks up the tall gable walls and defines the frame for the rest of the house. Trim was applied on top of the plywood siding so that clapboards, shingles or vinyl siding can be installed in the future without altering the existing trim.

A metal roof hides 4 in. of rigid insulation—
The metal roof is perhaps another result of my experience with farm buildings, but it was also a sound, economical choice for this house. A metal roof eliminated the need for another layer of sheathing and was quick and easy to install. In addition, the combination of a steep roof pitch and metal roofing virtually eliminates any snow and ice buildup.

Sandwiched between the roof decking and the steel roofing is a continuous layer of 4-in. thick rigid insulation with an R-33 rating (top photo, facing page). Any gaps in the butt joints were filled with expanding spray foam, which minimized air-leakage and air-infiltration problems. The roof panels are screwed to horizontal 2x4s that run on top of the insulation and are attached to the framing with long, heavy-gauge screws.

The steel roof panels, supplied by BHP Steel Building Products (E. 4111 Ferry St., Spokane, Wash. 99202; 509-535-0600), employ an interlocking-rib system, where the screws that hold one panel to the roof are covered by the overlapping rib of the adjacent panel. This system minimizes the need for exposed screws and hence the chances of roof leaks.

If I were to build this house again, I would would use a heavier-gauge roof. To save money, I

Bricks collect heat from the sun and the stove. A brick floor and half-wall serve as thermal storage to moderate temperature swings inside the house. Opening this central space to the roof is one of the strategies to making a small house seem bigger. Photo taken at C on floor plan.

let myself be talked into using 29-ga. steel, which was more flexible than I would have liked and shows some minor distortions of the flat panels— the sort of thing a builder notices but others might not. In retrospect, I would have used 26-ga. steel, but the roof's appearance is still pleasing.

The primary advantage to the roof system, in this case, is the efficient use of space. This design uses a high percentage of the volume inside the building by creating habitable space right under the roof (bottom photo, facing page). Volume efficiency is important for energy and resource conservation. It also makes building costs per square foot as competitive as possible. For these same reasons, this basic configuration has been used intuitively by builders for centuries. Admittedly, rigid-foam insulation is expensive. Deeper rafters or trusses would have allowed for less-expensive fiberglass insulation but would have required a finished ceiling, which would have added cost and was not the effect we were looking for.

A brick floor works as a thermal collector—
Inside the house, the main living space is organized around a brick floor and a brick half-wall that partially encloses a woodstove (photo above). The brickwork acts as a heat sink that stores radiant energy and improves the thermal comfort of the house. This construction helps to control uncomfortable temperature swings for much of the heating and cooling seasons. In ad-

dition, the roof overhang on the south elevation enhances the effectiveness of the brick mass by blocking most of the summer sun while allowing sunlight to reach the floor through a sliding-glass door for the entire heating season.

Because there's a large supply of fallen timber on the property, the woodstove is the primary source of heat. Several small electric heaters were also installed to keep the pipes from freezing when the house is not occupied.

A bargain at $45 per sq. ft.—The house was initially designed to be built for $40 per sq. ft., but in the end it came to $45, which included a reasonable profit for me, and which I think is still a bargain for John and Fran. Comparable houses in northern Idaho are being built for $65 per sq. ft. and up.

Since 1970 the median price of a single-family house has increased 375%, yet median family income in that same time has increased only 100%. This trend prohibits many hard-working families and individuals from entering the housing market. The challenge for builders is cutting costs while maintaining a suitable profit margin and providing lasting value for the homeowner. I'd like to think I succeeded in this case. ☐

Bruce Caswell has collected his master's degree and now works for Qualtim Technologies International in Madison, Wisconsin. Photos by Kevin Ireton except where noted.

A Romantic House

In this hectic, high-tech age, playful detailing and asymmetrical plans make a more comfortable home

by Jeremiah Eck

Combining old and new details. Although the steep roof and the wood siding are traditional details, on the southern elevation they're combined with a contemporary arrangement of windows that lets in light and adds some playful detailing. Photo taken from A on floor plan.

We live in an age of hyperrationality, where reason rules over intuition. Nowhere is this more evident than in the computerization of almost every aspect of our lives. Computers tell us what the weather will be, how much we have in our bank accounts and even suggest to many that the design of a house is a fully analytic process.

Our lives sometimes seem like a series of things to do on a list—and do quickly. I think there's an antidote, though, to our overregulated and hectic lives: a return to romanticism in our houses.

A few years ago I entered a competition for an ideal house of 1,500 sq. ft. Although this house was never built, recently I was able to design a slightly modified, enlarged version for Peter and Kathy Neely in Salisbury, Connecticut. The house, built by Jack Grant of Winsted, Connecticut, is a good example of how the plan and the details of a house can, in fact, be romantic.

Relating to the past—To begin with, the design of the Neely house makes reference to the architecture of the past but does not attempt to copy it. This is important because romantic houses are about the relation of the present to the past. This is not to say that the Neely house is nostalgic. That's what Disneyland is all about.

I was confounded to hear recently that a retirement community is being built in Florida in the "image" of a New England village. The experience and the product of three centuries of regional living in New England was to be built instantaneously in a region 2,000 miles to the south. Certainly our technology allows us to do that, but to what end? This is a false, technology-dependent romanticism and an example of sentimentality.

Arched windows with rectangular sash. The arched windows so prominent on the southern elevation (above) are actually an arched facade in front of rectangular sash, which cost considerably less than curved sash would have.

Bottom photo, this page: Kevin Ireton

The steep roof, the dominant chimney, the scaled-down windows and the traditional materials of the Neely house all suggest classic images of home, inspired by everything from 18th-century saltboxes to 19th-century Gothic-Revival farmhouses. But the open floor plan (drawing right), the extensive use of natural light and the configuration of windows and trim on the south elevation (top photo, facing page) all are contemporary.

Inspired by nature—The ultimate source of inspiration for romanticism is nature. In architecture, this inspiration often means that the shape of a house and its colors are compatible with its surroundings. Each side of the Neely house responds differently to the site. From the entry side on the north (photo above), the steep roofs and their green color blend with the low hills beyond, particularly between spring and fall.

The south side of the house is another matter. The house sits not quite at the top of a low, rolling hill and at the edge of a gently sloping meadow to the south. On the south side the house stands more erect (photo facing page), with the wall of what I call the living hall extending a full two stories. Unlike the north side, where the roof dominates to protect the house from the wind, the desire for sun and views across the meadow predominate on the south elevation. This large expanse of wall gives the Neelys a full 180° view and year-round exposure to the southern sky.

Because they are inspired by nature, the colors of romantic houses are seldom white, and the textures are seldom perfectly smooth. The Neely house has three exterior colors and three distinct textures. The roof is green, the cedar clapboards and the cedar sidewall shingles are natural brown, and the trim and the casings are beige. The green and the brown can be found in the surroundings, and the beige mediates the two.

As for textures, rough wood shingles are used next to the ground, defining the first floor of the house as coming from the ground. Clapboards, with their somewhat more refined texture, delineate the second floor, and the even flatter trim and the smooth medium-density overlay (MDO) plywood define the gable peaks against the sky.

Romanticism in plan and elevation—Romantic houses tend to have irregular plans as contrasted with formally centered geometric plans. Order is achieved through a balancing of irregular elements or space, not through strict symmetry. For instance, the Neely house is dominated by the tall living hall (top photo, p. 98). But that room is balanced by the length of the kitchen/dining/entry area that flows into it with only a partial visual and physical separation (bottom photo, p. 98).

This balance of irregular shapes can be achieved in other ways as well. The small, cozy loft of the Neely house (photo p. 99) balances the larger, open living hall.

Romantic houses can be small, too, because each activity or function need not have a distinct room or position in the plan. One of the problems

An open plan. *By consolidating the formal living room, the dining room and the family room into one central space—the living hall—the architect not only eliminated rooms, but he also reduced circulation space. The result is a small house (1,800 sq. ft.) that works well for a family.*

North

Second floor

Loft

Dn

Bedroom

Open to below

Bedroom

B

0 2 4   8 ft.

First floor

Master bath

Master bedroom

C

Up

Entry

Living hall

Dining area

Kitchen

D

Screen porch

A

SPECS

Bedrooms: 3
Bathrooms: 2½
Heating system: Oil-fired, forced air

Size: 1,800 sq. ft.
Cost: $100 per sq. ft.
Completed: 1993
Location: Connecticut

Photos taken from lettered positions.

A high ceiling signifies an important space. A two-story room, which the architect calls the living hall, dominates the interior of this house. The Rumford fireplace is surrounded by a board-and-batten wall composed of MDO plywood and pine astragals. Note the square windows: The arched shape so prominent on the exterior was created with an exterior wall that overhangs the windows. Photo taken from C on floor plan.

Long views make a small house feel bigger. The two-story height of the living hall (at the far end of the photo) is balanced visually by the expanse of kitchen and dining area that flows into it. Photo taken from D on floor plan.

of suburban houses today is that they are larger than necessary. Too often their formality or imagery requires spaces that are not used. The formal living room, for example, is an architectural relic. Even when I was growing up, children were banned from this room, and the furniture often was covered with plastic—almost as a precursor of the room's eventual demise.

Romantic houses tend to synthesize the use of many rooms into a few rooms. In the Neely house, the living room and the family room become the living hall. This also means less circulation space (hallways, doorways, etc.), which means a house can be smaller.

Romantic houses demonstrate the same balance or resolution of tensions in their elevations as they do in their plans. The dominant themes of the Neely house's exterior are the steeply pitched roofs and the large, almost theatrical, living-hall window. But those elements are balanced on one side by the lower pitch of the master-bedroom wing and on the other by small bay windows, one over the other.

By the way, if you look closely at the living-hall window, you will notice that the arched shape of the window is created by the exterior walls (bottom photo, p. 96). The windows are conventional rectangles. There also is a 2-ft. space between the exterior arch and the interior windows. This recession of windows behind the arched exterior wall helps shade the living hall from the southern sun. It also provides a transition between inside and outside and makes the window more interesting than it would otherwise be. And finally, creating the arches this way cost considerably less than buying custom-made, curved windows.

Such projections and recesses are common in romantic houses. Besides the living-hall window, many other examples occur in the Neely house. The entry porch, protecting one's arrival from rain, snow or wind, is carved out of the northeast corner. The window bay at the kitchen sink seems to reach out for light during those times of the day when you are most likely to be eating, sitting or working in the kitchen. The south- and west-facing screen porch off the master bedroom also is a recess in the overall mass of the house, providing both protection from the sun and privacy. Even the dormers offer interesting projections to a roof, but they occur only where necessary for headroom at the top of the stair or in a bedroom. All of these variations in the exterior facade enliven the house and give it a romantic playfulness, a sense of surprise not normally felt in flat-facade houses. Such unpredictability would go a long way toward relieving the dullness of the present suburban houses.

Playful detailing—Finally, romantic houses have details that evoke feelings, such as playfulness, warmth, softness and surprise. These are elusive notions, but what distinguishes romantic details is the personal nature of the feeling they seek to evoke. Such details are natural outgrowths of the other aspects of the plans and the elevations or of the projections and the recesses I discussed earlier.

For example, the chimney on the Neely house is not a simple straight run, single color, but it is made up of two colors with bricks set in at the corners. Such chimney details are not cheaper to execute than a simple chimney. If they were, we all would see them more often in new houses. But these details are not as expensive as you might think. Admittedly, recessing the corners of the chimney mass requires more time—and thought—on the part of the mason. But changing the color of some of the bricks to form a stripe certainly doesn't cost any more.

On the roof, two stripes, made up of a white and green blend shingle, cross a field of solid green. Both colors are standard three-tab shingles, so their compatibility wasn't a problem. Again this is not a more-expensive detail; it requires only some additional thought and some care in aligning the stripe with the gable detailing. This decorative detailing at the gable peaks has a half-circle shape that plays off the arch in the living-hall window. The detail is constructed of ½-in. MDO plywood and pine edging.

On the interior, there are other details I consider to be romantic. The two that appeal to me the most are the Rumford fireplace in the living hall and the board-and-batten wall around it. A Rumford fireplace is based on the formulas devised by Count Rumford in the late 18th century. You can find all you need to know about these fireplaces in a little reference book called *The Forgotten Art of Building a Good Fireplace* by Vrest Orton (Yankee Books). By its sheer size, the Neelys' fireplace lends an air of warmth to the living hall. The board-and-batten wall surrounding the fireplace is made up of MDO plywood with 1¾-in. stock-pine astragals applied as battens.

A dormer adds light and headroom. From inside the house, a shed dormer adds light and headroom at the top of the stairs. (Outside, the dormer adds interest to the facade.) In the background, the loft overlooks the living hall and serves as a music room for the Neelys. Photo taken from E on floor plan.

Does a romantic house work?—Does this romantic house really provide the Neelys with emotional sustenance and serve as an anecdote to these hectic, high-tech times? It seems to. The Neelys spend a great deal of time in their home now. It has become the hub for all of their family and holiday gatherings. Perhaps the greatest testimony to the house's success is that the Neelys haven't yet hooked up cable television.

Perhaps, just perhaps, our romantic intuitions are not all that bad in sustaining our lives. Of course, it would be silly to pretend that a building is merely a product of emotion; intellect too plays an important role. But when designing and building houses, we might want to consider our hearts before our heads, or at the very least, allow our instincts and intuitions to guide our intellects. □

Jeremiah Eck practices architecture in Boston, Mass., and is a lecturer in architecture at the Harvard Graduate School of Design. Paul MacNeely was associate architect on the project. Photos by Anton Grassel except where noted.

Economical by Design

Architects fashion a sophisticated house with a utilitarian heart for under $77 per sq. ft.

by Cathi and Steven House

Curve delineates rooms. An S-curve ceiling line separates the living room and the dining area. Painted pale blue in a house with otherwise white walls and ceilings, the curving wall above this line adds a distinctly contrasting shape to a rectilinear building. Photo taken from A on floor plan.

When Robert and Fran Stine first walked into our office, they were filled with doubts about whether they could afford to hire an architect to design their home. The Stines were living in an apartment across the street from our office, on San Francisco's Nob Hill, and for years they had walked by our office, pausing from time to time to study the models and the drawings of projects we put in our windows. When they were ready to build on their wooded lot in La Honda, California, a rural community on the peninsula 45 minutes south of San Francisco, they thought it was at least worth asking.

It may sound obvious, but our first task was to figure out just how much money the Stines would have for the construction part of building their house. After setting aside $15,000 for engineering and architectural fees, we had $100,000 left for the building.

Our preliminary tally of how big a house the Stines needed added up to 1,500 sq. ft. That meant the $100,000 construction budget would also have to include well, water tanks and septic field. Working with such a budget is not easy in this part of the country, but we took the job, hoping we'd be able to devise a prototype of an affordable house. We reasoned that if we kept the house simple, we could pull it off. We also decided to try using materials in such a way as to achieve more than one goal.

The spaces find their places—Once we had the budget figured out, our second task was to settle on the number and type of spaces we could include in the house while staying within the budget. In addition to the kitchen, dining and living spaces, the Stines needed a room that could be a study, family or guest room. They needed two bathrooms, a master bedroom and a bedroom for daughter Katie. The cars would go under a separate carport that included some storage space. And finally, the plan had to include a place for Robert's piano. He's a professional composer, and Robert's music studio needed to be private enough for him to maintain his concentration and to keep him from disturbing the rest of the household. Yet the studio also had to be centrally located for the times when he wanted to share his creations.

There's a reason why affordable houses have straight lines, a minimum of corners and square footprints. Corners cost money, and curved walls cost a lot more to build than straight ones—especially curved exterior walls that have to be made to stand up to the weather.

Square floor plans are more economical than rectangular ones because the square encloses more space than a rectangle for the same amount of foundation and wall. For example, a 20-ft. square house has 80 lin. ft. of wall and 400 sq. ft. of living space. A 10-ft. by 30-ft. house also has 80 lin. ft. of wall but only 300 sq. ft. of living space. So we chose a square footprint, 28 ft. (or seven sheets of plywood) on a side.

The living and dining rooms, along with the kitchen, the family room and a half bath, are downstairs (floor plan, right). The living and dining rooms are adjacent to one another, but they

House in a box. *The authors chose a square shape for the envelope of the house because it's the least expensive shape to build. Then to enliven the box, they varied the ceiling heights, emphasized the views with big windows and showcased the dramatic curving wall of the master bedroom as it cuts through the center of the house.*

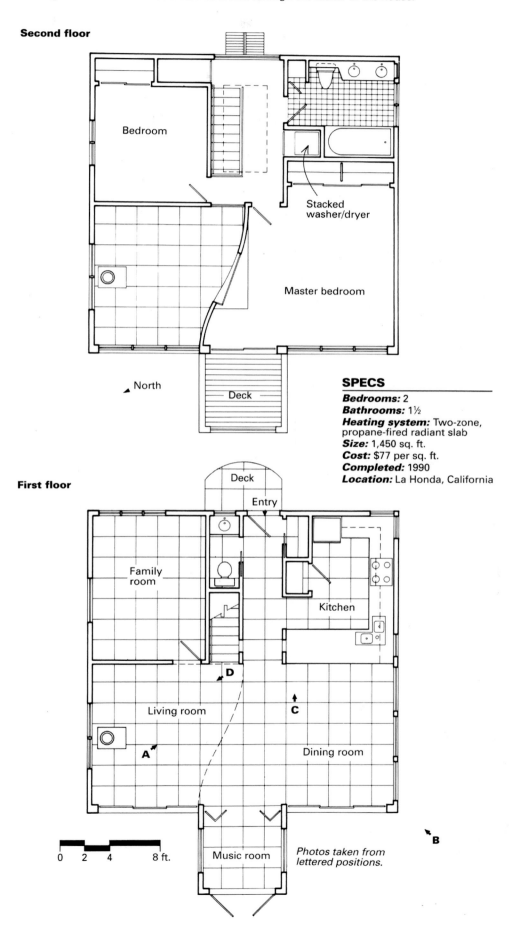

Second floor

Bedroom

Stacked washer/dryer

Master bedroom

North

Deck

First floor

Deck

Entry

Family room

Kitchen

Living room

Dining room

Music room

A

B

C

D

0 2 4 8 ft.

Photos taken from lettered positions.

SPECS

Bedrooms: 2
Bathrooms: 1½
Heating system: Two-zone, propane-fired radiant slab
Size: 1,450 sq. ft.
Cost: $77 per sq. ft.
Completed: 1990
Location: La Honda, California

Straight lines, crisp corners. Keeping it simple means straight lines and standard materials. On the west side of the house, 8-ft. sliding doors open onto the deck. The windows above them are off-the-shelf units that continue the vertical lines of the doors. The bump-out behind the cat is the music room, topped with a deck off the master bedroom. Aluminum extrusions trim the outside corners. Photo taken from B on floor plan.

are clearly separated by the curving line of the ceiling as it waves across the center of the house (photo p. 100). This is the only curve in the house, and it did cost more than a straight wall. But it's an interior wall made of simple materials—studs and drywall—so it didn't upset the budget.

The bedrooms are on the second floor, as are the full bath and the laundry. We tucked a stacked washer and dryer into a hall closet. The laundry is lit by a big skylight and a huge window in the hall, making this place a bit more inviting for one of life's less-exciting tasks.

Robert's music studio, large enough for a baby grand and an accompanist, became an 8-ft. square bump-out that protrudes from the west side of the house (photo facing page). The tiny studio has sound-tight doors that open to the living and dining rooms on one side and another set of French doors that open onto the deck for open-air concerts. The roof of the music studio is a deck off the master bedroom.

Walls, windows and floors—Wood-frame construction in California is typically sheathed in plywood methodically nailed to create shear walls that resist wind and earthquakes. Because we were required to have the plywood anyway, we decided to make it more than just a structural skin. By upgrading the material for a relatively modest increase in price, we had our exterior finish. The ⅝-in. plywood we chose is a resawn cedar, stained a soft gray to match the muted color of the boulders scattered around the property. The flat simplicity of the plywood makes a clean backdrop for the composition of the windows.

We selected stock aluminum windows and combined them into huge window walls that provide a view of the sky or the trees. For example, the 15-ft. tall window in the living room is composed of 10, 3-ft. square standard aluminum windows, which cost about $150 apiece (bottom photo, right). The resulting window looks far more complicated and dramatic than its modest price would suggest.

The operable windows take advantage of the site's natural air conditioning. When cool air from the nearby valley starts rising through the woods, opening a couple of windows funnels the breeze through the house.

The windows are set flush to the exterior wall and trimmed with drywall on the inside. The clean edges of the drywall around the windows make neatly carved openings in the walls, eliminating trim pieces that would otherwise clutter the composition and saving the expense of casings and the labor to install them.

To complement the brushed silver color of the aluminum windows and to keep the house form crisp, brushed aluminum extrusions trim the outside corners of the building (Extrusion #PCM7575 by Fry Reglet, 625 So. Palm Ave., Alhambra, Calif. 91803; 818-289-4744). Galvanized steel pipe handrails continue the clean look both inside and out.

For the sake of economy, we built the house on a concrete slab. The slab, however, also doubles as the finish floor. So we added a warm, rose-colored pigment to the concrete. Then contractor Jim Campi's crew scored the concrete on

Basic black. Black-laminate countertops and black cabinet pulls in the kitchen match the colors of the appliances and contrast sharply with the light straw color of the birch cabinets. The countertops extend into the window openings to become windowsills. Photo taken from C on floor plan.

2-ft. centers to make a decorative grid and troweled the concrete to a glass-smooth finish. This saved substantially on the cost of installing another finish on top of the concrete slab, with a result almost as beautiful as polished stone (bottom photo, right). Propane-fueled radiant heating in the floor makes it warm and inviting.

By the way, by using the concrete slab, we were able to put more windows in the house than typically allowed by California's tough energy code. That's because the slab acts as a heat sink, which conserves energy.

Colors and finishes—There is very little unpainted wood in the house, but what natural wood there is becomes a focal point. Bathroom and kitchen cabinets are birch plywood finished with clear lacquer to preserve their light straw color. The black-laminate kitchen countertop and the black cabinet pulls provide a cohesive backdrop for the matching black appliances (photo above). Open shelves next to the breakfast bar provide some conspicuous display space for special pots and mugs.

We picked industrial carpeting because it will wear well under this growing family, but careful attention was given to the look of the carpet. It's a Berber weave in shades of muted gray. Lighting inside is predominantly recessed cans with a few frosted glass fixtures selected for their clean lines. Industrial floodlights are used outside to illuminate the deck and the entry.

Privacy is not a problem on this isolated site, but to control the sun most efficiently, we selected vertical blinds in a soft gray fabric. The walls throughout are painted a matching soft gray—with the exception of the curving wall of the master bedroom above the living room. It's painted a soft turquoise.

The Stines didn't have any preconceived notions about the style of their house and entrusted us to develop its overall look. They did, however, request that it have clean lines and minimal

Tall ceiling. The living room isn't very large, but the room's 17-ft. high ceiling and towering windows impart an expansive feeling to the room. Photo taken from D on floor plan.

moldings. Its simple, cube shape is a logical outgrowth of that request, but it didn't mean that an inexpensive house has to be a modernist building. The components that we chose to spend a little extra money on—the curved wall, steel handrails and towering rows of windows—could just as easily have been spent on details to craft a simple house of another style. □

Cathi and Steven House are partners in the San Francisco, Calif., architectural firm of House + House. David Thompson was the project architect. Photos by Gerald Ratto except where noted.

Shade in the tropics. Roof overhangs of more than 6 ft. help screen exterior walls and windows from intense Caribbean sunlight. Rainwater collected from the galvanized steel roof is piped to a cistern for use later. Photo taken at A on floor plan.

Mango House

Deep roof overhangs and an open design help cool a house in the Caribbean

by Peter Mullen

Hurricane Hugo slammed into the island of St. Croix at dusk on Sept. 17, 1989. In the 12 hours that followed, Hugo thrashed its way along the spine of the island, traveling the 23 miles from east to west at a tortuous 2 mph. Hugo was a Category-5 hurricane, with sustained winds in excess of 150 mph, and the backside of the storm carried a cluster of tornadoes whose winds were estimated at 250 mph. No building on the island survived undamaged.

St. Croix, in fact, was devastated. The island had been green with tropical plants before Hugo; in its wake was a brown wasteland. Most buildings on the island were severely damaged. Many were destroyed. One of these badly damaged buildings was a single-story, three-unit dwelling

Framing details. **Roof overhangs are supported by eaves beams and diagonal braces.**

in the hills overlooking Christiansted. The building was next to a house I had designed a few years earlier for Elizabeth and Michael Kaiser. After Hugo, the Kaisers acquired the wrecked building and asked me to design a three-bedroom guest house on the same foundation.

A major part of my job was to design a house that took advantage of the climatic conditions on St. Croix. To keep the house comfortable, natural cross-ventilation was used, rather than an elaborate mechanical cooling system. The wood-framed second story includes 6-ft. wide roof overhangs to shield the walls and the windows from sunlight (photo above). And the new building is anchored solidly to the concrete slab and existing concrete-block walls so that the house

Bottom photo, this page: Peter Mullen

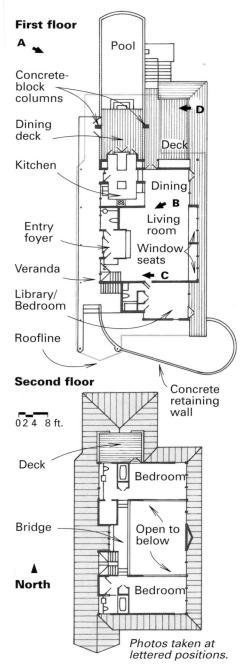

First floor

A

Pool

Concrete-block columns

Dining deck

Kitchen

Dining

Deck

D

B

Living room

Entry foyer

Window seats

Veranda

C

Library/ Bedroom

Roofline

Concrete retaining wall

Second floor

0 2 4 8 ft.

North

Deck

Bedroom

Bridge

Open to below

Bedroom

Photos taken at lettered positions.

Floor plan aids cooling
An open design, including a two-story living room vented at the roof, helps keep air moving inside the house. Wide roof overhangs shield windows and walls from intense sunlight, and big decks offer plenty of opportunities for enjoying the view.

Second-floor bridge. The two bedrooms on the second floor are linked by a bridge spanning the 25-ft. living room below. Photo taken at B on floor plan.

Nice stair, but the balustrade wouldn't meet U. S. codes. Photo taken at C on floor plan.

would better resist storms like Hugo that might strike in the future.

Using what Hugo left—Most of the demolition on the existing structure had been done by the storm. The flat, wooden roof and all the windows had been not-so-neatly removed by Hugo, leaving the concrete slab and reinforced concrete-block bearing walls capped by steel-reinforced concrete bond beams. It was my intent to use as much of the remaining masonry and concrete structure as I could. The original 51-ft. by 28-ft. building was divided into four bays, each about 12-ft. wide, by concrete-block bearing walls. I decided that portions of the two middle walls should be removed to open up the first-floor liv-

ing area. To complete the demolition, several interior non-load-bearing partitions were removed.

The remaining wall configuration provided an open first-floor plan that accommodates an entry foyer and a powder room, the living and dining areas, a kitchen and a library/bedroom with bath (drawing above). I maintained an existing 1-ft. level change in the floor slab but changed its location slightly to separate kitchen and foyer spaces from the adjacent living areas. The exterior walkway on the west side (the entry side) of the building made a perfect entry veranda when covered by a broad roof overhang. Beyond the kitchen is a covered deck leading to a swimming pool (photo p. 106). On the second floor, two more bedrooms, each with a bath, were placed

Drawings: Jeff Bellantuono

A deck for dining. Beyond the kitchen is a pool and a covered dining deck. The structure is supported by concrete columns and bond beams reinforced with steel. Photo taken at D on floor plan.

above the remaining bearing walls of the north and south bays. This plan left the two center bays (a total of about 25 ft.) open with a two-story living room between them. A wooden bridge, partially supported by ⅜-in. steel tension rods hung from the roof, connects the two bedrooms and provides access to a stair (top photo, p. 105).

It all worked on paper, but making this design a reality on an island 1,100 miles southeast of Miami, Florida, had its complications. When my architectural firm designed the Kaisers' main house a few years earlier, Michael and I experienced two problems: We never seemed to have the materials on site when we needed them, and there weren't enough skilled craftsmen working on the house every day. In taking on the new guest house, we were determined to avoid these pitfalls. My firm calculated the materials needed and ordered supplies from the states early enough to ensure a timely arrival on the site. Michael recruited quality craftsmen who were committed for the duration of the project.

As it happened, Michael was overseeing the restoration of his 19th-century house in Palm Beach, Florida, just as I was beginning to design the guest house. Working on the Florida job were three Finnish carpenters in their 50s, and Michael

asked them if they would build the guest house in St. Croix when their work in Florida was complete. They agreed, and I began design work confident that the house would be built skillfully. The carpenters were supervised by Torsti Laine, one of the Finns from Florida. The design included an upper story with an exposed timber frame and other wood architectural details, so their superb carpentry skills were critical to our success.

Cooling in the tropics—Big storms aside, the island's climate is as predictable as it is pleasant: 15-mph trade winds that blow almost constantly from the east, 12-hour exposures to cloudless solar radiation, a temperature range of between 62° and 94° and annual rainfall of 45 in. Natural cross ventilation is the ideal method for making houses comfortable in the tropics. The 360-day dependability of the trade winds allowed us to provide operable windows on windward and leeward sides to control the natural airflow through all rooms and obviate the need for mechanical systems. I did, however, include large ceiling fans in each room to aid ventilation on those rare windless days. The open, two-story plan of the house, with its rooms overlooking and interconnected with one another, further en-

hances the natural ventilation by introducing a chimney effect. Hot air rises two stories to a large exhaust dormer that removes the hottest air at roof level and induces cooler air to enter at the lower living levels.

Having introduced windows for ventilation and views, I added broad roof overhangs to protect them, as well as the exterior walls, from direct sunlight during the hottest part of the day. The second line of defense against the hot sun was insulation: 5½ in. of fiberglass batt insulation in the second-story walls and 2½ in. of rigid foam insulation in the roof. The foam insulation installed on top of the 1x6 T&G roof sheathing stops the heat, and the roof structure—some of the best craftsmanship of the Finnish carpenters— is open to view from the rooms below. Rooms that produce heat or odors, like the kitchen and the bathrooms, are located next to the leeward wall to provide a direct and natural exhaust.

Another climatic factor is rainfall, an important consideration in residential design on St. Croix. Caribbean roofs not only serve the traditional purposes of providing shade, insulation and shelter from rain, but they also provide surface area to catch potable water. The guest house, which the owners call Mango House, relies on a cistern that stores rain for its only source of water. Most houses on the island have similar arrangements.

Timber frame above—To make the best use of the carpenters' skills and to limit any additional load on the existing foundation, I designed the second floor to be of timber-frame construction instead of masonry. I thought that having a one-story masonry separation between the wood of the second floor and the voracious local termites would be enough. This, however, turned out to be another Northeastern practice that was not applicable to the Caribbean. Through research it became apparent that, in at least one stage of their lives, Caribbean termites fly. So having one story of concrete between wood and the ground didn't offer enough protection. My thoughts of building an exposed timber frame started fading to a pale shade of green as I visualized lumber treated with chromated copper arsenate (CCA).

My search for an effective alternative to CCA-treated wood led to the U. S. Forest Service experimental station in Gulfport, Mississippi, which had been testing a borate treatment for wood (see sidebar, right). One of the best features of this alternative to CCA treatment is that borate doesn't change the natural color of the wood. With the design work complete and construction documents in hand, the entire lumber list was established, cut in South Carolina, treated with borate in Savannah, Georgia, and shipped to the job site, all within two months. Because borate-treated lumber was a little more expensive than CCA-treated wood and not as resistant to weather, I opted for borate-treated lumber only where it would be exposed. In most other applications, and especially where the lumber would be in contact with concrete or exposed to the weather, CCA-treated lumber was used.

Key structural elements of the second-story are 6x6 timber columns that were anchored either to the existing concrete bond beam at the top of the first-story block walls or to the first-floor slab with prefabricated steel hold-downs and expansion bolts. The columns support the roof and provide resistance against lifting forces in high winds. To make a smooth transition from the 8-in. concrete-block walls of the first floor, the second floor was framed with 2x8s up to the level of the windowsills. Above that, walls are of 2x6 construction. The difference in the width of the outside wall created a 2-in. ledge where we installed a pitched water table around the perimeter of the house. The water table was capped with ironwood, a superior weather-resistant species.

Building the roof—With the timber columns and second-story walls in place, the next step was to build the roof structure. To each 6x6 timber column the carpenters attached a pair of 2x6 diagonal outriggers that reach up to support eaves beams (bottom photo, p. 104). The eaves beams are pairs of 2x12s with 2x spacers between them that support the 3x10 southern yellow pine roof rafters. The rafters cross the eaves beams 2 ft. from the outside wall and continue out another 5 ft. to provide about 6 ft. of shade around the building. All timber-to-timber connections were carefully notched and bolted and reinforced with specially fabricated steel splice plates. Wherever windows didn't get in the way, the exterior walls were reinforced with 1½-in. wide, 12-ga. steel diagonal bracing for increased rigidity and wind resistance.

Between each rafter—sandwiched between the eaves beam below and the roof sheathing above—I selected clear glass panels instead of more conventional frieze blocks. The glass seems to make the 40-ft. by 60-ft. hip roof float above its support system and brings light into what is usually the darkest part of a house—the space where the roof and the wall meet. The glass is held between a pair of 2x2s that are through-bolted to the rafters. The 2xs trap the glass and anchor the rafters to the eaves beams.

The roof over the 25-ft. living room is supported by a parallel-chord truss that acts as a structural ridge beam. The rafters and the decking were planed prior to installation, so no further finish was required. The roof is capped with corrugated steel roofing over the foam insulation and a layer of 15-lb. felt. The galvanized roof panels run from ridge to eaves without horizontal seams. The panels are attached to 2x3 purlins with screws and neoprene washers. I located the galvanized steel gutters about 1 ft. above the ends of the decorative rafter tails and provided drain lines to pipe roof water to the cistern below.

Sheathing and interior details—I wanted a stucco finish on the exterior of both the first and second floors, so structural sheathing was installed on the interior of the building. That's the reverse of the usual U. S. standard of applying drywall on the inside surface of exterior walls and plywood on the outside. I selected ½-in. straight-grain ash veneer plywood as the interior finish and shear wall. The plywood is nailed to the studs, and the nail heads are covered with cypress battens (bottom photo, p. 105).

The ash plywood with cypress base and vertical battens became the interior finish on the second floor. The wood got a light stain. The ash plywood was set flush with mahogany window and door casings so that the simple trapezoidal battens not only covered the joint between adjacent panels but also joints between panels and doors and panels and windows.

On the first floor, the concrete slab was covered with CCA-treated wood sleepers and 1x6 T&G cypress flooring. CCA-treated floor joists and plywood underlayment created the new bedroom floors on the second level, followed by the 1x4 cypress T&G finish floors. Extensive cypress trim, including base and crown molding, ties the part-stucco, part-wood construction of the first floor to the all-wood construction of the second floor. The wide window seats on the first floor, the mahogany door trim and stair treads and the ash-plywood kitchen cabinets are treated with AwlGrip, a two-part polyurethane product that stands up well to abrasion and sunlight (U. S. Paint, 831 South 21st St., St. Louis, Mo. 63103; 314-621-0525).   □

———

Peter Mullen is a partner in Mullen, Palandrani Architects in New York City, N. Y. Photos by Scott Gibson except where noted.

Borate treatment, an alternative to CCA

The construction of the guest house on St. Croix called for the use of treated wood to guard against the Formosan termites that are so prevalent on Caribbean islands. I wanted to expose timbers and roof sheathing, but the pale-green hues of wood treated with chromated copper arsenate (CCA) seemed inappropriate. The alternative was lumber treated with sodium borate, which is extracted from borax ore. The ore is mined in California's Mojave Desert.

Borate treatment has been used for 50 years in New Zealand, Australia and England to discourage decay and insect damage in building materials. Water-soluble sodium borate is introduced into the wood in one of two ways: either through dip diffusion for green wood or by conventional vacuum-pressure treatment for kiln-dried wood. In dip diffusion, freshly cut lumber is lowered into a vat of the borate solution where it soaks for a few minutes. The wood is then air dried for four to eight weeks. During this period the borate migrates through the wood, penetrating even the heartwood. The borate solution can even be sprayed on wood already in place as a remedial treatment for insect infestation or fungus, although this method is not nearly as effective.

U. S. Borax, Inc. (26877 Tourney Road, Valencia, Calif. 91355; 805-287-5463) sells the material used in the process and licenses companies to sell treated lumber under the Tim-Bor and Cari-Bor trademarks. Borate treatment does not affect the natural color of the wood, but it makes the wood toxic to insects and fungus. According to the company, the process eliminates harsh chemical treatments that might pose a danger to building occupants or to tradesmen. In addition, borate treatment doesn't change the workability of the wood; it increases the wood's resistance to flames; and it isn't corrosive to metal fasteners. Treatment is relatively inexpensive.

A disadvantage of the borate treatment is that the borate solution remains water soluble. As a result, borate-treated wood is not recommended for applications where it will be submerged in water or placed in contact with the ground. Nor would it be recommended for installation next to masonry surfaces, as a mudsill would be. According to U. S. Borax, however, the application of a water repellent finish (like a paint or a wood sealer) over the borate-treated wood allows it to be used in some exterior applications. The company also is trying to figure out how to fix the borate in the wood during treatment. —*P. M.*

The House in Alice's Field

An architect explains why he built a small house and what he had to give up to get it

by Robert W. Knight

My wife and I bought this land instantly, or at least that's how it seemed to me. We had looked at many pieces of property, and a number of them were okay. Indeed, we were ready to make an offer on one, but part of us was still looking. When we walked down into Alice's field, all parts of me stopped looking. But of course, it cost more than we had planned to spend. If there is a universal experience in building a house, it is probably this: starting out in the hole because the land cost more than you wanted it to.

After spending 25 years designing houses for other people, I have learned that probably the most important part of getting to where you want to go is the ability to focus on what *you* need and want. Be willing to spend the money

on that. But don't get trapped spending money on the stuff you don't care about. If you have dreamed of having a stone fireplace, you better have it. That doesn't mean, however, that you have to have granite countertops and Jacuzzis. For that first big decision, blowing the budget on the right piece of ground is never a mistake.

Why not a great big house?—So we have this wonderful hay field rimmed with old oak trees that slides down onto a peninsula in the Baga-duce River about halfway up the Maine coast. And the house needs to exploit it and live up to it, to be as wonderful as the site so that we enhance this place rather than detract from it. Sometimes, exploiting a wonderful site means putting up a huge house. But to my mind, that

would have been a mistake here. Out on the peninsula was where I wanted to build, but a big house would overflow the site visually. A little house would be just right.

Starting out short on cash added a financial incentive to the notion of small house, but it was a notion that Lucia and I had long entertained. We spend a good deal of time in the summer on an old wooden sailboat with about 40 sq. ft. of floor space. Because we find this space comfortable, it seemed to us that we would also be comfortable living in a house that fit around us the way our boat does.

There is a balance here. If you get too small, concentrating only on saving space, you can add complexity and expensive things such as built-in cabinetry to maximize your limited storage. These things can cost more than making the house a bit bigger.

We don't need a big living room—The first thing we realized was that we could do without the traditional living room. When people are in a living room, they sit around and talk, listen to music, read and watch TV. All this could be accomplished with an approximately 10-ft. by 12-ft. bay with built-in seating.

Standing on the building site, I knew I wanted a place to sit and talk that was surrounded by the view of the river. If this "living-room" bay projected into the view and had glass on all sides (top photo, p. 111), it would be all we needed. So the house's design started with this space. It never changed and anchored all of the other design decisions.

Opposite the living room is the kitchen (bottom photo), facing south, looking up the field and in control of the house. The kitchen needed to be bigger because we tend to get at cross purposes with each other when we are both cooking, so we needed two distinct work areas.

We had decided that we needed two bedrooms and two baths—upstairs would be ours, downstairs our son's room (when he is home for visits) or our guest's. So that leaves an entry space, an eating space and a bed/bath space to deal with on the first floor.

The building site is on the west side of the property, so in an effort to minimize the visual effect of our driveway bisecting the hayfield, the driveway hugs the western edge of the property as it approaches the house. This site organization led us to an entry on the west (floor plan, p. 110), so it made sense to include the eating space near the entry because both are public spaces, leaving the east for the downstairs bed/bath. Putting the dining area to the west also made it easy to put a screened porch on the northwest, where it belongs, giving us the afternoon sun in the summer when it is setting in the northwest, but not shading us in the winter when the sun is low in the south.

With easy access from the dining room (photo p. 112), the porch adds to the living space, encouraging lots of casual coming and going from porch to inside. It's important to use the relatively inexpensive space provided by decks and screened porches to augment the limited space of small houses.

The second floor is the master bedroom—Our bedroom is upstairs, and Lucia insisted on it being big enough (12 ft. by 16 ft.) for a comfy reading chair so that it can serve as an alternative living space if one of us wants to get away and be private (photo left, p. 113). There's also a wonderful bathroom on the south that is big

A big house would have been overwhelming. Along the north edge of Alice's field, Maine's Bagaduce River bends gently to create a narrow peninsula, a perfect building site with water views on three sides. Photo taken at A on floor plan.

Long views make a difference. The kitchen, dining area and living area are all open to one another, which allows long views that make the house feel bigger than it is. Photo taken at B on floor plan.

SPECS

Bedrooms: 2
Bathrooms: 2
Heating system: Oil-fired hydronic/hot air
Size: 1,326 sq. ft.
Cost: $111 per sq. ft.
Completed: 1996
Location: Brooksville, Maine

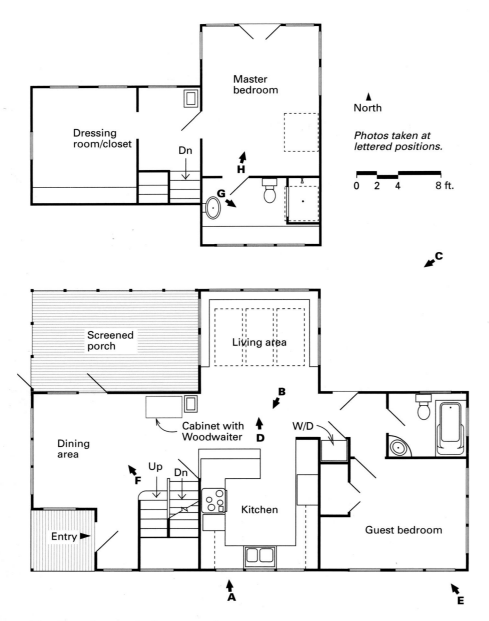

Most of the windows face the river. On the north elevation, you can see the living-room bay extending from the center of the house, as well as the French doors "leading nowhere" from the second-floor bedroom. Photo taken at C on floor plan.

Mostly a house to two people

To make the most of a small floor plan, the dining area, kitchen and living area all share circulation space. Also, the dining area opens onto the screened porch, which serves as extra living space during the warmer months. The upstairs is given over to the master bedroom, making it a private haven.

enough to have a sort of greenhouse for soaking up the sun and for long showers in the winter (photo right, p. 113). Showering there is like bathing in a jungle.

The rest of the second floor is a nice sunny landing at the top of the stairs and a big walk-in dressing room with all our storage on hangers, on shelves or in drawers but not behind a lot of expensive doors.

Yeah, but what's it going to look like?— While all this logical plan work was going on, the form that was emerging from the other side of my brain was of three simple gable forms that sort of slid together (photos above, facing page). I wanted simple forms that were not overly formal because the site dynamics suited a more relaxed house. Much as I like formal, highly composed houses, they look best on a neutral landscape, not competing visually with trees, rivers and hay fields. And I needed strong forms so that the house had a recognizable order seen from the road (about ¼ mi. away) and so that it didn't look like just a little blob (photo p. 108).

There are few houses along this shore because the farmers built up by the road and looked at and worked in the fields. The houses they built were mostly clapboard farmhouses, the best of them Greek revival. But our plan was developing a lot of corners and a lot of glass on the river side, both of which would conflict with the somewhat stiff requirements of the Greek-revival style. Greek revival would also lean toward costly decisions such as cedar-shingle roofs, expensive trim and paint. I could picture such a house there, but it felt wrong, like spending money on clothes that don't suit your personality.

What did emerge from these conflicts, after a good deal of back and forth, was inspired more

A 10-ft. by 12-ft. living room. To conserve space in this small house, the author reduced the living room to its essence: a comfortable place to sit. Just off the kitchen, the living area juts out like the prow of a ship to take in views of Maine's Bagaduce River. Photo taken at D on floor plan.

Three gable forms slid together. At 1,326 sq. ft., it's a small house, but it wasn't cheap. The author admits to spending money consciously on "glass and corners," enhancing the view from inside and from out. Narrow fascias delicately emphasize the roof forms. Photo taken at E on floor plan.

Dining spaces get the afternoon sun. A screened porch off the dining area adds useful living space without the expense of insulated walls. Note the bullnose drywall around the windows, which suits the simple lines of the house and also saved on the cost of trim. Photo taken at F on floor plan.

by the informal summer houses that people in Maine call camps. But I was not willing to have the house be completely anonymous, as though it had always been there. I wanted a certain design edge to reflect the fact that I'm an architect. Maybe that's why the windows are purple. The house shouldn't look totally off the rack, but it needed to be recognizable and welcoming.

Once those forms started to emerge, the decisions for shingles, roof color, trim color and everything else started falling into place. When you live with a design and it starts to work—when the house's personality finally emerges and the two halves of the design process become coherent—the small design decisions all fit neatly into place with little struggle.

The design I messed with the most was the roof edge (bottom photo, p. 111). A narrow fascia that angles slightly back was the key to get-

ting a house that felt sheltering and cozy—the vine-covered cottage that most people seem to have buried somewhere in their psyches—yet was simple enough to build that it wouldn't drive my builder crazy or create problems such as ice dams. Some delicacy of line, without a crazy amount of work.

Knowing when to save and when to spend—When it came time to decide about interior finishes, Lucia and I realized, somewhat to our surprise, that we had no objection to flush birch doors (as long as they were solid). That decision started us realizing that we both really like a lean, simple interior, which led us to use the bullnose drywall returns on the window jambs. They cost about $40 per opening, which was much cheaper than trimming and painting. This detail wouldn't work for lots of houses, but

Like showering in a jungle. On the south side of the house, the master bathroom doubles as a greenhouse, combating the effects of Maine's chilly winters with a tropical landscape. Photo taken at G on floor plan.

French doors but no balcony. Although hardly grand, the master bedroom is large enough for a comfortable reading chair and sports an extravagant pair of French doors that lead nowhere but let in lots of light and air. Photo taken at H on floor plan.

I think it works well here and sets the stage for the simple door trim that we used.

In the past when I specified flat board trim, I always included a shrink strip at the top. With biscuit joiners you can now butt door trim without shrinkage cracks. So a simple trim detail that would not have worked well a few years ago works now, fits in and is less expensive.

Where did we spend money? Glass and corners, good cabinetwork, door hardware and a Woodwaiter (W. Bruce Fowler Industries, 292 Queen St., Lennoxville, Quebec, Canada J1M 1K6; 800-290-8510), a mini-elevator that brings stove wood up from the basement. A masonry chimney because it's a gut response with me to have some masonry in the core of the house.

Upstairs in the master bedroom, the French doors to nowhere are a romantic need. I wanted to be able to get up in the morning and throw

open the doors. I didn't need to go out onto something, but I really wanted to throw open the doors, not crank them out. We consciously spent some money on that ... and I do throw them open (in the summer.)

What would I change?—I would put the washer and dryer upstairs in our dressing room; in busy family households, washers do well near the kitchen where they can be tended, but with no kids around it's simpler to keep them where your clothes are.

I would find someplace to recess the TV, which sits opposite the woodstove. The TV never bothered me before, but it feels clunky in this house. And I would figure out where to put the sound-system speakers instead of putting it off.

Would it be cheaper not to have a basement? Yes, on the this site we could have built a float-

ing slab and saved over $5,000, but that would have necessitated building a good deal of external storage at grade as well as a utility room, and I didn't want that. Also, a basement is the cheapest way to have a heated workshop, and I did want that.

Why it's called Alice's field—Our property was named after the lady we bought it from. When we were first looking at the land, our car got stuck in the field in a big rainstorm. After unsuccessfully trying to pull us out, our neighbor called the local towtruck. Listening to the conversation, I heard, "Richard, this is Mathew. Could you come over? The Knights are stuck in Alice's field." And so we are. □

Robert W. Knight is an architect in Blue Hill, Maine. Photos by Kevin Ireton.

Fitting into the landscape. At the end of a winding footpath, the three-building compound emerges in a clearing: the studio to the left, the central main house and the bedroom cabin at the right. Photo taken from A on site plan.

Three Buildings, One House

Separating the parts of a home into different buildings
connects the owners to their environment

by Jeffrey Prentiss

Dave and Carole Grumney live and work in Los Angeles—most of the time. Their second home is on Orcas Island, which is about as unlike Los Angeles as two places can be unlike. Orcas Island is the largest of the San Juan Islands, an archipelago in the middle of Puget Sound on the U. S.-Canadian border. The Grumneys bought their property, a small meadow gently sloping to a tiny beach and cove, backed by a steep forested hillside, because it offered a remarkable site upon which to build a peaceful retreat, a place to escape the frenzy of Los Angeles.

Given the beauty of the site, the last thing the Grumneys wanted to do was to stomp on local aesthetic toes. They wanted a house that weaved well into the natural site and altered it as little as possible. Having heard that I am a native of the islands and an architect who works well with site, the Grumneys asked me to design their island retreat.

A footpath instead of a driveway—The Grumneys wanted to avoid the type of situation in which, for convenience, one could jump directly out of the car into a protected building,

A transition from indoors to out. The main house's front porch, with its long steps, fieldstone fireplace and several doors, encourages outdoor living. Log supports add a rustic flavor reminiscent of the area's first settlements. The office is in the background, and having to walk outdoors to get to it from the other dwellings reinforces a sense of departure. Photo taken from B on site plan.

experiencing neither sun nor rain nor air movement nor shadows in trees nor whir of insects. So in Dave and Carole's case we left the cars at the property's edge and created a footpath that winds through the woods into the dwelling site (top drawing, right), enhancing the sense of discovery and arrival as you meander in. Yes, the footpath means that luggage and groceries have to be carried in, but in return some elemental quality of the site is preserved. This sets a tone for the ambiance of the spot. By the use of the winding footpath, we slowly disclose the destination, keeping the construction site relatively hidden until the path opens up to it.

You have to go outside—In formal neighborhoods, lawns, shrubs and fences demarcate property lines. The inhabited landscape is distinct from one house to another. At the Grumneys', we wanted to fit the structure into the landscape, blurring the distinction between the natural surroundings and the building.

Here, I first began to consider that the house might actually be a cluster of buildings, just as plants cluster in nurturing soils. By having space between structures, there would be more sense of integration of buildings and landscape (photos facing page). Separate buildings allow the landscape to wrap around them, which seemed an ideal way to minimize the impact of construction on the site.

The Grumneys wanted their home to address certain functions, and I separated the functions into the three strongest parts: public (cooking, laundry, guests, living room), work (the studio) and private (the bedroom). In the compound, the public space is centered between the studio and the bedroom (floor plan, right).

This separation of functions and structures places the Grumneys in continual contact with the environment. They need to leave the bedroom cabin each morning to get to the coffeepot and leave the coffeepot to go to work. As the day progresses, they must leave the work space to return for meals and socializing with their houseguests, then leave the social rooms to go to bed.

The property has a natural bowl-like contour, which is mirrored by the siting and massing of the buildings. Sited in a semicircle with the largest building in the middle, each building has a different view toward the channel, and the semicircular siting creates a sense of protection just like an original settlers' compound.

Simple shapes, simple materials—Architecturally, the buildings owe a lot to the old Hudson Bay Co. structures that dot the Pacific Northwest. These simple gable-roof structures were built from materials at hand: logs for walls, cedar shakes on the roof. I didn't want to replicate the Hudson Bay buildings, just work with the basic ideas: simple gable structures with lean-tos and porches attached.

To match the simplicity of the building forms, I specified materials that are simple, straightforward, strong and tactile. There is also a similarity of materials between interior and exterior, and all the structures are similar but not identical in use of materials and design elements. Maintain-

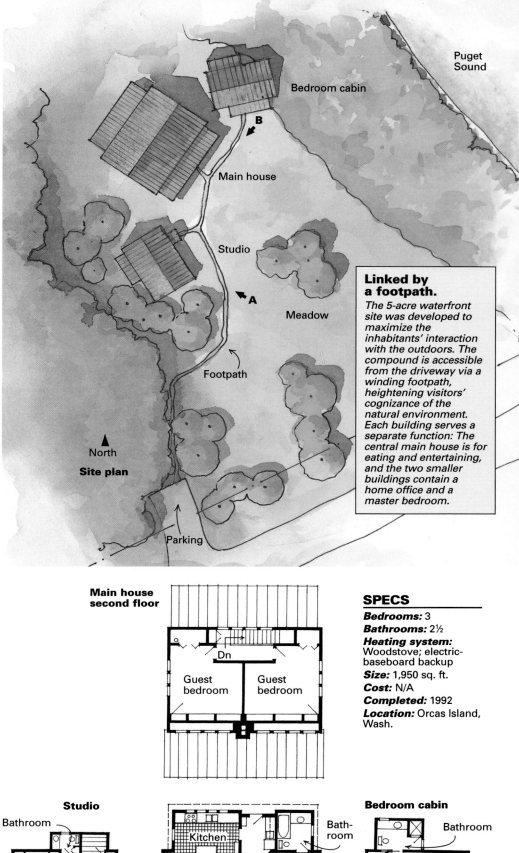

Puget Sound

Bedroom cabin

Main house

Studio

Meadow

Footpath

North

Site plan

Parking

Linked by a footpath.
The 5-acre waterfront site was developed to maximize the inhabitants' interaction with the outdoors. The compound is accessible from the driveway via a winding footpath, heightening visitors' cognizance of the natural environment. Each building serves a separate function: The central main house is for eating and entertaining, and the two smaller buildings contain a home office and a master bedroom.

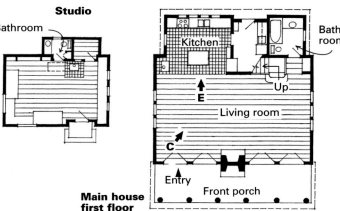

Main house second floor

Dn

Guest bedroom

Guest bedroom

Studio

Bathroom

Main house first floor

Kitchen

Bathroom

Up

Living room

Entry

Front porch

SPECS

Bedrooms: 3
Bathrooms: 2½
Heating system: Woodstove; electric-baseboard backup
Size: 1,950 sq. ft.
Cost: N/A
Completed: 1992
Location: Orcas Island, Wash.

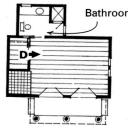

Bedroom cabin

Bathroom

D

In the main house. The center building is designed as a public area for entertaining family and friends. The living room has a pine floor and a cedar ceiling with 10x10 fir beams running into a clerestory light well, seen here in the upper right corner. Even though the windows are large, the covered porch and abundant trees darken the room. The clerestory windows over the porch roof brighten the living room. Photo taken from C on floor plan.

ing similarities among the buildings and between interior and exterior is another way in which the compound eases into the natural setting.

The colors and materials blend with the colors of the woodlands, not totally camouflaged but not glaringly contrasting either. For the exterior, horizontal shiplap siding was prestained in a natural weathered wood tone similar to the color of the aged bark of the surrounding trees.

At the porches, raw logs were used for the posts and the main-porch beam. The logs keep the house from appearing too finished and add the Hudson Bay-shelter character we were seeking. Unlike those old structures, these buildings have metal roofing instead of roof shakes, which were

too expensive and would create a fire hazard and need to be replaced too soon. Metal roofing fit the bill, and its dark green Kynar finish, the premium paint grade for metal roofing, fit into the natural surroundings.

To strengthen the sense of the roofs' mass, the cedar fascias are stained green, slightly lighter than the roofing. The green fascias add a layer of interest to the buildings, too.

For the chimney, Dave wanted a stone fireplace, and he chose local stone picked from the fields. The mason, Vern Landon, did a great job of packing two fireplaces—one facing the porch, the other facing the living room—back to back in a tight area. He also provided a couple of

shelves built into the chimney for use when cooking on the outdoor grill.

Viewing the outdoors—One of the most important aspects of these buildings is their large and plentiful windows. The compound worked well because all the rooms have light and views from several directions. To have as much interaction between inside and outside as possible, one should always be able to look out in several directions from a given spot, with each orientation of the windows giving a different view.

To this end, in the main house, there are four sets of French doors opening to the front porch. The front porch is like a long gallery operating as a transitional layer between indoors and out. Long steps spanning the entire front of the porch and the series of doors encourage people to move in or out anywhere along the south facade.

This long covered porch is also a place to inhabit: The roof provides cover for sitting outside during the Northwest drizzle; the fireplace allows outdoor living in the cool maritime climate. Combined, these two elements—the porch roof and the fireplace—yield the opportunity to experience outdoor sounds and movements without freezing to death from cold and wet.

In the main rooms of each building, light enters from every direction. The Pacific Northwest is often overcast, and the Grumneys' decision to keep almost all of their trees around and in the middle of the compound meant we could be into the dark and gloomies if we were not careful. Putting the porch all across the south facade of the main structure was not going to help either.

To offset the porch shadows, I designed clerestory light wells, framed at the second-floor level, that draw light into the lower floor (photo facing page). The ceiling beams run into the lightwells, which accents the massive 10x10 fir timbers.

These lightwells were created by narrowing the upstairs guest bedrooms, building interior kneewalls 3 ft. in from the exterior wall. The resulting taller kneewalls improved the bedrooms' proportions, and built-in bookcases in the kneewalls occupy what would have been lost space.

In the guest bedrooms and in the bedroom cabin (top photo, right), tall gable-end windows reach up to the cathedral ceilings. There are no collar ties. In the main house contractor Rick Delgarno used a structural ridge bearing on 6x8 window headers. In the bedroom cabin, a structural ridge bears on a 4x6 header high in the gable wall. The gable window is so tall that the header, which is horizontal, extends above the plane of the ceiling.

The windows we selected (Northwest Windows, 3227 164th Ave. S.W., Lynnwood, Wash. 98037; 206-743-4446) have Douglas-fir frames and sashes. The fir is sealed with oil to show off its golden glow, brightening the buildings while remaining in our natural-color palette.

Inside, natural wood was also the desired selection, but not so much that the interior became too dark. Wood floors, wood ceiling and wood trim on the natural-finish windows were enough. As an accent the stairwell is paneled in cedar with a fir railing and fir treads.

For the ceiling 10x10 fir beams cross at 5 ft. on center with T&G fir and hemlock car decking as the finished surface for both ceiling and floor. The large beams, although kiln-dried, checked far more than expected, but we found this an appealing look and kept them.

In the kitchen, painted cabinets of a traditional design brighten the house (bottom photo, right). A long low window above the counter brightens work areas and gives a view of the outdoors from the kitchen, another reminder to the Grumneys that the compound of buildings on the shore of Orcas Island is a long way from Los Angeles. □

Jeffrey Prentiss is an architect in the San Juan Islands and Seattle, Wash. Photos by Rich Ziegner.

In the bedroom cabin. This bedroom, a large closet and a small bathroom make up the bedroom cabin. The gable window's trimmer studs support a large header that supports a structural ridge, allowing for the open cathedral ceiling. The atrium door is one of a pair that open onto a small front porch. Photo taken from D on floor plan.

Kitchen located in main house. For the sake of economy, kitchen cabinets made primarily of medium-density overlay plywood (MDO) were selected. The door frames, while constructed of solid wood, were painted in a light color to brighten the kitchen. Photo taken from E on floor plan.

Dueling Towers
on the Carolina Coast

Designed by different architects, each of these houses
maintains its own personality within a powerful collective presence

by Chuck Dietsche

I f two cooks in the same kitchen is a recipe for trouble, then two architects designing separate halves of the same building should spell disaster. But just the opposite happened when I collaborated with Dan Costa, a Boston-based architect and friend, on a project to create a public beach access for a new resort village planned for Bald Head Island, North Carolina. Located 35 miles south of Wilmington, Bald Head Island and its rugged shoals form the notorious Cape Fear.

Two tall towers flank the path to the beach—Dan and I came up with the idea for the towers during a planning session with Kent

Mitchell, the island's developer, late in 1993. Kent, who is also an architect, wanted to create a distinctive building that would point the way to the beach access for his new island community, Harbour Village. But local development rules limited the amount of land for the beach access, and the cost of building a large community structure would have been prohibitive. So Dan and I volunteered to design and build two single-family houses that would create a kind of gateway to the beach in exchange for a break on the lots. The towers (photo above) would be connected with a trellis and a walkway to carry the public over the fragile dunes to the beach.

A landmark for land and sea. Built to mark the public access to the beach beyond, the towers are a keystone structure for the seaside village. Boat captains have come to use the towers as a range to help navigate the waters. Photo taken at A on floor plan.

Different stairs create different designs— For Dan and me, designing the towers became an instant source of friendly competition. The only rules of the game were that each tower had to be three stories high with a hip roof and that each would be built on a 20-ft. by 20-ft. footprint. We did not look at each other's plans until they were nearly completed so that we wouldn't in-

South tower (Tijuca)

North tower (Rapunzel)

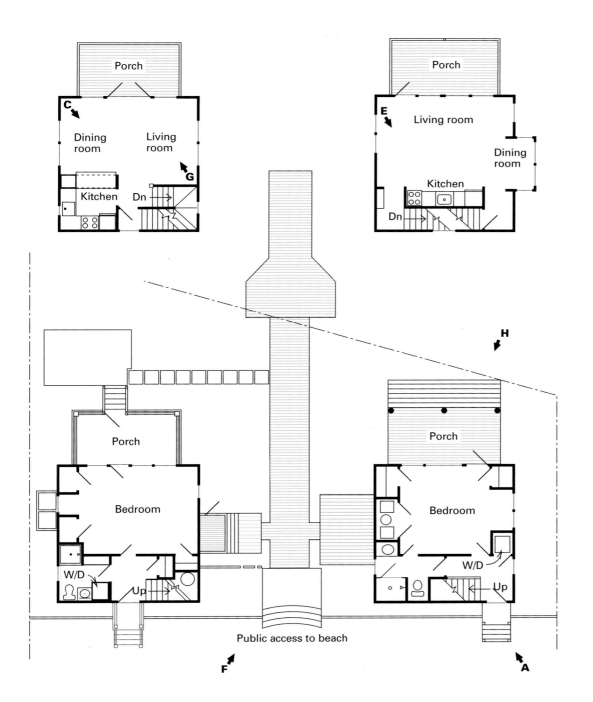

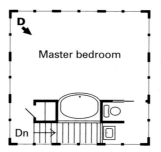

Public access to beach

SPECS

For each tower
Bedrooms: 2
Bathrooms: 2
Heating system: Heat pump/air conditioning
Size: 1,200 sq. ft.
Cost (north tower): $100 per sq. ft.
Cost (south tower): N/A
Completed: 1994
Location: Bald Head Island, North Carolina

North

0 2 4 8 ft.

Photos taken at lettered positions.

Two different towers grow up around two different staircases

Each architect began with a different idea on how best to climb the towers' three floors. The southern tower has a staircase that winds around one corner, creating an L-shaped floor space. The stairs in the northern tower are stacked in straight runs, leaving a large rectangular space on each floor.

Drawings: Mark Hannon

South tower (Tijuca)
Exposed framing, painted beadboard. The interior of this tower recalls New England beach houses with exposed rafters and wood walls. A bathroom with an inside window (above) is on the top floor. Photo taken at B on floor plan. A corner stairway (below) sets off a kitchen space. Photo taken at C on floor plan.

fluence each other's design. Each of the towers was designed with a bedroom and a bathroom on the first floor; kitchen, living space and dining space on the second floor; and the master bedroom and bath on the top floor. We also chose similar materials for the exterior roof and siding of each tower. But beyond these few basic items, not much else is the same between the two buildings.

The differences between the towers begin with two contrasting stair decisions (floor plan, p. 119). Dan's tower (the southern tower with the dark-green accents) has a stairway that winds its way around one corner, creating an L-shaped floor space. My tower (the northern tower with light-green and yellow accents) has two stacked, straight runs of stairs that leave a rectangular-shaped space on each level.

Dan's corner stair allows for a central entry on the first floor and a discreet kitchen separate from the large living and dining area on the second floor (bottom photo). With my stacked stair, the entry is off center, and the kitchen is linear, running almost the entire length of one second-floor wall (bottom photo, facing page). The two different interior layouts are reflected in the different exterior window patterns.

The towers' different personalities are even more apparent from the interior treatments. Dan's tower is named Tijuca, after a beach in Brazil where Dan and his sister Margot (who is also a part owner) summered as children. The simple woodwork, exposed ceiling joists, painted-beadboard paneling and furnishings seem to recall a far-off, simpler time.

I called my tower Rapunzel after the long-haired girl in the children's fairy tail who was held prisoner in a secluded tower. Rapunzel's interior is bright and brash with walls painted in bold, primary colors and simple moldings.

I say po-tay-to, you say po-tah-to—Although the window patterns are probably the most obvious exterior difference between the two towers, there are many other details that Dan and I included that complement each other's designs while creating a comfortable asymmetry.

Although we had agreed to use hip roofs on our towers, we never discussed overhangs. Dan designed Tijuca's roof with wide overhangs supported by large painted brackets that hint at the exposed structure inside. The larger overhangs on Dan's tower also create a slightly shallower pitch on the hip roof, but the eaves of the two

towers are lined up at the same height. The porches on the two towers also received different treatments. I chose not to put a roof over my second-floor porch to take advantage of the afternoon sun. However, I built solid sidewalls to cut down on the island's persistent breezes. The roof over Dan's porch steps down nicely from the wide overhangs that are above, and his more traditional railings create an intimate space for cool rocking-chair evenings (bottom photo, p. 122).

The porches on the first floor are even more different. My porch is approached with stairs that run its full width, drawing the eye into a visual ascent of the tower (photo p. 123). While I supported the porch structure with full cedar logs for a bold, rustic flavor, Dan's screened-in porch with its discreet entry and simple lines makes for a more private, quiet outdoor room.

The contrasting, complementary elements of our two designs are perhaps most evident in the trellis and public walkway where the two impish twins are joined (top photo, p. 122). As you stroll along the boardwalk, the fence and railing on Tijuca's side have strong classic details. The solid top rail creates a powerful horizontal line that points toward the horizon of the sea be-yond. Rapunzel's fence, on the other hand, undulates randomly in a playful mimic of the surrounding dunes.

A 360° view, the essence of the tower experience—At 1,200 sq. ft. per tower, these houses aren't exactly huge, but from the outside, the twin aspect of the towers doubles their impact. However, inside Dan and I had to work to make the houses feel as large as possible. And nowhere is this effort more apparent than in the third-floor bedrooms.

We each wrapped the third floors with a band of windows to take full advantage of the elevation and the view. Being able to look out to the horizon in every direction is at the heart of the tower experience. Also, the windows offer uniform lighting and refreshing cross ventilation throughout the course of the day.

Both Dan and I elected to have cathedral ceilings in the third-floor bedrooms, Dan staying with a theme of exposed rafters and beadboard (top photo, facing page). I chose to plaster the ceiling and paint it evening blue with gold stars scattered all over (photo right). Dan partitioned off the small section of the L formed by stairs for a third-floor bathroom. He put a window in the

North tower (Rapunzel)

Plaster walls and playful colors. A starry sky makes for a fanciful canopy above the master bedroom (above). Photo taken at D on floor plan. Straight stairs behind the kitchen (below) leave an open space for kitchen, living room and dining room. Photo taken at E on floor plan.

partition over the bed to let light from the bathroom filter into the bedroom.

My stair system left me with a large open space on the third floor, but there was no easy way to create a separate bathroom and still have the sweeping tower views I desired. So I opted for what I call the Poconos approach. I placed a whirlpool bath in the middle of the room between two towerlike structures, one of which forms a private area for the commode.

High winds and close calls—Many people question the prudence of building any sort of structure in a hurricane-prone area, much less a pair of tall, skinny buildings such as these. As architect as well as homeowner, I must confess that romance was the guiding force behind both the location and the design of the towers.

To counterbalance any romantic notions that might have been dancing in our heads, Dan and I made sure that we followed all recommendations made by our structural engineer, Rob O'Briant. The towers were built to withstand 110-mph winds, and last summer, hurricanes Bertha and Fran as well as two lesser tropical storms put Rob's structural expertise to the test.

The eyes of both hurricanes passed right over the towers, and a bolt of lightning from Bertha struck my weather station, freezing it forever at a wind speed of 99 mph, its highest possible reading. With some inexplicable luck and with much gratitude to Rob, our towers emerged from the storms with no major damage. □

Chuck Dietsche is an architect who splits his time between Wilmington, North Carolina, and Bald Head Island. Photos by Roe A. Osborn.

Trellis and walkway bridge towering personalities. Beachgoers who use this walkway experience the character of each building. The railings offer a straight, steady transition to sea on one side while the other side mirrors the playful lines of the dunes. Photo taken at F on floor plan.

Covered porch expands the living room. French doors open a window from the living room to the sea. The roof and traditional railing turn the porch into an intimate space that beckons you to sit and rock. Photo taken at G on floor plan.

Full-width stairs for a grand rear entry.
Stairs as wide as the rustic, open porch invite
the eye to climb up the northern tower. The
bump-out on the second floor is an asymmetrical echo of the porch roof on the other tower.
Built to withstand 110-mph winds, the two sen-
tinel towers were twice subjected to 100-plus
mph winds and have so far escaped serious
damage. Photo taken at H on floor plan.

A Little House with Rich Spaces

High-school students assemble an island vacation cottage with prefab panels

by Barry Griblin

A nearby high school has an ingenious approach to teaching basic construction methods. Each year a private sponsor is found to purchase the materials for a building project. For an extra 10% of the cost, the sponsor then receives a fully framed, prefabricated building that is ready to be erected on the site of their choice. In the past, projects have included cabins, carports, worksheds and other wood-framed structures of similar bulk and complexity.

A couple of years ago the class was set to build a garage when the sponsor suddenly withdrew. The class of 18 students was left without a project on which to develop practical framing skills. By the time my architectural office got a call to see if we had any ideas, the class had already started, and the students were growing restless.

Into the breach jumped one of my firm's clients. He owns a small farm on Pender, one of the Gulf Islands off the coast of Vancouver, B. C., Canada, and he'd been thinking about building a guest cottage. The cottage would provide accommodations for staff and colleagues from his publishing business, as well as for occasional guests and seasonal farm help.

My office has done a number of low-budget houses, including a couple of forays into the realm of affordable-housing competitions. Based on those experiences, my colleagues and I decided to apply our knowledge of modular-construction techniques to this particular project. The house we came up with is based on the universal module: the 4x8 sheet of plywood. As a result, the house is basically a plywood box. But even though it encompasses a scant 900 sq. ft., this little two-and-a-half story house is a barrack with aspirations.

The main floor (drawings this page) contains a living and dining space on one level and a kitchen with a sheltered entry on another (top photo, facing page). In the living area, a pair of built-in couches tucks into the corner (top photo, p. 127). Lit by windows and skylights, the corner is a cantilevered bay that projects beyond the line of the columns that bear the weight of the perimeter walls. The sloped glazing over the couches and the vaulted ceiling in the living room lend an expansive quality to what are actually small spaces. Upstairs, two compact bedrooms overlook the living room and share the

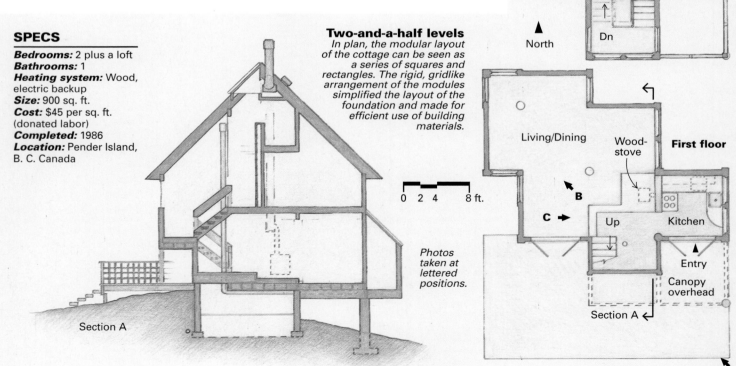

SPECS

Bedrooms: 2 plus a loft
Bathrooms: 1
Heating system: Wood, electric backup
Size: 900 sq. ft.
Cost: $45 per sq. ft. (donated labor)
Completed: 1986
Location: Pender Island, B. C. Canada

Two-and-a-half levels
In plan, the modular layout of the cottage can be seen as a series of squares and rectangles. The rigid, gridlike arrangement of the modules simplified the layout of the foundation and made for efficient use of building materials.

0 2 4   8 ft.

Photos taken at lettered positions.

Section A

Upper portion of closets

Loft

Loft

Upper portion of bedrooms

Upper portion of bath

Open to below

Bedroom

Second floor

Bedroom

Bath

North

Dn

Living/Dining

Wood-stove

First floor

B

C

Up

Kitchen

Entry

Canopy overhead

Section A

A

Drawings: Christopher Clapp

A simple cube with cutouts. A glazed canopy over the entry lets the sunlight reach inside the house where it can warm the concrete floors in the kitchen. The skylight at the peak of the roof illuminates the loft. The asbestos-cement roof provides a fireproof skin. Photo taken at A on floor plan.

Parked in the lot. The prefab panels were test fitted in the high-school parking lot atop temporary platforms (below). The panels were attached to one another with duplex nails for easy disassembly. The 8-ft. by 8-ft. panels were then trucked to the site and assembled by the class (right). Note how vertical and horizontal seams align. Horizontal seams will be finished with Z-flashings in the field, and verticals will be covered with corner boards and battens.

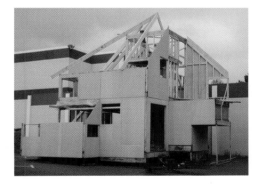

Bottom left photo, this page: Barry Griblin; bottom right photo: Karl Begrich

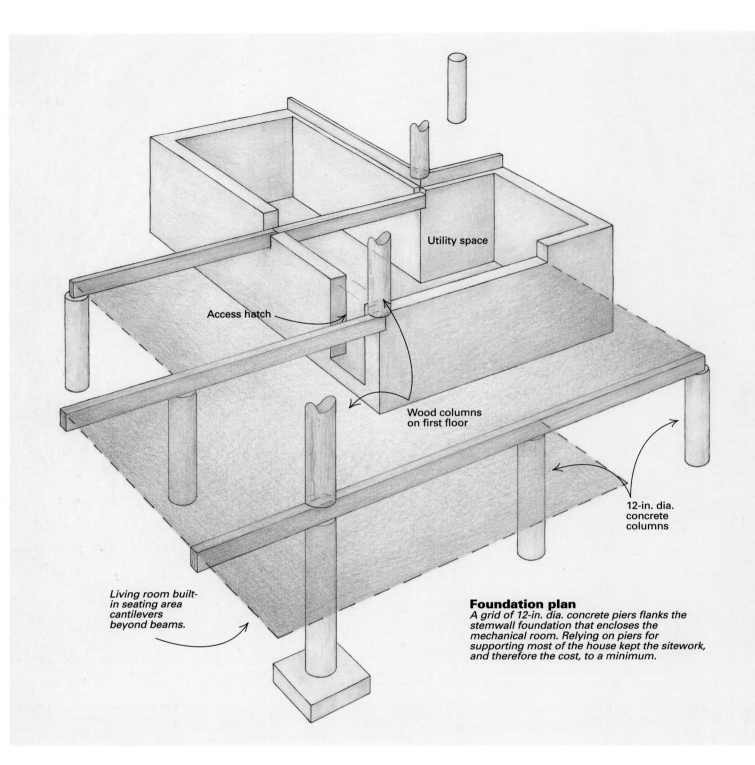

Utility space

Access hatch

Wood columns
on first floor

12-in. dia.
concrete
columns

*Living room built-
in seating area
cantilevers
beyond beams.*

Foundation plan
*A grid of 12-in. dia. concrete piers flanks the
stemwall foundation that encloses the
mechanical room. Relying on piers for
supporting most of the house kept the sitework,
and therefore the cost, to a minimum.*

large bathroom. A kid-sized loft, lit by skylights and reached by a ladder, adds another bunk and more open space to the stair volume.

Because the house is on a beautiful site, you want to be outdoors as much as possible. With that in mind, a large south-facing deck connects the house at the dining room to the hillside.

Modules in the parking lot—As requested by the instructor, Bjorn Hilstad, we designed the house to be built with platform-framing techniques. The house is made of 2x4 frames covered with T-111 plywood. After several sessions studying the working drawings and tallying up the necessary materials, Hilstad's class started cutting up the materials in the comfort of an en-

closed shop. Most of the panels are 8 ft. tall and 8 ft. wide (bottom right photo, p. 125). When covered with plywood on just one side, panels this size are still pretty maneuverable. Hilstad's class affixed the exterior plywood to the stick-framed walls. The interior walls, which are also T-111 plywood, were installed after the plumbing and wiring runs were completed.

The class worked through the fall fabricating the panels. Then they got a dose of construction reality by assembling the pieces in the school parking lot during a drizzly Vancouver winter (bottom left photo, p. 125). A wood base served as a temporary foundation for the house, and the panels were tacked together with duplex nails so that they could be disassembled easily.

The horizontal and vertical seams between panels align. In the finished cottage the vertical edges are covered with 1x2 battens, and the horizontals are separated with Z-flashings. Rough-sawn 2x8s conceal the seams where the walls come together at outside corners.

To spread the spirit of learning-by-doing a little wider, we arranged for an 18-wheel truck—piloted by a student driver—to transport the parts of the house to the site. The entire shell—numbered and disassembled—was packed into the truck's cargo bay. Then the truck headed for the ferry boat to the Gulf Islands.

The Gulf Island ferry's combination entry/exit ramp requires all vehicles to board at the bow and then circle around the vessel to exit. However, big trucks can't do this: They have to back onto the ferry. The pressure of backing a fully loaded driver-training semi-trailer into the darkness of a yawning ferry hull was not lost on the cheering passengers. The task eventually fell to the driving instructor, who finally made it after several attempts.

Energy saving on a tiny footprint—While the students were busy loading the 8x8 panels into the truck, a crew from the island began clearing the site. They had to take out a cedar tree and a large fir that stood within the perimeter of the house. Both trees were hauled off to the farm's simple but well-used sawmill to be turned into building materials for the cottage. The fir yielded columns for the living room, and the cedar was milled into battens and corner boards.

We try to keep excavations to a minimum on sloping, hard-to-reach sites. Instead of bulldozing a flat pad for a house, we would rather leave the terrain in its natural contours and build a house on piers. The uphill corner of this cottage sits atop a stemwall foundation that encloses a head-high mechanical room for the central vacuum and the water heater (drawing facing page). The rest of the house is carried by 12-in. dia. cast-concrete piers.

The house is heated by a woodstove that's centrally located against the half-wall that separates the kitchen from the living area (bottom photo, right). The woodstove puts out enough heat for all but the coldest days, when the backup electric-baseboard heating kicks in. But that's only a last resort. A fair amount of solar heat is collected by the concrete floor in the kitchen, as the sun streams through the glazed canopy that shelters the entry.

To take advantage of the heat that collects at the top of the stairs, we included a heat-redistribution system. It is simply an 8-in. dia. air duct that extends to within a foot of the skylight in the loft. A two-speed fan mounted in the top of the duct sends the warm air back to the first floor, where it's directed to a register under the stairs and to another register between the sliding doors and the dining table.

Getting rid of the heat in the summer is more of a problem than keeping it in during the winter. Right now the heat is exhausted directly through a hand-operated roof vent. But experience has shown that this 12-in. by 8-in. vent is too small to do the job without a mechanical assist.

The budget—We had $40,000 to spend on this house, and we did. That works out to about $45 per sq. ft., which would have been closer to $65 or $70 per sq. ft. without the donated labor of the high-school class. The materials we used were relatively inexpensive and should hold up well. The concrete floors and the plywood walls are industrial strength and in keeping with the working nature of the site.

So too is the asbestos-cement roof. But in retrospect, I don't think we would specify such a roof again. Our client wanted a fireproof roof skin, and from a durability point of view, the choice of asbestos-cement roofing made sense. The product is essentially inert and affords long-term,

Built-ins by the bay. **The combination of sloped glazing and a vaulted ceiling impart a lofty feeling to what is actually a small space. Photo taken at B on floor plan.**

maintenance-free protection from the elements. However, the possibility of asbestos inhalation required the installers to wear proper respiratory gear, clean their work clothes meticulously and continually hose down the work area to minimize dust. If we had to do it again, we'd specify fire-retardant treated wood shingles.

The comparative comfort and the newness of the cottage have overshadowed the farmhouse a bit. Now the old place seems a little too rustic, but the owner doesn't seem to mind. The earliest arrival on weekend outings gets first dibs on lodgings, and that's usually the owner. □

Barry Griblin is an architect in West Vancouver, B. C., Canada. Photos by Charles Miller except where noted.

Concrete floors. **The exposed-aggregate concrete floor in the kitchen spreads around the corner to the pad for the woodstove. A galvanized duct to the right redistributes heated air from the loft to a couple of downstairs heating registers. Photo taken at C on floor plan.**

Steep Lot, Narrow House

Plaster, concrete and weathered timbers come together in a cozy California cottage

by Jonathan Livingston

A traditional facade. A gently curving gable over a broadly arched entry leads to the front door of this three-story house. The living spaces are on the second floor, where the rooms are far enough above the street to enjoy a view of San Francisco Bay.

Wood is in short supply along the shores of the Mediterranean Sea. So houses that hug the seaside cliffs of Italy and Greece are mostly made of plastered masonry. Wood is used sparingly in these homes for rafters, beams and doors, and the chances are good that the precious pieces of wood have seen duty before—sometimes centuries before—in other buildings. The common denominator in these cottages is a cozy atmosphere created by basic, indigenous building materials used to make simple shapes that emphasize the structure of the building. The effect is timeless and handmade.

When Beverly Galloway began describing to me the kind of house she wanted, Beverly recalled the houses she'd seen on her many visits to Italy and Greece. She made it clear that she wanted her house to evoke a similar sense of structure and shelter but in a house that looked at home in northern California.

Three-story plan separates bedrooms—Beverly's building site didn't overlook a charming Mediterranean fishing village, but it had other attributes. A few years ago she bought a narrow, hillside lot in Point Richmond, a small town on the eastern edge of San Francisco Bay. From the top of the 30-ft. wide by 100-ft. deep lot, you can see San Francisco bracketed by the Bay Bridge and the Golden Gate.

Setbacks of 3 ft. on a side and 20 ft. in front and in back effectively dictated the footprint of the house and its placement on the lot. The plan arranges two bedrooms into a three-story house of roughly 1,600 sq. ft. (floor plan facing page). The bedrooms are separated by the living spaces on the second floor, which puts a premium on privacy. And because they both have their own bathrooms, each bedroom is, in a sense, a master suite—the perfect setup for overnight guests.

Over a meal at a Berkeley bistro, I sketched on the place mat while Beverly described what she liked about the local houses. As is usually the case, we had to keep the budget under control. Shapes and finishes had to stay simple. The image we kept coming back to in the sketches was reminiscent of the Normandy cottages that were built in the Bay Area during the 30s. Clad in stucco and arranged on narrow lots, these houses typically turned a gable end to the street. Often one of the rooflines curved upward to shelter a covered entry. We chose this form (photo left).

Thick walls, heavy timbers—The masonry buildings Beverly admired so much in Europe have thick walls that are revealed at windows and doorways. Thick walls impart a sense of sturdiness—not with a shout but with an occasional quiet reminder as you pass a window or go through a doorway.

Masonry walls, however, are a bad idea in the Bay Area because they fare poorly in earthquakes. So I built the thick walls out of framing lumber. An exterior 2x4 wall carries the weight of the building, and another 2x4 wall supports the interior plaster. The finished walls are 1 ft. deep, which leaves a large chase for wiring and a large cavity for insulation. Double walls bump up the price of the house because of the lumber cost and the labor to install them, so I limited their use to the second floor, where all public spaces are located. In the kitchen (photo p. 130), the thick walls provided ample opportunities for recessed shelves instead of over-counter cabinets.

The walls were finished with gypsum veneer plaster over Imperial Board gypsum lath (USG, 125 So. Franklin St., P. O. Box 806278, Chicago, Ill. 60680-4124). This kind of lath looks like drywall, but its surface is designed to anchor plaster.

The lath goes up the same as drywall. Then it's taped with fiberglass mesh and covered with a plaster veneer. The thick veneer covers all taped joints and smooths the irregularities of the framing. Then the finish color coat is applied. The velvet-smooth steel-trowel finish and integral color—in this case buckskin—produce an honest craftsmanlike finish that can't be matched by any painter. In my area, veneer plaster turned out to be the same price as smooth-wall gypsum board with a good paint job.

Douglas-fir timbers salvaged from a fire-damaged pier span the kitchen and the living-room ceilings (top photo, p. 131). I found the timbers at a local wrecking yard, covered with paint, tar and sea-gull guano. Before installing the beams, I cleaned them with a rented sandblaster. The clean beams were then inspected by an engineer to verify their structural integrity.

I also used Douglas fir for the doors and their casings. The fir is a soft wood that has an informal feeling. Its rich, golden-brown color goes well with the steel-troweled plaster walls and the gray concrete floors.

Concrete floors and radiant heat—The house is small enough that it could be heated by a radiant floor. Around here, radiant floors are typically made of concrete poured over a matrix of pipes that carry hot water. Then the concrete is finished with stone, slate, tile, wood or carpet. But the least-expensive method is to pour the concrete over the hot-water pipes, trowel it smooth and leave it. That's what I decided to do. The floor is 1½ in. thick, and it's supported by a ¾-in. plywood subfloor over wood floor joists.

I installed 1½-in. thick wood inlays in the concrete to serve several functions. They acted as screeds to control the thickness of the concrete, and they divided the slab into 7-ft. square units that were easy to pour and finish one at a time. Because this floor would be a finished surface, I decided to do it myself and take my time—no frantic scenes with a transit-mix truck for this job.

The sheer mass of this floor allows it to retain heat for a long time and helps regulate the temperature in the house. When it is hot outside, it stays cooler inside, and when the sun hits the concrete in the winter, it helps warm the home. There's more to tell about this kind of slab and its heating system than I have room for here. I'll be elaborating on it in an upcoming issue.

Sills and surrounds—Once the timber/plaster/concrete palette was established, I continued on with it to keep the detailing coherent. For example, the fireplace surround is made of cast-

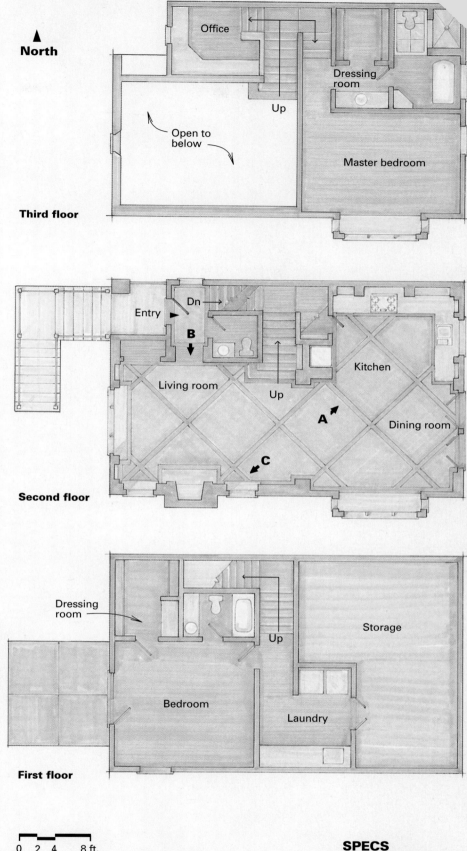

Two bedrooms, three floors. *The public spaces of the house are on the second floor, which enhances the privacy of the bedrooms on the first and third floors. The checkerboard on the second level shows the wood-strip pattern in the concrete floor.*

Photos taken from lettered positions.

0 2 4   8 ft.

SPECS

Bedrooms: 2
Bathrooms: 2½
Heating system: Gas-fired radiant slab
Size: 1,626 sq. ft.
Cost: $95 per sq. ft.
Completed: 1990
Location: Point Richmond, California

Drawings: Bob Goodfellow

concrete components that are secured to the plaster lath with latex-based mortar (photo right). The precast mantel, hearth and accompanying details cost about $250 (Concrete Designs, Inc., 3650 So. Broadmont Dr., Tucson, Ariz. 85713-5247; 602-624-6653).

The concrete fireplace surround set a style in the living room that I wanted continued in the windowsills. But I couldn't find prefab parts to use for them, so I made cast-in-place windowsills out of a rich concrete mix consisting of 3 parts sand, 1 part ⅜-in. gravel and 1 part cement (photo below). As shown in the drawing below, I lined the front edge of the forms with 4-in. wide crown molding to shape the decorative profile into the revealed edge of the sills.

To ensure easy release from the forms, I sprayed them with a little WD-40 before placing the concrete. I installed the sills after the plaster was in place, using liberal amounts of masking tape to make sure I didn't slurp any mortar on the finished walls. I used my orbital sander (without the sandpaper) to vibrate the forms, which took out most of the bubbles along the revealed edge. Then I let the concrete set up for a week before pulling the forms. □

Jonathan Livingston is an architect/contractor who lives on a boat in San Francisco Bay. Photos by Charles Miller.

Rough-sawn beams and smooth plaster walls. Salvaged timbers add weight to the living room. The fireplace surround is made of pre-fab cast-concrete components. Photo taken from B on floor plan.

Crown molding formed the edge. Cast-concrete windowsills in the 1-ft. deep living-room walls carry on the style established by the fireplace surround. The sills were cast in place. Photo taken from C on floor plan.

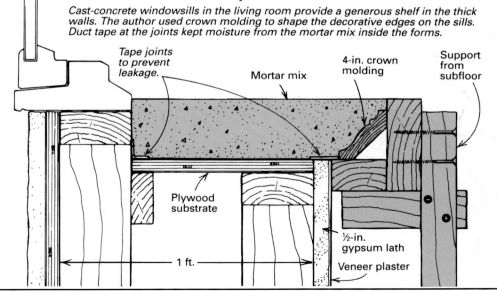

Cast-in-place windowsills

Cast-concrete windowsills in the living room provide a generous shelf in the thick walls. The author used crown molding to shape the decorative edges on the sills. Duct tape at the joints kept moisture from the mortar mix inside the forms.

Tape joints to prevent leakage.

Mortar mix

4-in. crown molding

Support from subfloor

Plywood substrate

½-in. gypsum lath

Veneer plaster

1 ft.

A comfortable home for two. The 720-sq. ft. loft above this garage is an inexpensive and practical starter home. Planned with expansion in mind, the garage has a mortgage payment about the same as rent for an apartment. Photo taken at A on floor plan.

The Garage as Starter Home

A future guest room or rental unit, living space over the garage is an affordable alternative to a fixer-upper or an apartment

by Ken Troupe

After I graduated from college and started work as an architect's assistant, the reality of northern Ontario's housing market hit home. I had big dreams but no money. I didn't want to rent an apartment, and I couldn't afford to buy a new home. A fixer-upper might start out cheap, but I couldn't predict just how much money I'd need to make it livable. This situation was frustrating; I worked with houses every day, yet I couldn't afford one that I liked.

The obvious solution was building my own home. I started by designing a three-bedroom starter home; then I estimated the cost and realized that even this modest home was way over my budget. I concluded then that I had to change my concept of a house completely. I tried to forget my previous notions of what makes a house, and I started my thinking all over again with the simplistic premise that a house is where you live.

I thought about what I needed from a house: a place to eat, to sleep, to bathe and to relax. I needed storage. My fiancée would soon graduate from university, so the house had to be comfortable for two adults. Of course, it couldn't cost much to build or heat. I wanted a house I could add to, and one with a low environmental impact. By the time I drew the final design, I had started my own contracting business, and I needed a garage for my tools and truck, too.

The rear dormer is the master suite. *To use the small space best, the bed is built into the dormer, and drawers slide out from under the bed. The window seat opens, and small doors access more storage areas under the eaves. High ceilings and an open floor plan keep this 24-ft. by 30-ft. loft from feeling cramped. The bathroom is the only separate room.*

A ▶

▶
North

Photos taken at lettered positions.

SPECS

Bedrooms: 1
Bathrooms: 1
Heating system: Woodstove
Size: 720 sq. ft.
Cost: $83 (Canadian) per sq. ft.
Completed: 1994
Location: Sudbury, Ontario, Canada

Thoughtful design makes a small house pleasant and efficient—My final design was a loft built atop a two-car garage (photo facing page). The 24-ft. by 30-ft. footprint yields 720 sq. ft. each for the garage and the living space. This space is small, and I kept it as open as possible to avoid a cramped feeling. Separate rooms for dining, relaxing and sleeping would have been tiny. Because there are no walls, these areas borrow space from each other and seem larger than

Interior stairs would have taken too much floor space. Exterior stairs lead to the loft and add a focal point to the front of the house. Photo taken at C on floor plan.

windows. The bathroom floor is ceramic tile, as is the floor that extends from the entrance to the hearth around the woodstove. The other floors are mill-run maple, a grade that contains some color variations. Mill-run maple is cheaper and, I think, more interesting than the No. 1 grade.

Bringing in the light and air—I put windows on all four sides to brighten the interior and to ventilate the house in the summer. A large north-facing awning window over the bed admits cooling evening breezes during summer's heat. Because of this window's location and orientation, I wanted to be sure there would be no equivalent breezes in the winter. This unit is double-glazed with a low-E plastic film between the panes that acts as a third pane. It has an R-8 insulating factor, about twice that of the rest of windows. It cost about a third more than a standard double-glazed window.

The other windows are double-glazed, low-E argon-filled units. All the windows are redwood-framed units made by Repla (482 S. Service Road E., Oakville, ON, Canada L6J 2X6; 905-844-1271). The two south-facing windows have fixed bottoms and operable top awnings so that hot summer air vents up high where it gathers. They were hundreds of dollars cheaper than fully operable units. With the high angle of the sun and our roof overhang, there isn't much unwanted solar gain in the summer.

On sunny winter days, however, these windows admit lots of free solar heat. For most of our winter, highs average about 14°F and go to a low of -4°F at night. On sunny days at this temperature, the house maintains an indoor temperature of 70°F with no heat but the sun. Once the days warm up to 30°F, solar gain increases the indoor temperature during the day. Recently, on a day like this, I left the house early when the indoor temperature was 68°F. When I returned shortly after lunch, the inside temperature had risen to 72°F solely from the sun.

Building for a cold climate—I used 16-in. deep wood I-joists to frame the floor between the garage and living area. They span the full 24 ft. front to back and eliminate the need for any supporting walls, beams or posts in the garage below. I spaced the joists on 24-in. centers and sheathed the floor with ⅜-in. oriented strand board (OSB). I insulated this floor with R-28 fiberglass batt insulation.

The roof and ceiling are conventionally framed with 2x10s. The ceiling angles are insulated to R-28, and the flats to R-50. An interior 6-mil polyethylene vapor barrier keeps humidity in the house and out of the framing, where it can condense and cause trouble. The exterior walls are framed with 2x6 studs 16 in. o. c. and insulated with high-density R-22 batts.

their measurements imply. Also, because I was planning a house for a couple, there wasn't as much need for privacy. The bed is built into an alcove under the back dormer, in full view of the living area (photo p. 133). The only separate room is the bathroom. Even here, I used a glass door with curtains to let light through and to maintain an open feel.

The stairs to the loft are outside the house (photo above). They add interest to the exterior, and they save interior space. I find the living space I gained to be well worth the extra snow I have to shovel.

Storage is important in a small house because clutter makes spaces seem smaller. I had to use space that would otherwise be wasted. Below the bed, I built in large drawers. Clothes hang in two closets to the side of the bed. The front dormer has a window seat that opens for stor-

age. Even the kneewalls at the eaves have doors that access additional storage under the roof.

I varied the ceiling heights to separate areas, to create moods and to add interest. Cathedral ceilings make the living and dining areas feel larger. Eight-ft. ceilings here would have made the whole house seem too small. I did use 8-ft. ceilings at the the back dormer where the bed is, at the window seat in the front dormer and in the bathroom to make these areas cozier.

A woodstove is the focal point of the living area and the main heat source, a hearth for the home. The kitchen is small, with few cabinets, but with a large country dining table. My fiancée and I don't cook much, and it didn't make sense to spend money on a kitchen we wouldn't use.

The casings are 1x4 and the baseboard 1x6 pine, both with router-rounded edges. I stained the trim a rich red color to frame the doors and

It takes about three face cords of wood a year to heat the house. The house uses about 3,300kwh of electricity per year, mostly for lighting, but also for the electric-baseboard backup heat. It takes 1,700 cubic meters of natural gas per year to heat the garage and the water, and to run the dryer.

An environmentally sound home—The house is heated with a Federal Convection Heater from Vermont Castings (P. O. Box 501, Bethel, VT 05032; 802-234-2300). It has an emissions rating of only 1.1g per hr., the lowest ever tested by the U. S. Environmental Protection Agency at the time that I bought the stove. Low-flow toilets, showerheads and sink faucets reduce water consumption, and the wood I-joists in place of conventional wood joists minimize wood use.

The house doesn't create much of its own pollution. The maple flooring and ceramic tiles at the entry and in the bathroom are inert. There is no carpeting that might outgas. With a house as tight as this, though, ensuring a supply of fresh outdoor air to replace stale indoor air is important. I installed a heat-recovery ventilator (Van EE 1000, Venmar Ventilation Inc., 550 Lemire Blvd., Drummondville, PQ, Canada J2B 8A9; 800-567-3855) designed for this small house size. Compact fluorescents provide most of the lighting in the house.

The small footprint of the house meant a minimal disturbance to the native vegetation. A single-story building the same size would have double the footprint, more foundation and more roof. It would have more surface area to lose heat, as well.

Affordable start-up—The house, excluding land, cost $60,000 (Canadian). The house can grow and change as my family grows and my needs change. I can easily expand off the back, connecting any future structure to where the bedroom is now. I'm undecided exactly what the future use might be, but there are several options. I could add extra bedrooms and continue the current use of the kitchen and living areas. Or the loft could become a master suite, an office or even a rental. I've already taken care of some big-ticket items, such as the garage, the driveway, the well, the septic and some landscaping. The mortgage is about the same as the cost of an apartment rental, and I own a home that is comfortable, efficient and pleasant. On cold winter nights, I hear the wind only a foot from my bed, and I watch the fire burn in the woodstove. In my own house. It's a nice way to fall asleep. □

Ken Troupe is a house builder in Sudbury, Ontario, Canada. Photos by Andy Engel.

A rain-screen wall lets the back of the siding breathe

The house is sheathed with ¼-in. oriented strand board (OSB). This is a common sheathing material in northern Ontario. It's cheaper and lighter than the ½-in. sheathing common in the United States, and it also provides plenty of bracing for our seismically stable area.

I covered the sheathing with 1-in. Fiberglass Glasclad (available only in Canada; Owens Corning/Fibreglas Canada, 4100 Young St., Suite 700, Willowdale, ON, Canada M2N 6T9; 800-463-7673), a rigid-fiberglass insulating board that's faced with housewrap and yields an additional R-4.5. I like Glasclad because it's highly permeable to water vapor. This means that water vapor easily continues on through to the outside instead of being trapped behind the insulation board. I butted the Glasclad to the windows and taped this joint and the seams between the panels with seam tape.

Next I screwed 1x3 vertical strapping to the studs, over the sheathing and the Glasclad. The reason is twofold. Glasclad is resilient and difficult to nail siding over.

The 1x3s compress the Glasclad for a more solid nailing surface.

Primarily, though, I wanted to create an airspace between the siding and the wall. Even on the best siding jobs, rain can get behind clapboards. Capillary action or high winds drive water into the tiniest of holes. The bottom of this airspace is screened to keep out bugs, but air circulates between here and the soffit vents. Water that gets behind the siding has a way out. This detail will keep the paint on the siding longer and minimize the chance that water will get past the housewrap and rot the framing.

Of course, these layers of Glasclad and strapping make it important to set the windows the right distance out from the sheathing. Get it wrong, and the clapboards run over the windows instead of butting to them. The Repla units I used are held in place by two or three angle brackets per side. These brackets adjust in and out on the frame so that I could set the window the exact distance from the sheathing that I wanted.—*K. T.*

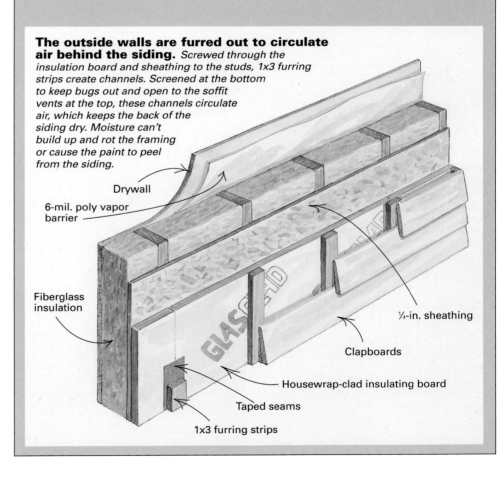

The outside walls are furred out to circulate air behind the siding. *Screwed through the insulation board and sheathing to the studs, 1x3 furring strips create channels. Screened at the bottom to keep bugs out and open to the soffit vents at the top, these channels circulate air, which keeps the back of the siding dry. Moisture can't build up and rot the framing or cause the paint to peel from the siding.*

Drywall

6-mil. poly vapor barrier

Fiberglass insulation

¼-in. sheathing

Clapboards

Housewrap-clad insulating board

Taped seams

1x3 furring strips

Variety wrapped in a small package. On the right, horizontal siding covers the private portion of the house; vertical siding is applied to the more public areas at left. The many textures have a big effect on a small house. Photo taken at A on floor plan.

Room Enough for Two

At 1,200 sq. ft. and $105 per ft., this compact house has the details and variety found in much bigger homes

by Scott Neeley

A mix of gable, shed and hip roofs. The red-metal roofing is the common element tying together the various rooflines of the house, which express the variety of uses within. Photo taken at B on floor plan

Paul Piersma and his wife, Amy, wanted just enough room to live comfortably. Just enough room in a small house with well-crafted details. Unfortunately, after looking all over Durham and Chapel Hill, North Carolina, they could find only big, bulky houses.

So in the summer of 1995, as Paul looked for alternatives, he approached me. Paul is a developer, and I agreed with him that the Durham-Raleigh-Chapel Hill Triangle area would be a good market to develop small, high-quality speculative houses. He decided the best strategy was to build a house for himself and Amy, using their house as a prototype and marketing tool for subsequent houses to be developed on other sites. Although the house would be unique to its site, the size, level of detail and use of materials would provide a model for future projects.

We focused on four areas: design; detailing and materials; energy efficiency; and environ-mental response (renewable resources and indoor-air quality). I designed for a construction budget of $105 per sq. ft., which was high relative to nearby speculative houses but well shy of the $125 per sq. ft. or more for a custom house.

The most radical aspect of the house is its size: 1,216 sq. ft., including a home office/loft. The small size isn't unusual for affordable or second houses, but it's the exception for an architect-designed primary residence. As such, it was consistent with Paul's and my view that building small is the first and best choice for new housing. Small size didn't mean skimping on quality.

Farm building inspires the elevations—Paul bought a lot in a wooded setting about 10 minutes from downtown Durham and Duke University. The site is listed in the county historic inventory and contains a simple, turn-of-the-century frame cottage and a tobacco barn. The countryside in the area is filled with similar to-bacco barns—tall, thin, gable-roofed buildings with vertical siding and metal roofs.

I wanted Paul and Amy's house to echo the shapes of the nearby historic structures. The house is composed of two simple volumes set in a line: a two-story, hip-roofed tower containing bedrooms and bathrooms, and a one-story, gable-roofed structure for the living and kitchen areas (bottom photo, facing page). At the rear of the house, a pair of shed roofs poke out to contain the dining room and screened porch (floor plan, p. 138; photo above).

Exterior details provide texture and interest—The two main volumes of the house share a front wall; I wanted to use different siding materials to set these volumes apart. I selected vertical board-and-batten siding for the one-story volume and 8-in. lap siding for the two-story

Ample variety packed into a compact floor plan

Within its 1,216 sq. ft., this concise house holds a loft/home office, a double-height living room, a screened porch, an intimate dining room, a galley kitchen, a guest room and two full baths. The house is divided into two main volumes. The two-story volume contains the private areas; the more public spaces, such as kitchen, living room and dining room, are in the one-story space.

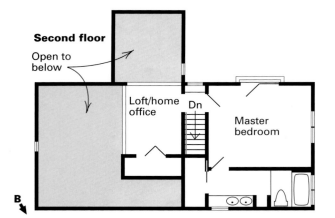

Second floor

Open to below

Loft/home office

Dn

Master bedroom

B

SPECS

Bedrooms: 2
Bathrooms: 2
Heating system: Radiant floor
Size: 1,216 sq. ft.
Cost: $105 per sq. ft.
Completed: 1996
Location: Durham, North Carolina

Photos taken at lettered positions.

North

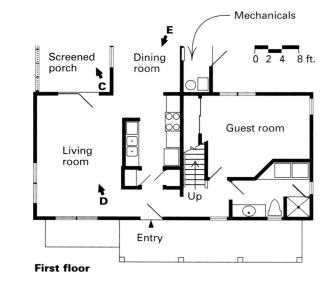

Mechanicals

E

Screened porch

Dining room

C

0 2 4 8 ft.

Living room

Guest room

D

Up

Entry

First floor

The porch extends the living room. Whenever the weather is mild enough, the living room can continue outside onto the screened porch. Photo taken at C on floor plan.

---

volume. The board-and-batten appearance was created by attaching cypress 1x2 battens at 8 in. o. c. over fir T-111 plywood (smooth-face, siding-grade plywood is not available locally). Cypress beveled 1x8 lap siding was selected for the tower. The difference between the siding materials varies from subtle to bold as shadows build and diminish.

I also chose a dark-red metal roof corrugated in a 5-V pattern for the house. However, the front porch, which connects the one- and two-story sections, is set off by a corrugated, galvanized metal roof.

Windows were another opportunity to distinguish the two volumes subtly. The gable-roofed living spaces are fitted with double-hung windows; the hip-roofed tower has casement windows. Large casement windows can appear blank and characterless, so I specified divided lites on the tall second-floor windows.

In North Carolina, concrete-block foundations are standard. Instead of the typical brick veneer over concrete block, I chose split-faced architectural block for the foundation walls. The walls were laid up with 8-in. block, topped by a 4-in. course.

Opening the living area—Large open rooms and lots of light belie the limited size of the house. The high ceilings and the oversize double-hung windows create a sense of spaciousness in the main living area (photo left, facing page). Axes visually extend spaces outside the house: the glass entry door, the galley kitchen and the large dining-room windows align (photo right, facing page); so do the living-room windows, the French doors and the screened-porch doors.

Exposed collar ties are set 4 ft. o. c. over the living room to stabilize the roof structure horizontally. The collar ties are built of 2x4s sandwiched between 2x6s held flush with the bottom of the 2x4s. This design provides a concealed cavity at the top of the collar tie for running cable to ceiling fans and lighting. The collar ties are wrapped in gypsum board.

The small loft above the kitchen serves as a home office (photo right, facing page). Here,

collar ties would be an obstruction because of the low ceiling height. Instead, a system of joists and wall studs resists the horizontal forces from the roof rafters.

Variety within a limited footprint—Paul expected well-executed details, something he found lacking in most speculative houses. This expectation resonated with my own belief that the best indicator of the real quality of a house is found in its smallest places. Good detailing means that materials turn corners and make transitions cleanly and logically, and that they are assembled in a way that creates rich textures and shadows.

Concrete is used as a finish material inside the house. The radiant slab was poured as a standard 5-in. thick reinforced slab and then scored in a regular grid. It was colored with a reddish-brown Epmar Stone Tone concrete stain (Epmar Corp.; 562-946-8781), then covered with plastic sheeting until construction was complete. Paul selected concrete for kitchen and bathroom countertops.

Drawings: Scott Bricher

Economy of space. Everything is close at hand. From the kitchen and dining room, it's a few steps to the living room. The home office floats above. Photo taken at E on floor plan.

Making small feel big. Just because a house is small and compact doesn't mean it has to appear small, as this high-ceilinged living room proves. The concrete floors are scored in a grid pattern. Photo taken at D on floor plan.

Custom millwork creates a sense of substance and luxury. All profiles are simple shapes in paint-grade poplar. I specified ⅝-in. thick baseboards and side casings. A ¾-in. by ¾-in. trim board caps the base, and the thinner side casings butt neatly into ¾-in. thick head casings.

The loft railing is designed to be sturdy but to appear delicate (photo right). Balusters are poplar 1x2s set on edge and double lag-screwed into the floor joists. The top rail is three 1x2s laminated together: two pieces parallel, the third perpendicular with a ⅜-in. by ⅜-in. reveal routed into both bottom sides.

Keeping an eye on energy efficiency—The house appears to face the road, but it is angled away slightly to face the south more exactly. A deep overhang shields the large south-facing and southwest-facing windows from the summer sun but lets in low winter sun. High ceilings and windows are set for cross ventilation.

Paul's goal was a high level of comfort and efficiency from heating and cooling systems. We decided on a radiant slab for heating and a heat pump for cooling. A gas-fired boiler heats water for the radiant slab, upstairs hot-water baseboard units and domestic use. An air-to-air heat exchanger was added to ensure indoor-air quality within the tight envelope.

We selected finishes for resource efficiency and indoor-air quality. Maple and poplar were selected for cabinetry and millwork, respectively; both woods are sustainably harvested in the United States. Cypress, which is regionally produced, was used for exterior lap siding, battens and trim. We limited the use of glues and construction adhesives inside to minimize potential offgassing, and we specified no particleboard or carpeting inside. The concrete countertops are low-tech, nontoxic items produced by a local craftsperson.

Appliances were selected with the same concern for efficiency. The Creeda (800-992-7332) Eco series washer and dryer and the Bosch (800-866-2022) dishwasher are highly rated for energy and water conservation. The washer and dryer are front loaders that fit neatly undercounter in the downstairs bathroom. □

Scott Neeley is an architect in Lincoln, Nebraska. Photos by Steve Culpepper.

An Island Homestead

Innovative timber-framing techniques make this home feel like a big farmhouse in a compact package

by Jill Fuerstneau Sousa

John and Carol Mosier had had many homes built for them over the years, but this one was to be their last. John was retiring as a corporate executive, and the Mosiers' two children were no longer living at home. Seeking a respite from the busy urban life they'd been living, John and Carol bought an old 14-acre farmstead on Whidbey Island in Washington state. It was time to simplify their lives.

To realize their vision of a simpler life, John and Carol decided to build a sturdy, timber-frame farmhouse, but at less than 2,000 sq. ft., the house would be just a fraction of the size of their previous homes. They wanted their new house to reflect the informal lifestyle that allowed the time and the resources for other pursuits.

The Mosiers' new home was to be open with the main living spaces and the master bedroom on the first floor and with guest accommodations upstairs (floor plans, p. 142). Carol also

Continuous interior spaces. The kitchen, living room and dining room all flow from one space into another. A woodstove is located in the 4-ft. bay that joins the living room and the dining room. Photo taken at B on floor plan.

Living room enjoys the view. With the main entry located on the other side of the house, the living room, dining room and master bedroom could be located on the side of the house with the best view. Photo taken at C on floor plan.

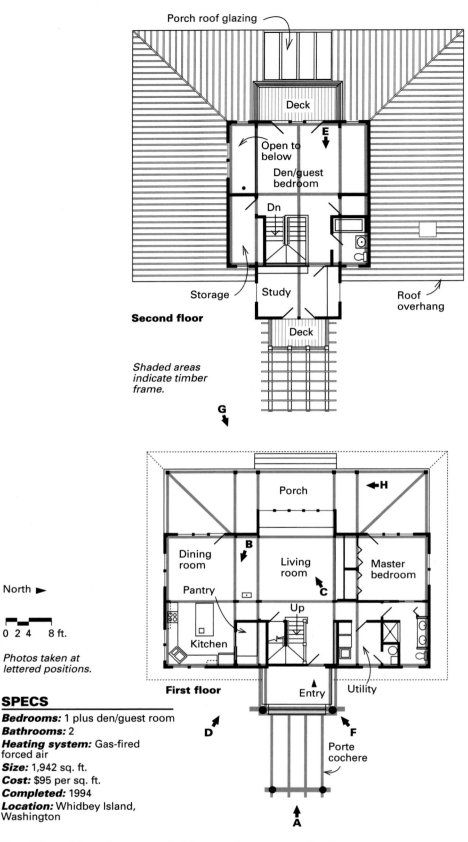

Porch roof glazing

Deck

Open to below

E

Den/guest bedroom

Dn

Storage

Study

Second floor

Roof overhang

Deck

Shaded areas indicate timber frame.

G

Porch

H

North ▶

0 2 4   8 ft.

Photos taken at lettered positions.

Dining room

B

Living room

Master bedroom

Pantry

C

Kitchen

Up

First floor

Entry

Utility

D

F

Porte cochere

A

SPECS

Bedrooms: 1 plus den/guest room
Bathrooms: 2
Heating system: Gas-fired forced air
Size: 1,942 sq. ft.
Cost: $95 per sq. ft.
Completed: 1994
Location: Whidbey Island, Washington

Traditional farmhouse outside, contemporary timber frame inside. *In keeping with other rural buildings on Whidbey Island, the single-story main floor of this house wraps around a two-story central section. The roof on the west side extends out over a full-length porch. Inside, the timber frame allows the spaces on the main floor to flow together.*

wanted one small, quiet room of her own, and John wanted a detached two-car garage with a woodworking shop.

Finding a different approach to the site—
The Mosiers' property slopes up toward the east from the main road. Their house would be built on a flat area near the top of the slope close to the site of a small, old farmhouse with outbuildings. The back half of the property is heavily wooded, framing the site and providing a buffer from the neighbors. To the west are views of a small lake and the rural island surroundings.

John and Carol envisioned a garden and small vineyard on this sunny west-facing slope. Unfortunately, the existing access to the property from the main road cut straight through the most desirable planting area. The problem was solved by obtaining permission to share a neighbor's right of way along the south side of their property. This new access gave the Mosiers an approach from the opposite side of their property.

Exterior design is borrowed from local buildings—The new driveway emerges dramatically from the woods at the back of the property and circles under a covered part of the driveway, or a porte cochere, off the entry porch that provides cover for rainy days (photo bottom left, facing page). With the entry on the eastern side of the house, the living room (bottom photo, p. 141), dining room and master bedroom could be located on the west side of the house, with uninterrupted views of the island countryside.

A covered porch stretches across the western face of the house with doors to the dining room and the master bedroom (photo p. 145). A glassed-in bay extends the living room in to the porch area, and part of the porch roof with clear glazing admits additional light to the living room. The kitchen is in the southeast corner of the house behind the dining area and overlooks the vegetable garden. In the southwest corner of the house, the dining room (top photo, p. 141) is open to the kitchen and the living room.

The form of the house was inspired by typical farm buildings on Whidbey Island. The central portion is two stories high with a single-story structure wrapped around it on three sides. On the fourth side, facing the woods to the east, Carol's small second-floor study extends out over the entry porch below. In keeping with vernacular island buildings, the roof pitch on the single-story parts of the house was kept shallower (3-in-12) than on the two-story central part (6-in-12).

Inside, the central section is flanked by 4-ft. wide bays running the length of the house on each side (floor plans left). These 4-ft. bays create spaces for auxiliary functions between the rooms on the first floor. The entertainment center and bedroom closets are in the spaces between the

Drawings: Mark Hannon

Roof without rafters

To simplify the timber frame, structural stress-skin panels span the distance from the ridge beam to the wall plates over an intermediate plate, eliminating the need for rafters (photo left, taken at D on floor plan). The ridge is supported by struts and tapered diagonal braces (inset, taken at E on floor plan) that leave an unbroken ceiling plane.

A pole-and-timber entry

The entry porch and a covered portion of the driveway, called a porte cochere (photo left, taken at D on floor plan), are framed with cedar-log beams scribe-fit to massive posts and Douglas-fir beams (inset, taken at F on floor plan) that hint at the exposed timber frame inside.

bedroom and living room. The wood-burning stove and hearth fit into the space between the living room and the dining room, and a walk-in pantry occupies the space next to the kitchen.

A roof without rafters—John and Carol wanted as much natural wood as possible in their new home, so timber-framing was a logical choice for construction. The Mosiers insisted on using recycled wood for the frame because of its environmental friendliness and for its rich look. However, they wanted to keep the timber frame simple and contemporary with as few knee braces and extra timbers as possible.

Jeff Arvin of The Cascade Joinery in Everson, Washington, helped us to simplify the frame by eliminating all rafters. Instead, the roof is spanned from the plates to the ridge beam (photo top left, p. 143) with structural stress-skin panels, which consist of a rigid-foam core sandwiched between two layers of oriented strand board with a layer of drywall on the bottom.

Eliminating the rafters results in an unbroken drywall ceiling in the house that reflects more light and gives the home a more contemporary feel (photo top right, p. 143). The ridge beam is supported by vertical struts resting on beams that span the central bay of each of the three main bents. Tapered diagonal braces support the vertical struts, creating the look of a king-post truss atop each bent section.

On the first floor, large diagonal cross braces connect the posts that frame the 4-ft. bays. This cross bracing gives the frame the lateral strength required to minimize the number of diagonal knee braces typical of traditional timber framing. The cross bracing was left exposed wherever possible, providing a distinctive design element in the house (bottom photo, p. 141). Between the living and dining areas, the cross braces provide a backdrop for the wood-burning stove.

The open entry porch was also timber-framed (photo bottom left, p. 143), but the walls of Carol's study above the porch were built only of stress-skin panels. Cedar-log posts a foot in diameter support the porch and porte cochere with two large cedar-log beams spanning the log columns (photo bottom right, p. 143). Heavy Douglas-fir timbers scribed to the log beams carry the study and trellis floor over the porte cochere. Part of the porte cochere is covered by

Owner-installed landscaping shows off the house. In addition to acting as general contractors, the owners of this house did many parts of the construction, including the landscaping. Photo taken at G on floor plan.

A protected porch. A covered porch extends along the west side of the house. Translucent panels in the porch roof let extra light into the living room. Photo taken at H on floor plan.

a deck off the study, and the rest is to be covered with clear fiberglass for weather protection.

The owners act as general contractors— From the start, the Mosiers were active participants in the construction of their home. For the first time in their many houses, they acted as general contractors and did many construction tasks themselves, including painting and landscaping.

John and Carol worked hard before the timber raising to have all the subcontractors lined up and ready to go once the frame was erected. The raising itself went smoothly and quickly, with the frame raised as wall sections rather than as bents in the traditional manner. Not having to place the rafters eliminated some of the time it normally takes to raise a timber frame. After the

frame was up, The Cascade Joinery crew enclosed the walls and roof in stress-skin panels. At the same time, a framing crew stick-framed the interior walls. The electricians and plumbers finished their work shortly after the framing was completed. All in all, less than a month passed from the time the timber frame was delivered to the site until the house was ready for drywall.

To keep up this hectic schedule, John and Carol had the advantage of living next to the construction site to oversee every detail. The small farmhouse that was on the original site and near the site of their new house was the Mosiers' temporary living quarters. After they had moved into their new house, the old farmhouse was sold to a young couple who moved the house to another site on the island and planned to renovate it.

With the old farmhouse removed, John and Carol could begin landscaping their property. They put in a large vegetable and flower garden and a perennial garden in the center of the circular drive. Off the west-facing porch, the Mosiers created a modest fenced-in yard surrounded with shrubs, trees and a small pond (cover photo). Carol has been raising a few turkeys and hens for eggs in another old outbuilding. Their next project is to put in that small vineyard on the sunny western slope of the property. The Mosiers look forward to toasting their new lifestyle with wine made from their home-grown grapes. □

Jill Fuerstneau Sousa is an associate at Johnson Partnership, an architectural firm in Seattle, WA. Photos by Roe A. Osborn, except where noted.

Comfort and Delight on a Low Mortgage

How one couple got the house they wanted for less than $100,000

by Ross Chapin

Bill Walton and Rita Lloyd faced a challenge. Unlike many of their peers, neither had bought a house in the early 1980s before prices shot up. Both had been single until they married in their early 40s, and neither had children. Their lives focused around bicycling and outdoor sports, and being renters gave them freedom for their lifestyle. But as newlyweds, Bill and Rita found the dream of owning a home irresistible.

Adding zest to a potentially dull facade. A band of red-cedar siding topped with painted MDO plywood squares enlivens the west wall. At the rear of the house, the shed roof over the window seat in the living room extends into a gable that shelters a hot tub. Photo taken at A on floor plan.

Bookcases and a window seat embrace the living room. A concrete-block fireplace surround finished with stucco frames the woodstove and acts as a heatsink to store the fire's warmth. A small door to the left of the woodstove is a pass-through for restocking the firewood supply. Photo taken at B on floor plan.

They began their search by looking at older homes within their price range. Problem was, these houses needed so much work that Bill and Rita would likely never see the road over a pair of handlebars again. They both wanted to center their lives around bicycling rather than house projects and thought that a new small house, designed and built on a budget, would be perfect. This type of house has been one of my passions, and that's how they came to me.

Keep it to $150,000—If they took advantage of Bill's Veterans Administration loan program, they could purchase a house and land for up to $150,000. Backing out the costs for the site, power, telephone, septic system, driveway, and design and finance costs left a construction budget of $94,000 for the house and a small garage.

Custom construction on this budget is tough to accomplish. For it to work, Bill and Rita had to take a hard look at their true needs and priorities. They met their goal in part because they were able to come to clear decisions. We started by considering the basic shape of the house.

Bill and Rita were most attracted to a 1½-story bungalow, with upstairs spaces tucked into the roof structure. Its stick-by-stick construction and less efficient use of space, however, costs roughly 15% to 25% more than a two-story house with 8-ft. walls and a roof supported by simple 2x4 trusses. A single-story house is also more expensive because it takes more roof and foundation to enclose the same amount of floor space.

General square-foot costs are just that: too general to mean much of anything. That's because the more costly support spaces such as kitchens and bathrooms, and the inescapable expenses such as septic systems, electric hookups and driveways remain roughly similar regardless of the size of the house. So to gain a clearer picture of where the money goes, I divide the house into parts and study them separately.

Basic living space, for example, may cost $50 to $70 per sq. ft. On the other hand, kitchens and bathrooms may cost $200 or more per sq. ft. because of their plumbing, cabinets and special materials. Stairways, decks and garages have different factors as well. And of course, material selections and details also play a major part in the cost picture.

I can get pretty close to calculating the cost of a house using these variable square-foot prices—

within 20% or so. But for a budget this tight, that isn't close enough. I think it's always a good idea to get the builder involved in cost evaluations as soon as possible. Builders are rich sources of cost-saving advice, if you ask early enough. In this case, Bill and Rita had chosen Richard Epstein while we were still developing the plan and details of the house. Richard had several cost-saving suggestions, such as including a pantry to take some of the function of more expensive cabinets. He also suggested that Bill and Rita provide sweat equity where they could: durational and pre-move-in cleanup ($1,500 savings), custom second-color painting ($1,000 savings), and garage finish (electrical, insulation, drywall and paint for a $4,000 savings). One suggestion that saved Bill and Rita several hundred dollars was to purchase freight-damaged and discontinued appliances at a factory warehouse.

By the way, if the builder hasn't been selected yet, I hire a professional estimator to itemize the costs of a project before we get into working drawings. At this stage of the game, we've decided on the basic shape and program of the house, and what the primary finishes might be. Even with rudimentary information such as this, a good estimator can get within 10% of the cost of the house. With this breakdown, clients can see how various materials, features and details affect the final price. It lets the client weigh the pros and cons of the details without getting too emotionally (or financially) involved. For a small house, this service typically costs about $400 in my neighborhood.

The conclusion after our examination was obvious. To meet basic needs while still having some room for quality materials and a few special design features, the construction systems had to be close to production-builder standards. Around here, that means slab-on-grade foundation, minimal corners, truss roof, composite siding, vinyl windows and minimal trim work—that is, a box. My design challenge was to make a small box look beautiful and feel spacious.

Thoughtful plan, straightforward construction—Regardless of its price, a house should relate well to its surroundings. I laid out the driveway around a large maple tree, with a walkway from the garage to the house through a grove of trees (photo p. 151). The entry to the house is from the northeast, away from the prevailing winter winds. The plan puts the kitchen, main bedroom and bathroom to the east, the living room and guest room to the south and west, and the utility room and stairway to the north (floor plans, facing page).

Many houses have an inefficient circulation layout. In this design, we placed the entry at the center of the house. The upper stair also lands at the center, minimizing the area for hallways. The walk-in closet on the second floor is separated from the bedroom, allowing one partner to sleep in while the other dresses. This layout also leaves the bedroom uncluttered with clothes. The angled interior (nonstructural) walls are a surprise, giving each room a unique shape.

Lots of windows, lots of counter space. By eliminating the overhead cabinets, the south and east walls of the kitchen were free to let in light. A walk-in pantry to the left of the stove makes up for the lack of cabinet storage space. Photo taken at C on floor plan.

Getting the most from the storage opportunities. On the left, a recessed shelf in the kitchen accommodates the dishware. On the right, a cabinet door behind the dining table leads to the space at the inside corner of the kitchen counters. Above the counter, the kitchen ceiling drops to distinguish the kitchen from the living room. Photo taken at D on floor plan.

The house is only 16 ft. wide, an economical 4-ft. increment allowing for a span using 9½-in. I-joists. Subtracting the width of the stairway and the 12-in. deep bookcase wall between the stair and the living room leaves a room that is only 11 ft. wide (photo p. 146). But the living room doesn't feel cramped because there are plenty of windows along the south wall, an alcove to the left of the fireplace stretches the space a bit, and at 9 ft. 5 in. the ceiling is about 2 ft. higher than any other ceiling in the house.

The frame is standard 2x6 stud construction at 24 in. o. c., with blown-in fiberglass insulation. This insulation system, by Ark-Seal (800-525-8992), added about $350 to the cost but provides significantly more heat-transfer resistance and will save money in the long run.

The roof is framed with trusses that have raised heels, which allow full-depth insulation where the trusses meet the walls (top drawing, right). We could have used attic trusses or a stick-frame roof system to create some storage space in the

The bump-outs make it work
Rectangular projections on the north and south walls make space for the laundry room/entry and a window seat in the living room. On the second floor, a big closet off the master bedroom doubles as a dressing room.

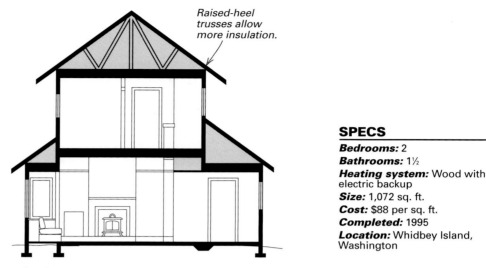

Raised-heel trusses allow more insulation.

Section

SPECS
Bedrooms: 2
Bathrooms: 1½
Heating system: Wood with electric backup
Size: 1,072 sq. ft.
Cost: $88 per sq. ft.
Completed: 1995
Location: Whidbey Island, Washington

▲
North

0 2 4   8 ft.

Photos taken at lettered positions.

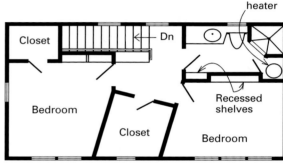

Water heater

Closet — Dn

Bedroom

Closet

Recessed shelves

Bedroom

Second floor

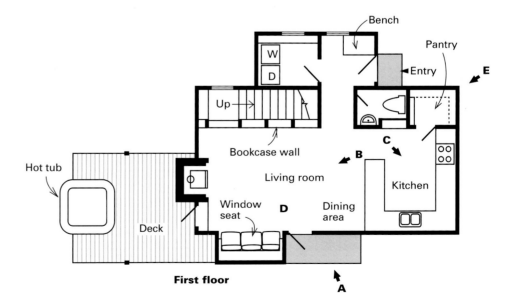

Bench

Pantry

W
D

Entry

E

Up →

Bookcase wall

C

Hot tub

B

Living room

Kitchen

Window seat

D

Dining area

Deck

First floor

A

attic, but either of those options would have raised the price of the house (about $1,000 and $1,900, respectively).

The house is built atop a slab-on-grade finished with paver tiles. We considered a basement but the high groundwater table made that option unfeasible. A basement will normally cost approximately $10 to $15 per sq. ft. in sandy soil, making it cost-effective space.

We considered putting a radiant-heating system in the slab, but the $4,000 bid would have precluded the woodstove and the hearth. Had we to do it again, I would have more closely examined the cost of a single-zone radiant system, with second-floor auxiliary electric heaters.

Softening the box—Without some detail to capture the eye, an unrelieved, two-story wall stands out like a blank billboard. Shed roofs are a good way to bring a tall wall back to earth. I used them on both sides of Bill and Rita's house. One shelters the entry; the other shelters the window seat in the living room. On the south side, the shed roof grows into a gable that covers the deck off the west end (photo p. 147).

Simple ornamentation and a variety of materials enliven a house at little cost. We used painted squares of medium-density overlay plywood to add a band of color above the kitchen windows, along with red-cedar board-and-batten siding to contrast painted composition siding.

Every room needs a focus. The focus of the main room in this house is the fireplace and surrounding hearth (photo p. 146). It brings a strong sense of order and symmetry. The stairway landing in the main room is part of the sitting circle.

Expanding the views—Window placement is key in expanding perception of space. In this house, we put windows along the sight lines at the entry hall and stairway landings. Most of the windows in the main room are placed along the long wall, visually widening the space.

In the kitchen, we did everything we could to maximize window area and to fill the room with natural light (photo left, p. 148). An adjacent

Separate buildings make a mini-compound. A winding driveway leads to what appears to be a garage, but is actually a bike shop/exercise room. Note how the roof extends on the right to shelter the lawnmower, ladders and a kayak. In the background, the front door enters the house in a shed-roofed bump-out that also contains the laundry room. Photo taken at E on floor plan.

pantry and recessed dishware shelf (photo right, p. 148) serve much of the function of upper cabinets, making way for large windows. We put the refrigerator under the counter, freeing wall space for windows. I have found that for a small household, a 6-cu. ft. refrigerator and a separate half- or full-size freezer meets most needs.

The garage is the other living room—Bill and Rita's garage was never intended to be a place for their car. It may serve that purpose for a future owner, but for Bill and Rita, it is a hangout space, a place to work on their bicycles, to listen to music, to exercise, to play darts and to read. Complete with a workbench, an old sofa, a refrigerator and a sound system, it is a getaway from the house (photos above, facing page).

The garage was a priority, and a number of other choices were given up to hold it in the budget. With the windows on the south and west walls and the glazed garage door (a $400 upgrade), it became a light-filled workspace.

Last year, Bill and Rita had 15 guests for Thanksgiving dinner. On that warm day, they set up a long sawhorse dinner table in the workshop and opened the overhead door. Cleanup was as easy as hosing down the floor. □

———

Architect Ross Chapin lives on Whidbey Island, Washington. Photos by Charles Miller.

Avoiding Wasted Space

A small three-story house in upstate New York
gets the most from every square foot

by Dennis Wedlick

ndy Ferrell and Dirk Lumbard's house is tucked away in the dense woods of an old retreat in the Catskill Mountains of New York. The house is only 22½ ft. wide by 29 ft. long (photo facing page). Arguably, it is the smallest possible house that can comfortably contain its variety of spaces—the kind you would find in a three-bedroom, two-bath house.

The house is small for two reasons. First, it had to fit within the owners' $120,000 budget, or it wouldn't get built. And second, the house had to fit as tightly as possible on the densely wooded parcel of land.

The trees on these hillsides are so dense that sunlight barely filters through them. In spring and summer, rivulets and creeks from the late snowmelt run down the hills in every direction. The moist, shady hillsides are the perfect habitat for the giant rhododendrons and ferns that grow rampantly. The darkness, humidity and vegetation give the setting a mysterious, almost primeval character.

Ferrell and Lumbard questioned whether they could, on a limited budget, build a new year-round home in this setting without destroying the landscape's primeval character. After all, each excavation for foundations, septic fields, wells, buried fuel tanks, and in-ground electric and telephone cables threatens the ruin of these woods. Our hope was to build the smallest

Standing tall. Centered in its forest clearing, this small house in the Catskills is designed to make the most of the forest's filtered daylight. Note how slight offsets in the walls and varying rooflines emphasize the different parts of the house. Photo taken at A on floor plan.

The dining room lights up the second floor. Facing south and west, the dining room acts as a big light trap, capturing the sunshine and bouncing it into the adjacent spaces. Photo taken at B on floor plan.

Bedrooms: 2, plus a writing studio
Bathrooms: 2
Heating system: Propane-fired baseboard radiators
Size: 1,690 sq. ft.
Cost: $69 per sq. ft.
Completed: 1996
Location: Forestburgh, New York

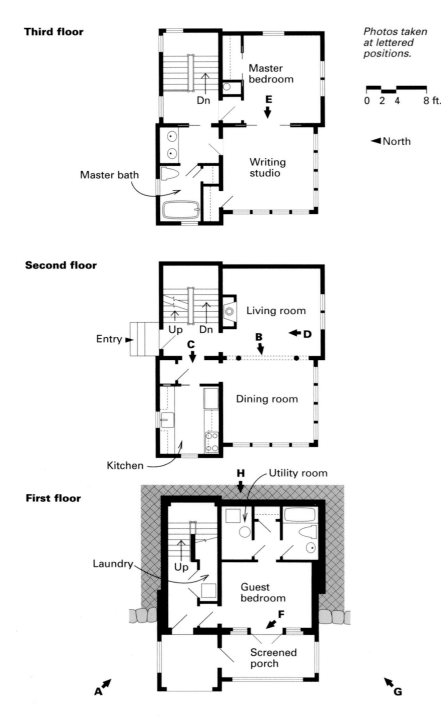

Third floor

Master bedroom
Dn
E
Master bath
Writing studio

Photos taken at lettered positions.

0 2 4   8 ft.

◄ North

Second floor

Living room
Up   Dn
Entry ►
C   **B**   ◄ **D**
Dining room
Kitchen

First floor

H ─ Utility room
Laundry
Up
Guest bedroom
F
Screened porch
A   **G**

A small footprint lessens the impact on the landscape

Notched into a west-facing hillside, the Ferrell/Lumbard house takes advantage of the slope by tucking the first-floor level into the basement. Sited to catch the light, the south and west walls have abundant windows, unlike the north and east walls. On the third floor, the writing studio can become a third bedroom by closing the sliding doors.

home possible to minimize disturbance of the existing landscape.

Reduce each room to its minimum size— Rather than assume that each room needed to be of a certain size, Ferrell and Lumbard had to consider smaller spaces to suit their requirements: three separate sleeping rooms (one of which would double as a writing studio); two full baths; an easy-to-climb staircase; a living room with a fireplace; a separate dining room; and a kitchen that could be closed off from the rest of the house. In addition, the house needed plenty of storage, a laundry room and a covered porch. A house that Ferrell and Lumbard were familiar with that met these requirements was over 2,400 sq. ft. My goal was to keep the new house under 1,300 sq. ft. aboveground, or about 50% of that size.

Fortunately, the slope of the site worked to our advantage, allowing for a partially exposed basement in which comfortable living spaces could be located. This was instrumental in keeping the house's footprint small because the more levels in the home, the smaller each level needs to be. It reduced the home's footprint, and site disturbance, by a third (floor plans, left). Although building a house on a hillside may sound more difficult and therefore more costly, using the basement for more than utilities and laundry far offsets the extra expense.

I began my design by considering the minimum requirements for each room, starting with the most restrictive space: the stair hall. To meet the owners' requirement that the staircase be easy to climb, I used a switchback stair design, which provided a comfortable intermediate landing. I chose an 11-in. tread with a 7-in. riser, which resulted in a staircase with a gently climbing slope. Finally, because the staircase would run along an outside wall and because some of the living space was to be in the basement, I needed to use a wider-than-normal staircase for the two upper levels. This is because a masonry basement wall is much thicker than the insulated wood-stud wall it supports. The minimum stair width is required against the basement wall, resulting in a wider stair above. The resulting stair-hall dimensions were 7 ft. 6 in. wide by 13 ft. long (floor plans, left).

This width is also the minimum for a separate galley-type kitchen, which the owners wanted to keep meal-making messes out of sight from the dining room. A basic galley kitchen calls for two 2-ft. deep counters separated by a 3-ft. 6-in. aisle (photo left, facing page). With the width set, I considered the minimum length of the cooking space. Its three major components are the stove, the sink and the refrigerator, which ideally are located apart from each other, separated by counter space. In the shape of a triangle, the sink is best set at the center of one counter with the stove and refrigerator flanking the opposite counter.

Again working with minimal dimensions, I placed the 30-in. stove 6 in. in from the south wall to allow for a comfortable position when cooking. A 4-ft. long counter between the stove and the refrigerator provides workspace, with cabinets above and below for food storage. The total length of 10 ft. worked perfectly for the opposite counter, with a 36-in. sink cabinet centered between two 42-in. cabinets for utensil storage. By adding a 3-ft. wide vestibule and coat/broom closet to these dimensions, I ended up with a rectangle the same size as the one that contains the stair and the entry hall.

Consider the furniture—To determine the width of the living room (photo bottom right), I considered that a grouping of a sofa and two chairs could easily fit within a 9-ft. by 9-ft. square. Adding a fireplace to this arrangement required at least 4 ft. (30 in. to allow for the depth of the smallest zero-clearance fireplace and another 18 in. for the depth of a hearth). This added up to 13 ft., a perfect square. To complete the grid, the dining room (photo p. 153) was also made 13 ft. square. In reality, a dining room need not be as wide as it is long, but its length cannot be much less than 13 ft. if you want to seat six with a sideboard comfortably.

Now I had a pair of roughly 8-ft. by 13-ft. rectangles, and a pair of 13-ft. squares to fulfill the requirements of the living/dining/kitchen floor. This grid worked equally well for the second floor. Of course, the stair hall remained the same above as below. On top of the living room is the main bedroom. Closets sliced 30 in. off this square, leaving a 10-ft. 6-in. by 13-ft. room—perfect for a queen-size bed and dresser.

Above the kitchen was generous space for a bathroom. I divided the bathroom into two

No wasted space. Yes, you can fit a complete range of full-size appliances, along with adequate counter space, in an 80-sq. ft., galley-style kitchen. Photo taken at C on floor plan.

In the living room, simple moldings used well. A picture molding circles the room at 7 ft., creating the illusion that the ceilings are higher than their standard 8 ft. At the fireplace, tapered shoulders and wide crown moldings impart a sense of massiveness to what is otherwise a basic gyp-board box. Photo taken at D on floor plan.

Working in the treetops. On the third floor, a writing studio wrapped in windows opens onto the master bedroom. Photo taken at E on floor plan.

The downstairs bedroom has its own outdoor connection. A screened porch off the first floor makes a secluded getaway for guests, and diverts attention from the underground nature of basement rooms. Photo taken at F on floor plan.

spaces, with the toilet and tub in one area and a pair of sinks in the other. With this arrangement, the latter space could double as a hallway to the room above the dining room, which worked well as a writing studio (photo above center).

In the basement, the same dimensions allowed another bedroom and bath, and room for laundry and utilities. Also, enough space remained for a covered porch (photo above left) tucked under the dining room and kitchen.

Offsets and rooflines emphasize the parts of the house—Designing the house to be tall rather than wide suited not only the preserva-

tion of the woods but also echoed the natural aesthetics of the tall, columnar trees that compose it. With each room dimensioned to fit over another, I could assign each stack of rooms its own architecture, as if the house were not one structure but rather a combination of four. To do so, I needed to jog the grid slightly, which you can see in the floor plan. The resulting corners cast shadowlines that help to make the parts distinct from one another. By making each part distinct, the exterior of this house is given the variety and interest of a much larger house.

I also assigned each stack of rooms its own roof form. The trick to using different roofs adja-

cent to each other is avoiding valleys, which are potential water collectors. I created a gabled-roof L-configuration for three of the structures. For the remaining one, in the southwest corner, I set a nearly flat roof at a lower height than any gable. In this way, water could always flow down and off without interruption.

The rooms beneath the flatter roof are the study and dining room. Facing south and west, these rooms have nearly all-glass walls with 6½-ft. tall double-hung windows spaced tightly together. By the way, these windows cost minimally more than the 4-ft. tall versions, but they add substantially to the style of the house and

Boulders hold back the soil. The inevitable byproduct of excavating rocky ground is rocks—or boulders in this case. Rather than see them as a nuisance, builder Larry Cronk rearranged them as retaining walls and planters. Photo taken at G on floor plan.

The east wall turns its back on the cold. In contrast to the open nature of the south and west walls, the north and east sides of the house are mostly solid, well-insulated wall. Photo taken at H on floor plan.

quantity of light that they admit. Inside, the dining room and study are virtually open to the adjacent rooms on the east side of the house (the living room and the master bedroom), letting the light and views penetrate into them as well. For both visual contrast and insulation, the outside walls on the north and east sides have few windows (photo bottom right).

Use materials that age gracefully—The house is clad in simple cedar siding that is lightly treated with a weathering stain, and the roofs are covered with inexpensive asphalt roofing. All windows and doors are painted wood and of

standard sizes, which kept these costs to a minimum. The basement walls are concrete block. Where they are exposed, the blocks alternate in height to give the wall some pattern.

I had originally specified cast-concrete retaining walls for the east and west sides of the house. But our builder, Larry Cronk, had a better idea. He stacked the boulders that came out of the basement excavation into ledgelike embankments that seem as natural to the site as the moss that grows on them (photo top right). □

Dennis Wedlick is an architect in New York City. Photos by Charles Miller, except where noted.

Index

A

Additions:
  duplex, 41
  third-story, 66
Appliances, energy-efficient, 139
Arts-and-Crafts style:
  house in, 29
  remodeling in, 87

B

Balconies, Arts-and-Crafts style, 10
Baseboards, corner details for, 61
Bathrooms:
  colorfully painted, 41
  divided, 154, 155-56
  efficient fixtures for, 44
  as greenhouses, 110, 113
  "Japanese," 33
  for limited space, 27, 29
  north location for, 93
  in separate buildings, 33
Beach houses, twin towers of, 123
"Beaches," before fireplaces, 32, 35
Beams, salvaged, 129, 130
Bedrooms:
  guest, basement, 154
  half-walled, 94
  as living rooms, alternative, 109
  screened porch off, 156
  separate building for, 115
Benches, built-in, 21, 22
Blockwork:
  with alternating brick sizes, 152, 157
  houses of, 81
  sandblasting, 78, 79
  split-faced, 26, 29, 136, 138
  walls of, vents for, 81
Bookcases:
  beneath stair, 40
  in stairwell, 23
Brickwork, neatly detailed, 19, 21, 22
Bridges:
  over dunes, 122
  suspended interior, 105
Building:
  cost-cutting tricks for, 148
  by owner, costs of, 49
  by students, 127

C

Cabinets:
  alternatives to, 148
  plywood, medium-density overlay, 117
Cabins, post-and-beam summer, 91
California, zoning ordeal in, 26
Ceilings:
  beamed, 21, 23
  of car decking, 116, 117
  cathedral,
    corbeled beams in, 82, 86
    with off-center ridge, 84, 86
    varied-height, 83, 84
  collar ties in, gypsum-wrapped, 138, 139
  curved drywall, 100, 103
  pine, white-tinted, 38, 39, 40
  plastered, with applied stars, 121
  varied heights for, 134
Chimneys:
  metal exterior, 77
  two-toned, with set-in bricks, 97, 99
Clerestories, light-well, 116, 117

Closets:
  as dressing rooms, 110
  north location for, 93
  walk-in, 148, 149
Colors:
  ladding, to concrete, 17
  choosing, 40, 41
Columns:
  logs as, 114, 116
  paired 4x4s, 15, 16
Concrete:
  coloring, 17
  gridded colored, 100, 103
  paint for,
    epoxy, durability of, 53
  stained, 139
  over tires and mesh, 50, 53
Cooling:
  by convection, 44
  design for, in tropics, 107
Countertops:
  concrete, 34, 35
  cutting boards for, sliding
    cantilevered, 34
  for eating, 109
  marble, radiused, 86
Courtyards, creating, 38
Cutting boards, removable cantilevered, 34
Cypress, for siding, 139

D

Decks:
  off bedroom, 76
  cantilevered, 48, 49
  fireplaces for, 19, 22
  formal, 72, 77
  importance of, 109
  roof, 44
  rooftop, 51, 52, 53
  second-story, off bedroom, 71
  trellis over, with corbeled beams, 85, 86
Design:
  for actual needs, 113
  for blending in, 61
  with camera-captured views, 75
  for compactness, 95, 113, 152-57
  around compound, 117
  for cooling, 107
  for development prototype, 139
  for economy, 103
  for hurricane resistance, 107
  for low budgets, 81, 151
  modular, 79
    4-ft., 54
    with plywood, 124-25
  for rainy gray climate, 57
  "romantic," 99
  solar, 95
    for rainy gray climate, 57
  in squares vs. rectangles, 101
  three-story, 152-57
Dining rooms:
  light-lit, 153
  shrinking, 109, 112
Doors:
  French,
    in angled bay, 74, 76
    8-ft., source for, 86
    interior, 86, 87
    to nowhere but out, 113
    transoms over, 82, 86
  garage multilite, into garden, 33, 35
  retractable translucent, 55, 56
  sliding, of sandblasted glass, 65, 66
  See also Hardware.

Dormers:
  shed, over stair, 99
  stairway, gabled, 18, 20
Driveways, siting, 109
Dryers, upstairs location for, 113
Drywall, bullnose returns for, 112, 113
Dumb waiters, for wood transport, 113

E

Earthquakes:
  foundations for, concrete-pile, 46-48
  masonry walls for, 128
Eaves:
  Arts-and-Crafts-style curved, 26, 29
  fiberglass translucent, 54, 57
Eckerman, Michael, fireplaces by, 82, 86
Energy conservation, design for, 139
Energy efficiency, design for, 135
Entryways:
  in bump-out, 149, 151
  gabled, 18, 20
  overhang for, 85, 87
  pole-and-timber, 143
  recessed, Arts-and-Crafts style, 10
Exercise rooms, garage doors for, glazed, 150, 151

F

Fascia, narrow, 111, 112
Finishes:
  bleaching-oil, 13
  exterior, 61
    color-preserving, 87
  interior, spray, 90
  penetrating-oil, for trim, 87
  sunlight-resistant interior, 107
Fireplaces:
  Arts-and-Crafts-style, over steel insert, 29
  asymmetrical, 61
  "beach" before, 31, 32
  block,
    sandblasted, 80, 81
    stuccoed, 147, 148
  concrete, coloring, 17
  concrete-block, 31, 32
  fieldstone, 116
  hearths for, cast-concrete, 131
  inside-outside, 19, 21, 22
  olivine, 10, 12
  as room dividers, 60
  Rumford, 64, 66, 98
  small, 64, 66
  stone, in horn-of-plenty motif, 82, 86
  surrounds for, cast-concrete, 130, 131
  zero-clearance, 155
    in bay, 74, 75
Flooring:
  car decking as, 116, 117
  painted, 60, 61
  plywood panels for, 45
Floors:
  brick, as thermal mass, 95
  concrete,
    colored, 12, 13
    exposed-aggregate, 127
    pigmented, 56, 57
  concrete-gridded, 100, 103
  concrete-stained, scored, 139
  glass-block, 31, 33, 35
  hinged, to rise upright, 35
  insulating under, 94

Footings, concrete pre-cast, 94
Forms, release for, WD-40, 131
Foundations:
  block, split-faced, 136, 138
  for cantilevered post-and-beam, 68
  concrete-pile earthquake-resistant, 46-48
  pier-and-grade beam, 126, 127
  post-and-grade beam and gravel, 94
  upon tires and mesh, 50, 53
Fountains, stone-masonry, 82, 86
Framing:
  exposed, 120
  on rim joists, steel-post supported, 47, 48
  2x4s, thinner, 95
Frieze blocks, windows as, 105, 107
Furniture, built-in, 21, 23

G

Gables:
  curved, 26
  small, 18
  tripartite intersecting, 111
Garages:
  doors for, glazed, 150, 151
  driving design, 27
  as starter houses, 135
  See also Porte cocheres.
Gardens, rooftop, 41
Gazebos, steel, with walkway, 67, 70
Glazing:
  efficient, source for, 45
  sloped, 125, 127
  triple Heat Mirror low-e, 45
Greenhouses, bathrooms as, 110, 113
Guest houses, garages as, 135

H

Hardware, for doors, sliding, 66
Heating systems:
  electric,
    baseboard concealed, 44
    for bathrooms, 29
  for small houses, 36, 38, 39
  wood-stove, 95, 135
    and air duct, 127
    low-emissivity rated, 135
Heat-recovery ventilators, for small houses, 135
Hot tubs, exterior, 147
Hot-water systems:
  electric instaneous, 44
  energy-efficient, 44
Hurricanes:
  design for, 107
  engineering for, importance of, 122

I

Inglenooks, raised stone, 10, 12
Insulation:
  for block wall, 79
  board, fiberglass-wrapped, 135
  fiberglass, blown-in, 149
  rigid, for roofs, 94, 95
  for tropics, 106
  under-house, 94

J

Joinery, abutting edges in, emphasizing, 87
Joists, wood I-, for deep insulation, 134

K

Kitchens:
  Arts-and-Crafts style, 25, 28
  corridor, Arts-and-Crafts style, 86, 87
  galley, minimal, 56
  islands in, concrete, 34, 35
  open, timber-framed, 141
  small,
    angled bay in, 75
    galley-type, 154, 155
    open, 98
  tiny, 134
  for two cooks, 109

L

Laundries, in bump-out, 149, 151
Lighting:
  from stairwell, 63, 65, 66
  suspended, over work space, 80, 81
  valences for, redwood, 80, 81
Living rooms, requirements for, basic, 109, 111
Lofts:
  over dining rooms, 69
  sleeping, 30, 31
Logs, as interior elements, 31, 34, 35

M

Mantels, cast-concrete, 131
Membranes, copolymer alloy-nylon, 44
Metal connectors:
  corner-brace, 53
  in post-and-beam, 68, 69
Moldings:
  crown,
    dropped, 155
    over fireplace, 155
  PVC pipe as, 45

O

Offices, separate building for, 115
Oriented strand board, ¼-in., source for, 135

P

Paint, epoxy, durability of, 53
Pantries, as cost savers, 148
Partitions:
  designing, 66
  partial, 44
Pavilions, rooftop, 36, 41
Plaster, gypsum veneer, lath for, 129
Plates, doubled, advantages of, 13
Plywood:
  as exterior siding, 102, 103
  as flooring, 45
  house of, 124-25
  T111, as sheathing-siding, 95
Polyurethane, paint, two-part sunlight-resistant, 107
Porches:
  arched corbelled entrance to, 72, 77
  covered, 121, 122
  importance of, 109, 113
  screened, 138
    off bedroom, 156
  for seaside cabin, 114, 117
  timber-framed, 142, 144-45
Porte cocheres, rustic, 140, 142, 143

Post-and-beam:
  with metal connectors, 68, 69
  for open plan, curved, 71
  piers for, concrete, 89, 90
  summer cottage in, 91

R

Radiant-floor heating systems:
  propane, in concrete slab, 103
  propane-heated, 32
  simple, 129
  for small houses, 36, 38
Rafters, exposed, Arts-and-Crafts style, 8, 10
Railings:
  caps for, bridle-jointed, through-tenoned, 10, 11
  for decks, 85
  metal, 67
  simple, 15
  steel galvanized, 100, 102, 103
  steel-rod minimal, 105
  1x2s, for loft, 139
Ranges, in concrete counters, 34
Redwood, finish for, color-preserving, 87
Remodeling, Arts-and-Crafts style, 87
Renovation, of row house, 66
Rental units, garages as, 135
Ridge beams, lowered, 57
Roofing:
  galvanized, 67, 71, 104
  glass, trellis support for, 85, 86
  metal, 30, 95
    corrugated, 138
  for roof decks, 44
  shingle, stripes with, 96, 97, 99
  translucent, over entry, 145
  for tropics, 104, 107
Roofs:
  for cold climates, 81
  deck, tiled, 49
  for deep insulation, 135
  with eave beams, braced, 104, 107
  fascia for, narrow, 111, 112
  gable, 17
    with smaller gables under, 83
  hip,
    with clerestory windows, 88, 89, 91
    overhangs with, 121
  insulation for, rigid, 94
  overhangs for,
    as shelter, 151
    in tropics, 104, 107
  rainwater catchment for, 104, 106
  in series, 58, 59, 61
  shed rooms on, 150
  of stress-skin panels, 143, 144
  timber-framed, 93

S

Saltboxes, shingle-style, 77
Saunas, Japanese-American, 33
Screens:
  shoji, in bathrooms, 33
  See also Doors: sliding.
Sealers, finish, spray, 90
Sheathing:
  as siding, 95
  for wind resistance, 53
Shelves, recessed, 130, 131
Shingle style, saltbox, 77
Shingles, exposure of, alternating, 13

Siding:
  board-and-batten, 15, 16, 17, 138
  cedar, 152, 153
  clapboard, 138
  plywood,
    exterior, 102, 103
    smartening up, 95
  relief panel in, painted plywood, 147, 150
  rough-sawn vertical, 67
  texture of, varying, 96, 97
Skylights:
  gabled, 31, 35
  in peak, 125
Slabs, for tropics, 107
Sofas, built-in, 21
Solariums:
  as heat sink, 57
  vents for, 56, 57
Stains, exterior, 61
Staircases:
  comfortable, small, 154
  design for, contrasting, 120, 122
  exterior, to upper apartment, 134
  load-bearing, 53
  spiral, as space saver, 27, 28, 29
Storage:
  overhead compartments for, 44, 45
  planning for, 39, 66
  strategies for, 39, 40, 133, 134
Stress-skin panels:
  for roofs, 143, 144
  for walls, 144
Stucco:
  for low maintenance, 53
  in tropics, 107
Studios, music, 101, 102, 103

T

Termites, borate treatment against, 107
Terraces, rooftop, building, 36, 38, 41
Thermal mass, concrete slab as, 103
Tilework:
  granite, 87
  mixing, 17
  over radiant-floor heating system, 38, 39
Timber-framing:
  double plates in, 13
  with recycled beams, 13
  for small house, 13, 140
Toilets, Swedish low-flush, 44
Towers:
  as design element, 45, 53
  finding heights for, with raised camera, 75
  with garden top, 36, 41
  shingle-style, 77
  twin, on the beach, 118
Trellises:
  over deck, 85
  between houses, 122
Trim:
  biscuit-joined, design offerings of, 113
  exterior, aluminum extruded, 102, 103
  finish for, 87
  interior, finish for, 87
  particleboard, 38, 39
  poplar, painted, 139
  redwood, 87
Trusses:
  exposed, 25, 29
  parallel-chord, 105, 107
  for roof savings, 148, 149

V

Ventilation. See Heat-recovery ventilators.
Vents:
  cone, source for, 44
  ridge, source for, 81
Views, previewing, with camera on pole, 75

W

Walls:
  for deep insulation, 135
  furred-out, for air circulation, 135
  half-, as thermal mass, 95
  interior, stained plywood, 105, 107
  masonry, earthquake-proofing, 128
  retaining, boulders as, 157
  retractable translucent, from garage door, 55, 56
  semi-circular, with post-and-beam, 68
  of stress-skin panels, 144
  See also Partitions.
Washing machines, upstairs location for, 113
Water, catchments for, roof, 104, 106
Windows:
  aluminum, 67, 68, 71
    stock, 102, 103
  arched, aluminum-framed, 67, 69, 71
  Arts-and-Crafts-style, 29
  bay, angled, 72, 74, 77
  clerestory,
    above fireplace, 75
    in hip roof, 88, 89, 91
    for ventilation, 57
  corner, with cantilevered plates, 13
  double-hung, tall, 153, 156-57
  Douglas-fir, source for, 117
  fixed, with operable tops, 134
  as frieze blocks, 105, 107
  gable-end, 117
  for historic renovation, 62, 65
  insulated, low-E, 134
  low operable, for ventilation, 44, 45
  muntins for, designing, 71
  rectangular, arched facade over, 96, 98
  returns for, angled, 44, 45
  round, 33, 113
  transom, 25
  windowsills for, cast-concrete, 131
  wrap-around, 63, 66
Window seats, in bump-out, 146, 149
Wiring, chases for, in ceiling, 138
Wood preservatives, borate, 107
Workshops, garage doors for, glazed, 150, 151

The articles in this book originally appeared in *Fine Homebuilding* magazine. The date of first publication, issue number, and page numbers for each article are given at right.

8   **A Compact Timber-Frame Farmhouse**
October/November 1996 (105:98-103)

14   **A Cost-Conscious House in North Carolina**
Spring 1996 (101:52-55)

18   **Simple, But Not Plain**
Spring 1995 (94:40-45)

24   **A Craftsman-Style Cottage on a Tiny Lot**
Spring 1995 (94:76-81)

30   **A Little House in the Big Woods**
Spring/Summer 1997 (109:98-103)

36   **A Duplex With a Rooftop Garden**
December 1996/January 1997 (106:76-81)

42   **High Living in a Small Space**
Spring 1993 (80:68-71)

46   **A Small House on a Rocky Hillside**
June/July 1993 (82:78-81)

50   **Building Small and Tall**
October/November 1995 (98:78-81)

54   **Sunspace House**
Spring 1995 (94:68-71)

58   **Small House, Simple Details**
April/May 1995 (95:94-97)

62   **A Town House Opens Up in Philadelphia**
April/May 1998 (115:78-82)

68   **A Mountain Retreat**
June/July 1995 (96:75-79)

72   **Shingle Style Meets Saltbox**
Spring/Summer 1997 (109:66-71)

78   **A Small House of Concrete Block**
December 1994/January 1995 (92:66-69)

82   **A Redwood Remodel**
December 1994/January 1995 (92:90-95)

88   **Summer Cabin in the Land O' Lakes**
June/July 1996 (103:86-89)

92   **A Small, Affordable House**
December 1995/January 1996 (99:74-77)

96   **A Romantic House**
June/July 1994 (89:86-89)

100   **Economical by Design**
April/May 1994 (88:54-57)

104   **Mango House**
December 1993/January 1994 (85:72-75)

108   **The House in Alice's Field**
Spring/Summer 1997 (109:50-55)

114   **Three Buildings, One House**
October/November 1994 (91:66-69)

118   **Dueling Towers on the Carolina Coast**
Spring/Summer 1997 (109:80-85)

124   **A Little House with Rich Spaces**
February/March 1994 (86:72-75)

128   **Steep Lot, Narrow House**
June/July 1994 (89:72-75)

132   **The Garage as Starter Home**
December 1997/January 1998 (113:84-87)

136   **Room Enough for Two**
February/March 1998 (114:94-97)

140   **An Island Homestead**
April/May 1998 (115:110-115)

146   **Comfort and Delight on a Low Mortgage**
June/July 1998 (116:88-93)

152   **Avoiding Wasted Space**
June/July 1998 (116:106-111)